13 Days of Terror

13 Days of Terror

Held Hostage by al Qaeda Linked Extremists —A True Story

Greg Williams

New Horizon Press
Far Hills, New Jersey

New Horizon Press
P.O. Box 669
Far Hills, NJ 07931

Greg Williams
        13 Days of Terror: Held Hostage by al Qaeda Linked
        Extremists—A True Story

Cover Design: Robert Aulicino
Interior Design: Susan M. Sanderson

Library of Congress Control Number: 2002112729

ISBN: 0-88282-229-2
New Horizon Press

Manufactured in the U.S.A.

2007   2006   2005   2004   2003   /   5   4   3   2   1

Dedication

This book is dedicated to my sons, Bryan and Gregory, Jr. My love for you and the memories of our precious little time together gave me the reason to carry on.

Author's Note

This book is based on my actual experiences and reflects my perception of the past, present and future. The personalities, events, actions and conversations portrayed within the story have been reconstructed from my memory and the memories of participants. In an effort to safeguard individual privacy, I have changed the names of certain people and, in some cases, altered otherwise identifying characteristics. Events involving the characters happened as described; only minor details have been changed.

Table of Contents

Acknowledgements ix

Prologue 1

Introduction 9

Part I

Chapter 1   Early Dreams. 23

Chapter 2   The Path of Destiny 31

Chapter 3   Nightmares 39

Chapter 4   Shades of Prophecies. 67

Chapter 5   The Island Nation 81

Chapter 6   Cebu 103

Part II

Chapter 7   A Trip to Nowhere. 125

Chapter 8   Living With Fear 143

Chapter 9   Every Day a Gift from God 175

Chapter 10   The Gates of Hell 201

Chapter 11   Facing Evil 221

Chapter 12   A Worthless Hostage 237

Chapter 13   Delaying the Inevitable 261

Chapter 14   Darkness and Light 279

Afterword 299

Glossary 309

Acknowledgements

First, I owe a great debt of gratitude to Dr. Joan Dunphy and her staff at New Horizon Press for their interest in my story and the invaluable guidance they have given me in shaping the finished product. I am extremely thankful for my agents at Sedgeband Literary Agency. It is their belief in my story and their tireless efforts in finding me the right publisher that has made this book possible.

I want to thank my wife, Nheni, whose love and support gave me the courage to put down in words what was a nightmarish part of my life. I am especially grateful to Pastor Don Lyon for his personal and spiritual support. It is the power of God's will through Pastor Lyon and Faith Center Church in Rockford, Illinois, that convinced me to use my story to bring hope and encouragement to others.

I must also thank Dennis Jordan and Brenda Moorhous for being the most shining examples of what true Christians are. My thanks also to Pastor Rick Thomas of Abundant Life Christian Center in Florida whose example encouraged me to dedicate my life to the Lord's work in the Philippines. It is Pastor Thomas who recommended me to

Pastor Sumrall in Manila and thus started me down the path of God's plan for me.

I am grateful to my brother, Brian, for taking me in when I had nowhere else to go after leaving the Philippines. And I will forever be grateful for the love and understanding of my mother and father who, after they learned the truth about my circumstances, embraced me again and bought me a computer, giving me the tools to write my story.

Most of all I thank God and our Lord Jesus Christ for the many blessings that have been bestowed upon me.

Blindsided

I was a stranger in a strange land. As I looked around, I saw that I was the only Westerner in a vast sea of Asian faces. Pale-skinned Americans and Europeans stuck out in a country like the Philippines, especially here in Cebu, an island in the southern part of the country where the people are a mix of glossy topaz colored Polynesian and Spanish ancestry. Standing on the sidewalk, I felt men and women staring at me. Obviously, most of them were assuming I was "a rich American" and were going out of their way to be pleasant and attentive. Women especially glanced at me with curiosity and interest. Their eyes lit up as if I were the most handsome man they had ever seen. Having just come through a bitter divorce after my wife left me, I had to admit, it was very flattering. Of course, I knew that to most of them, I represented money and possibly a free ticket away from the poverty and hardship of their lives. At the very least, they probably hoped that I would spend money on them, for the basic necessities.

As I came to find out, in addition to the harsh, desti-
tute states of their families, many Filipino women were not
treated very well by the men. Rape and abuse were common.
The seemingly kind blue eyes of a foreigner spoke not only of
a few luxuries but of other more caring environments, real or
imagined. Yet, I had no intention of becoming involved at this
point with another woman, no matter how attractive. I had
come to the Philippines on a spiritual quest.

Standing outside my hotel I took a moment to reflect
on this mission. Only a few days before, I had been in America.
Now I was on my way to an even more remote island than this
one to do God's work. I would be helping the impoverished
children there get good meals to eat and decent clothes to
wear.

Tired but excited, I felt ready for the coming boat trip.
It would be exciting to learn about this beautiful land and its
people. I thanked God for this opportunity to renew my spirit,
and most of all, for giving my life purpose and making it feel
meaningful again.

As I stood there in the bright sunlight, cars and motorcycles sped by spewing black clouds of smoke into the air.
Many of the women who walked by wore handkerchiefs over
their noses and mouths, apparently trying to filter the dust and
exhaust fumes. Around me people were hurrying to and fro,
just as they would during the morning rush hour in the United
States. The only differences here were people's appearances
and modes of transportation. Almost every Filipino who came
near me smiled pleasantly or nodded. Some spoke English and
called out, "Good morning" or "Maayong Buntag" in their
native tongue, making me feel welcome.

Suddenly, hearing some commotion, I turned around and saw the woman called the "Blind Prophet" with whom I would be making my pilgrimage. As she emerged from the hotel, I marveled to think that I had not even met this woman until a week ago, and now, I was following her into the remote countryside of this foreign land. "God works in mysterious ways," I murmured.

A party of about ten other people circled around the Prophet. This was her entourage—a number of aides and supporters who helped carry out her work. I spotted my new friend Remy among them and he flashed me a broad smile.

Though we had met after I arrived in Cebu, I felt quite close to Remy. He was an outgoing young Filipino man, in his early twenties, married with a two-year-old child. Trim and muscular, he had the appearance of a handsome, well-conditioned boxer, yet had a surprisingly gentle manner. Remy seemed always on the lookout for my welfare. He acted like my own personal bodyguard, keeping me informed ahead of time about things of which I should be wary. Already we shared a mutual respect and understanding of each other. He was fast becoming the closest thing I had to a good friend.

"It's time," he said walking up to me, "to leave for the port in order to catch a ferry to the island." Two cabs drove up. The Prophet and her entourage split up between the two cabs and climbed inside them. There was no room for Remy and me, so we stayed behind to hail a third cab.

"Do you know the way to the ferry?" I asked Remy as the other two cabs drove away.

"Yes, yes," he assured me. "I have lived in Cebu all my life. Don't worry."

Another five minutes passed before we were finally able to flag a free cab. Getting inside, Remy gave the driver instructions and we were off.

After about fifteen minutes of the cab maneuvering through heavy traffic, we approached an area clogged with cardboard and wooden shacks. Rising above this shantytown, in the blue morning sky above the rooftops, were the tops of masts and communication antennae from ships anchored in the port ahead. The driver, like most cab drivers, seemed to have his own little detours around traffic to get us where we needed to go. As I watched, he deftly pulled the taxi out of the mass of cars inching along and turned right down a side street. We found ourselves heading toward a long row of boxcar-type containers that had been unloaded from a freighter. Once we were driving among the containers, the driver slowed the car down to a crawl and peered down the alleys formed between the rows of containers, searching for a faster route. He had seemed to know where he was going, but now it appeared he was having trouble finding his shortcut.

As I turned to Remy to ask him about the time of the ferry's departure, the cab abruptly came to a lurching halt. There were no seatbelts and Remy and I were thrown forward by the sudden stop and bumped our heads on the seats in front of us. As we rubbed our foreheads, looking at each other with confusion and trying to figure out what happened, the driver let out a strange sounding yelp. Remy and I turned and stared with astonishment through the front window of the cab. A bunch of tough-looking men waving assault rifles, some wearing bandanas across their faces, others wearing black ski masks, quickly surrounded our vehicle.

"Is this the Port Police?" I asked Remy uncertainly, wondering why government officials would be dressed in this manner.

"No, I'm afraid they are bandits," Remy whispered.

I leaned forward in horror, disbelieving what I was seeing. As the men pulled open the doors of the cab, the first thought that came to my mind was that we were being robbed. *This can't be happening,* I kept thinking. I watched in shock as the cab driver was brutally yanked from his seat and thrown violently against one of the shipping containers. Almost simultaneously another man reached in and pulled out Remy. The bandit on my side of the cab screamed loudly and waved his AK47 rifle at me, indicating I should get out. As I stood up outside of the cab, I lost sight of what was happening on the other side of the car. I could only hear men screaming at Remy and the cab driver.

At that moment the man who had threatened me, raised his rifle only inches from my face and pointed it right between my eyes. I felt the blood drain from my face and my fear was so great, I thought I would urinate in my pants. It was like a scene in a nightmare from which I could not awaken. Only this was real. A few seconds later I heard a loud thud. Then someone on the other side of the cab yelled in pain, but I could not move to help. I could only stare at the rifle pointed at my head, praying that the man holding it would not pull the trigger.

Time stood still. I was frozen in place, unsure what to do. Then I felt a sharp pain in the back of my head and realized I had been hit from behind. I fell to my knees, my hands instinctively reaching out in front of me to break my fall. I was aware of some sort of cloth being pulled over my head and tied tightly around my throat. I could not see. *My God,* I thought, *are they going to hang me?*

I gasped for air through the cloth. Then I felt someone drop a rope over my shoulders and pull it tight around my mid-section, pinning my arms at the elbows against my sides. At almost the same instant someone pulled me to my feet, grabbed my hands and tied them together in front of me. As I struggled to breathe, the men pulled the ropes tighter until all I could do was scream in pain.

"Ahhhhhhh!" I protested loudly. Someone untied the cloth around my throat, pulled it up to my nose and stuffed a piece of cloth into my mouth, causing me to gag. Then they pulled the hood back down and retied it.

Although the rope was being held tight, I was no longer being pushed, pulled or hit. I stood shakily and listened to anguished cries coming from Remy and the cab driver. There was yelling and then loud thuds; I assumed they were being beaten and tied up. Their cries turned to muffled moans as the sound of fists and guns pummeling their bodies reached me. Had their heads been covered also or were they able to see the men attacking them? For a brief moment, I wondered why I was not also being beaten.

Then my mind went back to a more immediate problem: I could not breathe. I struggled to take air in through my nose. Suddenly a voice with a heavy Filipino accent yelled into my right ear, "YOU, YO FOLA ROP! NOW! EY YO PATAY!" My mind raced, trying to figure out what he was saying to me. I wasn't certain, but I thought he had told me to follow along wherever they took me or I would be very sorry.

My heart froze and my legs turned to jelly. "NOW!" he yelled louder. "EYYO PATAY! Or you will die!" His new threat was clear and shook me to the bone. I felt the rope pulling me and began to take small lurching steps in that direction. *God help me,* I thought, as I stumbled forward amidst the yelling and muffled moans of pain. Although I was too stunned to understand it, I had just been taken hostage. My life was about to become a living hell.

Introduction

Situated at the crossroads of the Pacific Ocean and South China Sea, the Philippines was called by patriot Jose Rizal "the Pearl of the Orient Seas." The earliest inhabitants were believed to be Negritos and Mongols from the Asian mainland who arrived approximately 30,000 years ago. Between 1500 and 500 B.C., five separate migrations of Indo-Chinese settlers occurred and were followed in 500 A.D. by a steady migration of Malayans. Traders from Persia, China and India also passed through the archipelago, creating a diverse ethnic, religious, political and cultural landscape. The rise of Islam throughout the Middle East and Asia in the thirteenth and fourteenth centuries soon spread to Southeast Asia and found ready converts. At the beginning of the sixteenth century, the arrival of Spanish and Portuguese fleets in the region brought a new religion: Christianity.

Made up of thousands of islands, the archipelago was inhabited by many small tribes, each ruled by a different chief, or Raja. In 1521, Spanish explorer, Ferdinand Magellan, and his expedition landed on the island of Samar. Naming the archipelago San Lazaro, Magellan claimed the lands for Spain. He soon met and was welcomed by two Rajas who brought him to the island of Cebu to meet the chief, Raja Humabon. Humabon also welcomed Magellan and even accepted his religion. Along with hundreds of Cebu residents, Humabon was baptized a Christian by Magellan's missionaries. In return, Magellan offered the Raja assistance in fighting Lapu-Lapu, a rebellious leader of the nearby island of Mactan. During battle, Magellan and many of his men were killed. Lapu-Lapu would become revered by many for being the first Filipino chief to resist foreign intruders.

Without Magellan's leadership, tensions rose between Raja Humabon and the remaining members of the Spanish expedition. The explorers decided to return to Europe. Despite heavy losses, their ship was laden with enough spices to more than cover the costs of the voyage and give the Spanish crown a substantial profit. With one successful expedition completed, Spain sent subsequent trade missions in 1525 and 1542.

Anxious to truly establish control over sea routes to Asia, Spain sent a fourth expedition in 1564 to establish a Spanish colony on the islands. Appointed first Governor-General by King Philip II, Miguel Legazpi settled on the island of Cebu and named the colony the Philippines after his leader and benefactor. Despite an unsuccessful attempt by a Portuguese fleet to take over the colony in 1568, Legazpi persevered. In 1571, he selected Manila as the capital and continued developing an extensive network of trade from Asia, through the Philippines, to Mexico and finally to the Spanish colonies in the Americas. Ruling from Manila, Legazpi and subsequent civil leaders chose to govern indirectly through the local tribal chiefs. They created a feudal system in the countryside with a landed elite and landless tenants—an economic structure that created social discontent and political strife for centuries to come. At the same time, missionaries traveled throughout the colony spreading Christianity and converting nearly the entire population to Roman Catholicism. A priest was stationed in each village to serve as not only the religious leader, but a representative of Spanish authority. Thus religious orders and landholders became the two pillars supporting and controlling local communities in colonial society.

Under Spanish rule, men between the ages of sixteen and sixty were required to work forty days each year on public projects without pay. Most Filipinos were poor, uneducated and landless, yet under the medieval feudal economy were required to pay taxes to landowners, the church and Spain itself. Moreover, despite the existence of a land-owning class and local tribal chiefs, Filipinos were barred from holding any positions of power in the central government. Discontent steadily rose, particularly among the lower classes.

Although the threat of invasion was constant throughout the seventeenth century, Spain ruled the colony in almost complete isolation until 1762, when the British invaded and took control of Manila. British control lasted only until 1763 with the end of the Seven Years' War in Europe and the Treaty of Paris restoring Manila back to Spain. However, the repercussions of the British invasion were a potent blow to Spain's power. It opened up the region to more competition for trade from European rivals, weakening Spain's control of the local trade routes. This influx of European trade also introduced to the region's people contemporary Western political ideas. Furthermore, it demonstrated to the Philippine people that the Spanish could, in fact, be defeated.

Though it took several decades, discontent turned into rebellion as multiple uprisings against Spanish rule arose in the middle to late 1800s. One of the most well-known opposition leaders from the period was José Rizal. A man of many talents, Rizal was a medical doctor in training, poet, philosopher, sculptor, scientist and folklorist who spoke several different languages. While completing his medical studies in Madrid, Rizal became interested in anthropology and set out to discredit the racist notion of Filipino inferiority through scientific study of the history of the Malay people. He later wrote two novels, *Noli me Tangere (Touch Me Not)* and *El Filibusterismo (The Subversive)*, exposing the authoritarian nature and abuses of the Spanish government and clergy. Banned in the Philippines, the books were smuggled into the country and widely read. Rizal returned to the Philippines in 1892 and started a group dedicated to national independence. Shortly thereafter, Rizal was arrested and exiled by Spanish authorities for inciting revolution.

On the night of Rizal's arrest, the Katipunan, a secret nationalist brotherhood was founded. Based on Masonic rites and principles, the organization's goal was independence through any means necessary, including armed resistance and terrorist assassinations. Over the next several years, the group grew to 30,000 members until, in 1898, Spain learned of their existence and began arresting any person suspected of associating with the Katipunan. Jose Rizal was tried again for sedition, found guilty and executed. News of his death resulted in armed insurrections throughout the country. After months of skirmishes, Emilio Aguinaldo, who had risen to become the new leader of the Katipunan, agreed the group would lay down arms and leave the country.

However, in 1898, with the outbreak of war between Spain and the United States, Aguinaldo returned to the Philippines to support the Americans, thinking they would grant the Philippines their independence after the Spanish-American War. Aguinaldo's rebel forces routed the demoralized Spanish troops and seized Manila. On June 12, 1898, Aguinaldo declared the Philippine's independence; yet it soon became apparent that the United States was not going liberate the islands. A peace treaty was signed between Spain and America, ceding the Philippines (in addition to several other Spanish colonies) to the United States for twenty million dollars.

Filipino nationalists were incensed at the arrogance of the two imperial powers bargaining with each other for the island nation. On January 23, 1899, Emilio Aguinaldo proclaimed a constitutional government and the First Philippine Republic. The United States refused to recognize Aguinaldo's authority and on February 4, 1899, Aguinaldo declared war on United States forces in the islands. This resulted in two years of bloody battle. Aguinaldo was captured in combat on March 23, 1901. He agreed to swear allegiance to the United States and called on his soldiers to lay down their arms.

Recognizing the determination of the Filipino people to gain their independence, the United States government began preparing the Philippines for self-rule. To achieve this goal, American political institutions were introduced, beginning with a two-house legislature in 1916. An act separating church and state was implemented. The Philippine economy was opened to Western markets and classrooms were built to provide improvements in education. In 1935, the Philippines became a self-governing commonwealth and Manuel Quezon was elected President. A ten-year transition period, to end in 1946, was established during which the country would prepare for independence. The Philippines were on their way to total self-sufficiency when Japan intervened.

On December 8, 1941, just ten hours after the attack on Pearl Harbor, Japan bombed the Philippines from the air and invaded the island on December 22. Both American and Philippine troops joined together in resisting the invasion until 1942, when many of these soldiers were killed, imprisoned or were forced by starvation and illness to surrender. Forced to retreat, General Douglas McArthur vowed, "I shall return." In October 1944, McArthur did return to the Philippines with fresh troops who, along with local resistance fighters, engaged in fierce battle with Japanese troops, driving them from the country. When the firing had ceased and the smoke had cleared, most of Manila, where some of the heaviest fighting occurred, was leveled. An estimated sixty thousand Americans and one million Filipino lives had been lost in the years of battle.

As a result of the war, the country was heavily damaged and was suffering an internal organizational breakdown. Yet despite the shaken state of their country, the Filipino people wanted independence and were granted it by the United States on July 4, 1946. The country officially became the Republic of the Philippines. In 1962, the official Independence Day was changed from July 4 to June 12, to commemorate Emilio Aguinaldo's declaration of independence from Spain in 1898.

The taste of freedom from foreign rule was bittersweet for the people of the Philippines. The early years were dominated by the United States' assistance in postwar reconstruction. The communist-inspired Huk Rebellion (1945-53) complicated recovery efforts before its successful suppression by President Ramon Magsaysay (1953-57). With the execution of domestic reform programs and the expansion of Philippine ties to its Asian neighbors from the succeeding administrations of Presidents Carlos P. Garcia (1957-61) and Diosdado Macapagal (1961-65), the country gradually began to stabilize and progress.

Yet, in spite of this, lawlessness would soon sweep over the Philippines. It began during the eventful first term of Ferdinand E. Marcos (1965-86) who was reelected in 1969. Accusations of dishonest campaigning, favoritism and bribery roused criticism of Marcos from many. With an economy unable to grow as fast as the population, discontent was on the rise, along with labor strikes and student protests. Using these and other events as the reason, Marcos declared martial law in 1972, suppressing democratic institutions and restricting civil liberties among the citizens. Corruption and favoritism were rife under Marcos' presidency, which further led to a downward spiral in the country's economic growth and development. Marcos suspended the regular congress and replaced its members with a national assembly of his choosing under a newly created constitution in 1973. He used the military as his personal political machine and, along with his wife and supporters, developed monopolies in agricultural, manufacturing and financial sectors, bilking the nation's economy of billions of dollars. The unrest in the country was successfully held at bay by Marcos' administration until the assassination by a military escort of opposition leader Benigno Aquino in 1983. Thus began Marcos' downfall. His corrupt reign officially ended with the election of Aquino's widow, Corazon Aquino, in 1986. Under Aquino's administration, civil liberties and democratic institutions were restored to the country; however, there were also attempted coups led by members of the military.

One leading opposition group that first emerged during Marcos' administration and continued its resistance against the government through the 1980s was the Moro National Liberation Front (MNLF). They traditionally had equated the right to carry arms with their religious heritage and were suspicious of the government's intentions toward them. Organized by Abul Khayr Alonto and Jallaludin Santos, the MNLF's mission was to make the southern islands of the Philippines an independent state.

Fighting for an independent Moro nation, the MNLF received support from Muslim backers in Libya and Malaysia. Destruction and casualties, both military and civilian, as a result of guerrilla warfare were heavy and an estimated 50,000 people were killed. The government used a variety of nonmilitary tactics and announced economic aid programs and political concessions, along with incentives such as amnesty and land to those who would put down their arms. The government's programs plus a sharp decrease in the flow of arms from Malaysia set back the Moro movement. The conflict began to wane in the late 1970s and the MNLF tried to embrace popular politics and made peace with the government. However, not all of the members of the MNLF were in agreement with its party's decision. Some stayed with the group, pushing them to continue opposition to the government, while others broke away voicing their dissent.

A young, charismatic, Islamic Filipino, Abduragak Abubakar Janjalani formed a group in 1991 called the Abu Sayyaf, which was implacably opposed to peace initiatives between the government and the MNLF. The name, Abu Sayyaf means "Bearer of the Sword" in Arabic. Their goal: a sovereign Muslim state in the southern Philippines. Janjalani was said to have close ties with other Islamic radical leaders, many of whom he became acquainted with when he joined Afghanis in their fight against Russian occupation. From the beginning, Abu Sayyaf has been involved in armed resistance. This is not unusual in the southern islands of the Philippines where groups have been fighting the Catholic majority for thirty years. In 1995, the Abu Sayyaf was implicated in the assassination plot against Pope John Paul II, who was, at the time, visiting the Philippines.

Janjalani's militant group's funds came from front organizations heavily linked to the international terrorist organization al Qaeda. When Ramzi Yousef, the man convicted of bombing the World Trade Center in 1993, came to the Philippines, he was hosted by Janjalani, with whom he had trained in Khost, Afghanistan. Yousef told Janjalani that he wanted to attack United States airliners in the Philippines using Abu Sayyaf members.

The majority of the group lurks deep within the extreme southwest hemisphere of the Philippines—surrounding the islands of Basilan, Sulu and Tawi-Tawi. Both the BBC and the White House say that many of the Abu Sayyaf have close ties to mastermind terrorist leader, Osama bin Laden. Janjalani first met and worked with bin Laden while studying in Libya and Saudi Arabia before fighting in Afghanistan. Bin Laden's brother-in-law, Mohammed Jamal Khalifa, reportedly met directly with the group. Because of these past ties and strong suspicions that the group still receives funding from al Qaeda, the United States has become more heavily involved in scrutinizing the region.

Although the group sometimes abducts Filipinos, they prefer to kidnap Westerners for whom they can claim more ransom. In fact, one spokesman for the Abu Sayyaf said, "We have been trying hard to get an American, because they may think we are afraid of them. We want to fight the American people." The Abu Sayyaf's long-standing affection for the Pakistani terrorist, Yousef, is reflected in the fact that they demanded Yousef's release from the United States, where he is held, as one of their conditions for releasing an American hostage. However, American leaders refuse to negotiate with the terrorists. Yousef is still in jail serving a 240-year sentence, keeping him in solitary confinement for the rest of his life.

Calling them common bandits and thieves, the Philippine government also has refused to negotiate with the Abu Sayyaf. When the government made this declaration, a wave of bombings and kidnappings followed. In April 1995, Janjalani launched his first full-scale attack and destroyed the center of Ipil, a predominantly Christian town, taking away thirty hostages and killing fifty-three civilians and soldiers. The group grew in number when a peace agreement between the government and the MNLF was made in 1996, in which the MNLF renounced the idea of an Islamic state, leading disgruntled separatists to join the more radical Abu Sayyaf.

In December 1998, Janjalani and his radicals clashed with police on Basilan Island and he was killed. A power struggle within the regime ensued, with Janjalani's younger brother, Khadafy Janjalani, emerging as the new leader of the group. He is on the "Most Wanted" list of Islamic radicals sought by the United States government. Since then, the group has split into three rival factions. Although the army has captured and killed many of the guerrillas, that hasn't stopped the remaining ones' thirst for kidnappings and demanding hefty ransoms.

In 2000, the group became the center of international attention, when they kidnapped twenty-one people, including foreign tourists from a Malaysian resort and transported them to the Abu Sayyaf's main base on Jolo Island. The hostages were eventually released by the group for the hefty sum of twenty million dollars, which, according to the military, served as a means of arming the rebels for new guerrilla warfare.

Their group's next newsmaking act was the capture of two American missionaries, Martin and Gracia Burnham, and a Filipina nurse, Deborah Yap, in 2001. The hostages were held under the leadership of Abu Sabaya until June 2002, when Philippine troops trained by United States advisors seized the opportunity to attempt a rescue. The plan backfired, leading to a shoot-out and the deaths of Martin Burnham and Ediborah Yap. Gracia Burnham survived but was wounded in the leg from crossfire. Two weeks later on June 21, Abu Sabaya was spotted by Philippine naval forces in the waters off Sibuco. A gun battle ensued and Sabaya was shot and killed. After the guerrilla murderer's death, United States President, George W. Bush, praised Philippine President Gloria Macapagal Arroyo for her victory in the war against terrorism. "There was a group of killers named Abu Sayyaf in her country. They kidnapped, they killed. And today, their leader met his maker, thanks to one of our coalition partners."

In addition to taking hostages, the Abu Sayyaf has also made bomb attacks on Roman Catholic churches and airports. Thus, in its war on terrorism outside Afghanistan and Pakistan, the United States has identified and targeted the group, placing a five million dollar bounty on the leaders of Abu Sayyaf. In addition, marines, pilots and engineers, numbering over one thousand, are training and supporting Philippine troops to combat guerrilla insurgencies. The United States has also sent to the Philippines surveillance and satellite technology to locate, track and eliminate these terrorist guerrillas.

In 2002, as the Philippine government continued trying to crack down on terrorist activities within its borders, the United States was also monitoring the Abu Sayyaf's moves, hoping to stop any related terrorist threats. And as 2003 unfolds, the United States has stepped up its efforts to eradicate the Abu Sayyaf after new attacks on missionaries and the bombing of Davao airport in the southern Philippines. After coming to an agreement with President Gloria Macapagal Arroyo, Pentagon officials announced in late February 2003 that American troops would soon be deployed to the Philippines to join Philippine forces in active combat "to disrupt and destroy" the remaining members of the Abu Sayyaf. Meanwhile, the Abu Sayyaf is hiding, deep within the thick foliage of the Philippine jungle—waiting for the right opportunity to strike back.

However, seven years earlier, in 1996, little news of the serious political instability of the region reached Western ears and the threats of hostage-taking by Abu Sayyaf terrorists was only vaguely known. Thus, Greg Williams was largely ignorant of the peril he might face when he boarded a plane to the Philippines. He naively believed he was simply answering a call to aid a Christian missionary in helping the poor of the beautiful island country, never realizing the mortal dangers lurking in his future...

Part One

Chapter One

Early Dreams

Almost every day of my early childhood seemed filled with awe and delight. Perhaps it was the adventurous nature I had back then that was the beginning of an insatiable curiosity about the world in which I lived. But like everything else in my life, every new discovery appeared to come at a price. And the older I became, the more serious and painful the cost seemed to be.

I grew up an ordinary American boy in a middle-class family. We made our home in a small Midwestern town in Illinois. My childhood was a very normal one, despite the fact that I witnessed some bad times between my mother and father, and I had a little brother with whom I have always wanted to be closer.

My brother and I have always loved each other and tried to be supportive despite our differences, but the truth is we have always been two very dissimilar people. However, in our youth, we had many good times together like the days we

played football after school and the many other games we
played in our neighborhood with the local kids. It was fun to
have a brother who was a companion and could participate in
those childhood adventures.

But all was not play. As a child, doctors found that I had
serious allergies. After testing me, one physician jokingly told
my mom, "Your son is allergic to everything God put on earth!"
And so I was required to have three injections every week for
about three years. The aggressive immunization program gave
me the ability to consume normal things like milk and corn.

My allergies contributed to some pretty miserable sum-
mers and it seemed each year they got worse, forcing me to
take heavier and heavier doses of antihistamines just to
breathe. But I persevered and I did not let the allergies keep me
from participating in sports and playing in the many parks that
dotted our town.

During my childhood I learned discipline and how to
take care of myself. My mother was a meticulous housekeeper
who taught both my brother and me how to do laundry and
other housecleaning chores. The efficient organizational skills
and cleaning procedures I learned from my mother served me
well later in life when I became a leading manager and teacher
of housekeeping, laundry and facilities management in the
health care industry.

I learned mental toughness and physical discipline
from my father and further honed those skills playing baseball
and wrestling on the high school varsity teams. For me, sports
were a great way to learn about life. I learned teamwork,
sportsmanship and how to prepare physically and mentally for
facing opponents.

Young and feeling indestructible, I stubbornly refused to let my imperfect health keep me from achieving my goals.

My time in school was both exciting and terrifying. Because I was shy and introverted, I often became the butt of others' jokes or pranks. But I tried to take such incidents in stride. I developed a good, healthy sense of humor about myself and tried not to be confrontational. However, I lost my temper and actually participated in a physical fight when I was in grade school. It happened the day I found a ten-year-old boy beating up my little, eight-year-old brother during recess. Afterward I regretted raising my fists in anger, but in the end I felt my actions were justified. Besides, it felt good to defend someone I loved.

Childhood days came and went. By junior high school I was enjoying the mounting challenges that were facing me in the classroom, in social spheres and on playing fields. But unlike my one fight in grade school, I had a showdown with another bully in junior high school which turned out very differently.

One day a boy who was known as a troublemaker in our school tripped me while I was going up the stairs. I reacted in a very measured way, ignoring the boy and calmly going about my business. Yet, as I continued up the stairs and down a hallway, the bully followed and began taunting me. When he shook his finger in my face, I suddenly lost my cool. Grabbing him by the arm, I swung him into some lockers.

Both he and the kids around us were shocked by my move. Recovering, he put his fists in the air ready to fight. The kids in the crowd forming around us began cheering for a scuffle.

"I hope he kicks his ass!" said one boy. I thought they were talking about the bully, but then I heard both a boy and a girl rooting for me to their friends: "The blonde haired kid is the good guy!" they whispered excitedly. I was shocked to hear that I was the favorite in the contest.

With fire in my eyes I raised my fists. We circled each other waiting to see who would throw the first punch. Then the bully, pointing to my head, stated, "You're just a stupid towhead!" making a joking taunt about my blond hair.

It was such a ridiculous statement that suddenly I felt sorry for him. I dropped my hands, looked him in the eye and said, "Grow up and stop acting so stupid." I turned my back on him and walked away leaving the boy stunned and the group of kids in the hallway both surprised and a little disappointed. It was during that encounter in my junior high school hallway that I realized violence is not the right answer when responding to people who are both ignorant and narrowminded. From that point on, I had found a philosophy by which I wanted to live my life.

In high school I made up my mind to work harder and shoot for a college education. I went from a C student to a B+ student during my sophomore year. Although I had begun to discover girls, athletics was still my passion. I worked hard to be a better student and an even better athlete. In my junior year I joined the wrestling team and was a bit surprised to find myself undefeated midway through the season.

My year in wrestling continued with exciting landmarks. Once I went to a meet where I competed with some of the top wrestlers in the state and I won the tournament championship. My Dad and I were very proud when we cut out an article in the local newspaper about my unexpected win. I began looking into wrestling scholarships to help me get into a good college.

But then my right shoulder began to ache. It was something that developed slowly over several weeks, but it reached a point where the pain really bothered me during wrestling moves. Doctors X-rayed my shoulder several times, but could never find anything wrong with it. I continued wrestling with only one arm fully engaged and with my shoulder still bothering me, yet I still won. Finally, another doctor performed a series of extensive tests which showed much more damage than was previously thought. He performed orthopedic surgery a few weeks later. I still carry the screw and two staples which hold my shoulder together. Though I tried to return to sports the next year, it was discovered that I also had joint weakness. Sadly, I was not able to continue wrestling. It was during my recovery period that I discovered a new outlet: playing the drums.

That was the year I also found that my passion for the opposite sex was growing. Even so, I aspired to have high morals and ethics. I did not drink or do drugs. My life as a teenager was a cornucopia of new adventures, sports triumphs, sports injuries, girls and rock and roll. It was a wonderful time in my life, despite painful physical injuries and the even greater pains of my first few romantic heartbreaks.

I will never forget the words my father spoke to me at that crucial period in my life. They still inspire me to this day: "The best thing you can do with your life is to help other people." I took his words to heart and made many of my early decisions based on nonviolence and caring about my fellow human beings.

In my last year of high school I finally was able to save enough money to buy a good drum set. As I began planning my career in music, I tried to learn the skills that would later help me succeed.

During the summer after I graduated from high school, I became part of a three-piece band. The unusual thing about this group was that we were not interested in just playing other artists' music to get jobs. We vowed to be original and create our own music. At first, this did not help us to get gigs. But after much persistence and some good promoting, our band finally went on tour and won several "battle of the band" contests.

My career took off from there. I put college on hold and was soon living the dream of a rising rock star. Recording and touring became goals that I would eventually reach and surpass. After a good outing with my first band, I went on to join other groups, some achieving a good deal of success.

And, of course, I had no shortage of female admirers. I also felt that I was helping people by inspiring them with the music that I played. It was an exciting and satisfying time.

Eventually I found success in both concert bands and more commercial bands that toured major clubs throughout the country. I rubbed elbows with famous musicians and became successful enough in two different bands which garnered our own agents, road crews, limousine services and even fan clubs.

I was able to resist, most of the time, the women, drugs and craziness that went on during those tours. But I had begun drinking to loosen myself up. I thought I had my drinking under control until one fateful night at a club in Champaign,

Illinois. I was preparing for our last set around midnight when, as I sat down on my stool and went to reach for my drumsticks, I realized I could barely see anything. I had become so inebriated that I could not function, let alone play an instrument. It hit me like a ton of bricks, one of those moments in life that you never forget.

I sat there staring at the blurred drumsticks in my hand and realized that I was in trouble. The very type of person I had tried so hard not to become was emerging from within. It was a revelation, and even in my drunken stupor, I knew that I had to take drastic action.

I stopped drinking immediately and fortunately our tour ended shortly after that. When I came home, I began to question whether I really wanted to be a musician. I recalled the many people that I had met in the clubs and how every new town seemed to have the same faces. The drunken, horny, sad people that I saw every night had the same characteristics, no matter where we played.

I realized by then that I was not really helping others with our music, because I was playing in places where drinking, drugs and sex were like a plague that infected the people who gathered there. How could I feel good anymore about what I was doing? I had come to a crossroads in my life. After almost three years on the road, I was burned out. I needed a change.

A few nights later while I was waiting for sleep to overcome me, I had my first vision.

Out of the darkness over my bed a glowing
light appeared and a strong but tranquil voice

spoke to me. It told me to change my life, change everything about it and go in a totally different direction.

The voice told me that the peace and satisfaction I was seeking did indeed lie in helping other people. "Go South, far away from your home and seek out a place where you can become part of God's work."

It was a manifestation so clear and true that I had no doubt in my mind that the vision disclosed the right path for me. Suddenly, I remembered a man with whom I used to work who had moved to Florida. He had mentioned once in passing that his company was looking for potential employees who could relocate to Orlando. At the time, I was fully immersed in my music career and thought nothing of his comments. Now, tired of traveling in snow and ice storms and concerned about continuing a career that kept me immersed in a bar culture of sex and alcohol, my heart jumped at the chance for this new start in a new place far to the south which I hoped would be the very destination told about in the vision. I felt my prayers were answered.

The next day I told my parents about my new plan and to my surprise, they seemed genuinely enthused about the idea. However, they tried to tell me to be realistic about my chances for success and to not put too much stock in the vision I'd experienced. Nevertheless, I was absolutely confident that my dreams for the future now awaited me in Florida.

Chapter Two

The Path of Destiny

Like many of the strange twists of fate my life has taken, my move to Florida ended up not being what I thought it would be. From my parents' home in Illinois, I spoke to the man in Orlando who set up a tentative meeting with me the following week. But he told me something that gave me pause. He said, "Our wages here in Orlando are not like the North. You might try Fort Lauderdale first, because their hospital wages probably will be higher."

I took his advice. Through a contact in Fort Lauderdale, I was hired at a hospital there and given two weeks to get my affairs in order in Illinois and move. Once again, despite some initial roadblocks, things seemed to have turned out for the best. I was starting a new and exciting life in the south, just as the vision instructed.

It seemed during that period I could do no wrong. Working hard, I found my new field to be challenging and renumerative. In addition, I felt I was doing something good with my life by helping others.

While working in the hospital in Fort Lauderdale I was blessed to meet people who saw something special in me and advised me to get into supervision and management. I was referred to a contract company that, at the time, was the world's leading cleaning service for hospitals. Their Christian philosophy and caring attitude matched my own.

Thanks to their leadership and friendship, I became a good manager and leader of people. I could feel the wonder of God's powerful touch with every step I took. As my career kept climbing to new heights, I married and settled down to raise a family. I worked even harder to build a solid reputation. I won some awards and reached a point in my life where I could say "I am a success." Headhunters and other companies constantly contacted me in order to entice me with new job offers.

But there was a down side to my success during those years also—the steady strain of long hours at work with little personal time.

One night, after a seminar, I had a drink with some friends who invited me to a bar near the hotel where the seminar was held. Even though I hadn't had a drink since my musician days, I didn't think there would be much harm in having one with friends. What I didn't realize was the allergy medicine I was taking at the time dramatically exaggerated the effects of alcohol. After I left the bar I was pulled over almost immediately by a policeman who asked me to get out of my car. He then did a few tests to see if I was impaired. I was. In fact, I was glad that he stopped me, because I was beginning to feel strangely.

However, I was less pleased when I was arrested and taken to a jail where they had me take a Breathalyzer test. I tried to explain that my disoriented state was caused by the mixture of prescription medication and alcohol that impaired my responses, but the police paid no attention. A few days later I was convicted of driving under the influence and had to pay a fine and perform community service. It was a humiliating experience.

Though I took responsibility for being partially at fault and not learning the side effects of my medication, I felt that my punishment was far too severe for this misjudgment. My faith in myself and in the fairness of our judicial system was shaken. It was a traumatic emotional event that had a very negative effect on my self-esteem. However, my life went on and I was eventually able to recover from the embarrassment and humiliation of the conviction. It did not affect my career, but I began to feel depressed. At the time, I thought that my recurring nightmares and negative thoughts were caused by the arrest incident. In retrospect, however, I now believe that this was the beginning of the onset of a hereditary form of depression.

Soon my job began to lose its appeal. I felt I needed something new and more challenging so I decided to make another change in my career and location. I accepted an employment offer from a good hospital in Miami and threw myself into my new job feeling again the excitement of starting over. The depression seemed to fade as I got my life back on track and my success at my new job brought more responsibilities and rewards. Even though I was working hard, I wanted children more than anything. My wife and I decided we were ready to start a family.

A short time later, my workload increased even more when I became involved with computerized facilities management, because the person originally given the responsibility at our hospital did not have the time to do it. My success in this new area soon attracted more headhunters seeking me out to work for other organizations. But I decided to stay at the hospital that so far had treated me very well.

My wife and I soon had a baby on the way and I felt again like I was on top of the world. My biggest goal, that of being a successful businessman and good father, was about to be reached. I remember thinking, *If I die now I will be happy!* I had a lovely wife, a great job, money, status, prestige and soon I would also have a child. I felt I had everything a man could want. But as they say, be careful what you wish for. I made the mistake of thinking that I had finally made it.

Soon after our child was born my wife experienced severe postpartum depression. Her deeply sad state of mind did not last for just a few months, but for over a year. Our relationship began to break down from the strain of her depression, having a new child and a job that kept me out of the house much of the time. Though I didn't realize it at the time, my depression was returning as well. Soon, I started feeling dejected and eventually, hopeless. I did not understand what was happening to me. I blamed myself for not appreciating the good life I had and could not understand why I had become so unhappy. However, between the pressure of my demanding career and the responsibilities of being a new father, I was coming apart emotionally. My wife, who was having her own emotional difficulties, became terribly withdrawn. Then one night when our son was two, he developed a high fever.

My wife went to the pharmacy to buy him some medicine. While she was gone, he had a seizure.

While I waited for my wife to return, I grabbed our cordless phone and put my son into the empty bathtub. Still holding him while he was convulsing, I ran cool water over a washcloth and then held the washcloth to his fevered head. With one hand holding his head up and the other holding the washcloth, I watched helplessly as his body continued to twitch violently. When the cool water from the washcloth didn't help, I freed one hand, picked up the cordless phone and dialed 911.

An operator took the call asking what was wrong. I could only say, "Please come fast! My son is convulsing from a fever. Please hurry!" In no more than three or four minutes, I could hear the siren of the ambulance on its way to my home.

I watched as paramedics worked on my son, but even after several minutes he was still convulsing. I felt powerless to help and could only pray to God that my child would live and not become brain dead.

My wife pulled up just as the ambulance was driving away to go to the hospital. Despite the quick thinking on my part and the immediate arrival of the paramedics who applied emergency measures, our son was still convulsing. I feared that there was a strong chance he would not make it. I blamed myself, feeling that I had not done enough, fast enough. It was an agony of helplessness I will never forget. In her own pain and anguish and helplessness, my wife turned her anger about the situation on me. I also believe she lashed out because she felt she should have been home at the time. Like most new mothers, I think she felt that if she had been there things might have turned out differently. Realistically, her presence or lack of it made no difference and although I tried to tell her that, she still felt badly. She was afraid about what might happen to our son and, like me, had difficulty dealing with her emotions.

During the next twenty-four hours, my son was put into a drug-induced coma. We watched and prayed for him to show signs of life. And then miraculously, slowly and surely, he came out of the coma on his own. After running tests, the doctors said our son did not suffer any brain damage. But his recovery was long and slow, even after we were able to bring him home.

With a sick child and deteriorating marriage, things were looking so bad I could see no way out. My depression worsened and I felt as thought I were trapped in deep, dark pit. Finally, I decided that it was best for everyone, including me, if I was dead. One night, I took all the sleeping pills and medication that I could find in the house and decided to end my life. A cold, calm feeling swept over my body as the drugs took hold. I was no longer conflicted for the first time in a great while. And it felt good.

My wife found me and I woke up in a hospital with tubes down my throat and nose, gagging and vomiting. I was very sick, but I did recover and was transferred to an adjoining psychiatric hospital. After a week, I went home.

Within days my wife made it clear that our marriage was over. With a heart that was breaking and the cloud of depression still hanging over my head, I moved out and rented an apartment. I tried only to concentrate on my treatment. I told myself I had to get well for my child's sake. Even though I was lonely, I began to regain at least part of my former self. I returned to work and threw myself into my job, trying my best to support my dependents. But during the divorce my depression returned and my financial woes piled up. Still, somehow I went on. Time passed.

When I wasn't working on my recovery from depression, I was concentrating on work. After avoiding social engagements and dating for quite some time after the divorce, I began to feel very lonely. Then one day on a business trip, I met a young Latin American woman who seemed to be both old-fashioned and a good Christian. Thinking she might be the right antidote to help me pull my life together, we married and I brought her to Florida to live with me.

But my financial problems didn't shrink, they grew. Having reached a point where I was unable to pay my debts, I filed for bankruptcy so that I would be able to provide for my new bride and my child from my first marriage. It was a time filled with many mixed emotions as I struggled desperately not to repeat the same mistakes I had made in the past.

Unfortunately, my new marriage was rocky from the start. Now my life became a difficult balancing act trying to keep my new wife happy while spending time and money supporting my child and treating my own depression.

Late one night while in the bathroom, I broke down and went to pieces emotionally. "Why Lord?" I sobbed as I knelt on the cold tile floor of the small room. On my knees in the bathroom that night I prayed and cried and cursed my luck because of the difficult problems I was facing. I kept asking God why this was happening to me. Finally, seeking comfort, I turned to the Bible and, with the passage of time, things began to get a little better. The enjoyment I got from my work and from my new married life, helped my depression to lessen. My wife and I soon had a baby, a son, which helped to further fuel my growing contentment. But just as I was enjoying happiness again, another cruel twist of fate was skulking around the corner.

Chapter Three

Nightmares

The beginning of the end began for me during the first week of November 1993. It was a normal week at work except for some safety issues that I observed while making rounds in the hospital. A construction project in the hospital was being supervised by the engineering department and facilities management. I came upon construction materials being stored in one of the hospital stairwells blocking the fire exit, a violation of fire safety laws.

I reported the problem to the engineering manager and the facilities manager in the hopes that it would be taken care of. But after several days and two trips to their offices the material had yet to be moved. I knew that the hospital could be fined if this was discovered by city officials.

Finally, at the end of the week, out of frustration I took the problem straight to the administrator of the hospital. He told me he would look into it. Later that Friday, he called to inform me that he had discussed the problem with all involved and that the material would be moved by that following Monday. I was relieved that at last some action would finally be taken over the weekend.

That Monday, I arrived around 6:00 A.M. and began catching up on some paperwork in my office. Around 8:00 A.M., Tom, my assistant for the dayshift, came in. We chatted about the weekend and numerous work-related topics. Before making our morning rounds in the hospital, I asked Tom to come with me while I checked the stairwell where the construction materials had been illegally stored. I felt that there might still be some clean up required and I wanted him to be there with me to assess how to assign this task.

We made our way to the first floor walking down the corridor to the stairwell to inspect it. Opening the door from the hallway into the stairwell we found that indeed most of the materials had been removed as promised. However, in addition to the normal dirt and dust I expected to be left behind, there were long, thin pipes still lying on the floor along the wall. Then Tom and I peeked around the corner under the stairs and saw more pipes and debris.

Backing away from the underside of the stairwell, I turned toward Tom and said, "Look, there's more debris." Taking another step backward I suddenly slipped on one of several pipes that lay on the ground behind me. My legs flew out from underneath me and I fell sideways against the wall, my body twisting awkwardly backward as I slumped to the ground.

As I sat there stunned by what happened, I felt a sharp pain shoot up my back and down my leg. Trying to get to my feet, the pain shot through me again. In agony, I fell to the floor. "Oh my God!" I blurted out, as Tom rushed to my side and tried to help me up.

I sat there frozen, in pain and gasping. "I can't move. This is excruciating!"

"I'll go get help," Tom said and rushed out of the stairwell. He and several other hospital employees showed up a few minutes later with a wheelchair. They helped me into the chair and then Tom pushed me over to the Emergency Department.

During the next couple of hours X-rays were taken and I was given medication for the pain. But when the doctor came back to report on the X-rays, he did not have good news. "You have a badly herniated disc in a very unusual place in your back," he explained. "I can see now why you are in so much pain." The doctor then went on to give me three choices: 1. Go home and try to rehabilitate the injury with rest and physical therapy. 2. Have surgery on my back with a recovery period of as much as a year. 3. Have laser surgery on the damaged disc, which was less invasive and would help me get back to work within months. The laser would shave away the protruding disc, thereby relieving the pressure on the nerves.

I chose option #3 in the hopes that I could get back to work as soon as possible. The surgery was scheduled for the next week.

Unfortunately, during the surgery the doctors hit an artery and I began bleeding profusely. They could not complete the procedure until they had transfused me with massive quantities of blood and stopped the bleeding. Then the procedure was hastily completed, but proved not to be successful. Several nerves had been damaged which would eventually lead to my being disabled years later. I have never blamed the doctors for this. After working in hospitals for much of my life, I know that sometimes these things happen. After a couple of weeks, I went home to recover.

Eventually, after about four weeks I was able to use my computer to work from home. There were numerous monthly and weekly reports that needed to be completed and only I could do them. I made sure that I kept in daily contact with the staff so as to keep up to date on events and the record keeping necessary to provide reports to the hospital administration. By the third month of my recovery, I convinced my doctors that I could return to work.

I had two bosses. Roger was employed by the independent company that contracted me to work for the hospital. He supervised my work since his company was the one that paid me.

Prior to moving to Miami, I had had a very successful career with this company at another hospital. When I moved to Miami and again began working for the company, they reinstated my benefits based on my previous seven years of service. Unfortunately, I would soon find out that the company and many of the managers had changed. It was not the same people-oriented company that I had left years before.

My other boss, Don, was the administrator of the hospital. This was the customary arrangement between a contract service company and a hospital. On a daily basis I reported to Don as he was my on-site boss. Only when it came to company policies did I have to get Roger, my company boss, involved. But there was always a monthly meeting in which all three of us would meet to discuss progress and plans for the future.

During the year following my accident and surgery, I noticed a different attitude from Don. It was as if he was trying to put some distance between us. There was a lack of appreciation and gratitude for the extra effort I had put in to compensate for my time on medical leave.

I kept asking myself why he and some other hospital administrators seemed to have less confidence in me. Were they embarrassed about the accident that had happened to me in their hospital? Why would they treat me this way when it was my work in the hospital that had almost cost me my life?

Was that the very reason that they were now treating me in such a standoffish way? Was it because they felt the hospital could be held liable, because the hospital doctors had botched my surgery? I also found out later from a laboratory technician that during my back surgery I had been given the wrong type of blood. This was another shocking revelation and further fueled my doubts.

As the year progressed I tried to accustom myself to the strained, alienated relationship I felt had developed between my bosses and me. I did all that I could to continuously improve on my work. But then one evening the unthinkable happened.

While preparing for the arrival of some VIP visitors, I performed a walk-through of the meeting facilities with Don. There were a few minor problems including a spot on the carpet of the meeting room. I personally went over these items with my night manager who was quite capable of carrying out any requests I made of him. But given the important nature of the visitors, I made sure that I returned later that evening just to check that the spot in the carpet had been removed.

It was about 8:00 P.M. when I arrived at the hospital. I went directly to the meeting room to check to make sure the cleaning had been done properly.

Some things had been completed, but the spot was still visible. I contacted the night manager and we talked about the problem again. He assured me that it would be cleaned up before he left that evening.

After reviewing all of the other preparations being made for the VIP arrival, I was confident that all was going well. Like many similar occasions before, I had no reason to doubt that everything, including the spot on the carpet, would be properly taken care of. After a personal appeal by my night manager that I should trust him and that everything would get done, I finally left for home.

The next day all hell broke loose. Don blasted me for not being there to personally supervise the spot cleaning. He refused to speak to me and branded me irresponsible for this first and only lapse in my performance. Although this man was the same administrator who had failed to get the construction material out of the stairwell where I fell and injured my back, he was turning a minor problem into a huge ordeal.

Suddenly, I was a scapegoat for one small mistake and from that point on I tried in vain to speak to Don in person to rectify the matter. But he always refused, instead hiring Mark, another administrator, to be his assistant and to whom I now had to report. Especially since my performance evaluation a month before this incident indicated my continued above average performance, I had a growing suspicion that I was being set up to be fired.

I was reminded of similar incidents I had witnessed as a manager in the past. I remembered how some administrators would simply not like the look of an employee and then find reasons to fire the person. This was morally wrong, but I had seen it happen time and time again with hospital administrators who were intoxicated with their own power. I had become skilled at dealing with these big egos on a daily basis.

I also recalled that some past employees who had been hurt on the job were subsequently mistreated by management. Some managers viewed those employees more as potential liabilities rather than valuable workers. One manager to whom I reported once told me, "Start a paper trail on him and let's get him out of here." I felt this manager's only reason for firing the unsuspecting employee was the manager's fear that a lawsuit would soon be coming. It was a very cold business approach toward a very human problem. And now I found myself on the receiving end of it and felt dejected. About that time, my back and leg pain began escalating, returning to the level I had experienced just after my accident. And on top of that, my second marriage was beginning to fall apart.

During those difficult months, while I struggled to get back the faith of my superiors, my wife put our infant son in day care and began working. She was growing distant and our relationship seemed to sour. Maybe she was frightened by my sudden frailty in body and mind. Maybe it was just her strong-willed, independent nature that began to steer her away from me and toward other goals.

Of course, her rejection was for me a double blow. I had experienced a similar coldness when my ex-wife had become depressed and withdrawn after the birth of our child. Then my own depression returned rendering me incapable of thinking clearly about myself and my life. I began to truly believe I could not be either a good father or a good husband.

My behavior became erratic and highly emotional. I went from crying spells to fits of anger. I was afraid that I again would need to be hospitalized and blamed myself for everything that was going wrong both in my marriage and my life. For even my career success, something I felt I could always count on as a source of strength, was crumbling. In addition, I felt betrayed by my own body. I was becoming crippled physically and emotionally. I had never felt so helpless and vulnerable.

Realizing I needed professional help, I went to a nearby clinic. As my doctors tried to address the deterioration in my physical and mental condition, they ended up telling me that I was becoming disabled. Disabled? It was a word that I could not bring to my lips. Not me! No, it was just not possible!

And worst of all, I was too embarrassed and ashamed to discuss the details of my problems with my parents and friends. I didn't want them to know what I was going through. I simply could not swallow my pride and tell even those close to me the embarrassing details of my misfortunes. Meanwhile, I was losing sensation and strength in my left leg to the point where I sometimes could not walk. I kept telling myself the mental anguish and physical paralysis were just temporary. They would go away. My pride would not allow me to face the reality of what was happening to me.

Finally, thinking that if I could improve just one major problem, things in general might get better, I arranged for marital counseling. Because we had a small child, my wife and I needed desperately to try to save our marriage. My wife agreed to go, but we only attended one session.

The counseling session was a complete disaster and then on top of this, the counselor simply gave up. He told me, "Your wife is overwhelmed with anger and resentment and I do not think it will be beneficial to continue our sessions." I was crestfallen; I thought the purpose of marital counseling was to get the two people's feelings out on the table instead of keeping them bottled inside. My feelings of hopelessness and depression were now compounded.

For the next several months my wife and I lived our lives in mechanical and emotionless ways. I was miserable. But thanks to the medication I was taking I managed to hold on to my sanity. Depression or not, I was determined to take care of my children. During those trying times my church and my bible were my only sources of emotional support. Without them I would surely have cracked under the weight of all my problems.

But the worst was yet to come.

On Christmas day, the final blow fell. After unwrapping gifts with our child, my wife announced that she was taking my son and moving out. When I asked her why, she said she just wanted to be free.

I was crushed by her announcement. The timing seemed incredibly cruel. But worst of all, once again, my child was being taken away from me. Still wearing a back support and barely able to walk, I was in a panic. I called the police while she was trying to leave with our son. When the police arrived, I cried, "My wife is kidnapping our baby!" I blurted it out in my hurt, upset state of mind. But the police told me there was nothing they could do. It was not against the law for a mother to take a child and leave a husband.

And so, my world came crashing down. I felt dazed, angry, sad and confused.

For the next several weeks I could not shake my incredible sense of loss and heartbreak over what happened. I tried in vain to keep in touch with my wife and see my son, but she seemed to be avoiding me.

Soon I found it increasingly difficult to even get up in the morning. One day at work I finally broke down and told Mark, my new boss, about my predicament. He was aware that I had been struggling with my back and leg pain and that my physical condition was deteriorating; however, he had had no knowledge of my troubled marriage. Now, learning that my wife had left me, Mark seemed very sympathetic to my distraught emotional state.

Meanwhile, my financial situation was getting worse and worse. I moved to a smaller place and held a couple of garage sales in order to raise money. The money I got was just a temporary bandage and my work was suffering because of the emotional turmoil I was in. Mark had given me a day off here and a day off there trying to help me deal with my situation. I felt he was the only one who seemed to have any sympathy for what I was going through.

One day, I received notice from my wife that she was filing for divorce. Now added to my despair was the cost of retaining a lawyer and negotiating with my wife about my visitation rights with my son. I also now had to pay child support to both my children's mothers and my salary had drastically shrunk.

I didn't know what to do. I had already filed for bankruptcy once a few years earlier in order to have enough money to pay child support for my older son and to provide a decent life for my new wife and child. Now I was drowning in legal expenses, medical expenses, childcare expenses and both of my ex-wives were suing me to get more money.

My doctors told me that I should be able to get a short leave of absence due to new labor laws dealing with disabilities. With my doctors' encouragement and the knowledge that there were now laws protecting me, I felt safe in approaching Roger asking for a "Reasonable Accommodation" at work due to my depression and partial paralysis. With my emotional stability collapsing, I really needed some time to recuperate. The next day I explained to Roger that the depression I had been suffering hadn't abated. I asked for a leave of absence, but he said they couldn't spare me that long.

Not being able to get him to agree to that, I then asked Mark about taking a week of vacation that I had coming. I explained that I had a number of appointments with doctors and lawyers that had piled up. He was more than understanding and said, "Do it. You deserve some peace."

Unfortunately, Roger, the boss who worked for the contract company, was not as accommodating. When I told him that Mark had agreed to let me take my vacation week, Roger was hesitant about allowing me to do it. But since my hospital boss had already approved the request, there was not much Roger could do. He knew that I had over two weeks of vacation coming and since I was only requesting one week of it, arguing against it seemed rather unreasonable.

My vacation was a little over a week in length, but it did have a therapeutic effect on me and I returned to my job feeling better. But the very first day back I had another emotional shock.

While in my office I received a phone call from my company boss who proceeded to question the reasons for my vacation. I explained again that I had needed to complete a number of appointments and take some time to relax. But Roger pressed me again about the exact details. I was insulted that he suddenly was treating me like a child who had to explain his actions. "Look, I took care of personal business," I said.

Then he began pressing me about where I went. To which I answered that I did not feel I needed to disclose such details of my personal life to him. He shocked me by saying, "If you do not tell me where you went and what you did by the end of this week, you will be fired!"

In frustration I turned to Mark, the only other person at work that I thought I could trust. I sat down with him and explained what Roger had said to me. He seemed surprised. At the end of our conversation, Mark told me he was sure that this problem could be worked out. I will never forget his last words to me. He said, "Go home, cool off and just don't do something stupid."

Try as I might, I could not believe Mark's reassurances. As I drove home from work that day I could feel myself coming apart. I could not control the tears that poured from my eyes. My mind felt like it was going to explode. My body was shaking uncontrollably.

I barely made it to my door when I became nauseous, weak and faint. I felt that I was on the verge of a nervous breakdown and might do "something stupid" like attempt suicide.

Hopelessness and sadness overwhelmed me. Waves of despair washed over me reducing me to a quivering, crying mass of raw nerves.

For a long while I sat in the dark agonizing. Why were my wife and now my employer treating me so badly? Was I that awful a person?

I tried going to bed hoping I could get some rest. I knew that if I did, my problems would probably seem much smaller in the morning. But I was too agitated to sleep. After turning and tossing for hours, I took several sleeping pills to reduce my emotional agitation. I had no intention of killing myself. I was angry and hurt but not stupid. I would not give anyone the satisfaction of getting to me so badly that I would end my life. Soon my problems faded away into the bliss of a deep, soothing sleep.

I awoke to find my assistant, Tom, standing next to my bed, shaking me. In a groggy voice I asked, "What are you doing in my apartment?" He told me that I had left the front door open.

"I knocked for a while but there was no answer, so I tried the door and walked in. We were concerned about you, because you didn't come to work this morning or answer the phone." He explained that the administrator had sent him to my house to check on me. "It's late afternoon now, time for a shift change at the hospital."

I could not believe I had slept so long, but I could not seem to move out of the bed.

Tom peered down at me. "Are you alright?" he asked nervously.

"I'm fine, I'm fine. I'm just very sleepy."

"Okay. Could you give me your keys to our office filing cabinets? I need to get some things."

"Sure," I groggily replied. "They're over there on the bureau."

He told me not to worry about work and that he would see me the next day. As he left I drifted back into a deep sleep. Some time later, I was again awakened, this time by knocking at the front door. Slowly I made my way from the bed to the door and to my surprise I found an ambulance crew standing there.

"Are you okay?" one of the medical technicians asked me.

"Yes, I am," I said, a little confused about their presence. "Why are you here?"

They said someone had called about me and asked that the paramedics come and check me out just to make sure I was okay. Again I told them I was fine.

The events that occurred in the next twenty-four hours were so absurd and outrageous, they could have been a scripted comedy of hilarious proportions. In addition to all I had been through with my botched surgery, my divorce and my job problems, the circumstances of that day conspired against me in a most incredible way.

The paramedics asked if they could come in and check on me. I didn't see any harm in that and believing they were just trying to do their jobs well, I invited them to enter. Immediately after letting the paramedics in they started checking my vital signs. They asked what I had taken to sleep and I told them some sleeping pills, assuring them that I had no intention of killing myself. After looking over my medications and asking me several questions the ambulance crew looked as if they were satisfied, but then they did something that greatly affected my future.

One of the paramedics asked me if I would go with them to the hospital just to make sure I was okay. "Why?" I asked. "I'm fine."

He insisted saying, "It's just a precaution; we just want to make sure."

"Okay," I said, relenting. "If you really feel it's necessary." It turned out to be a very big mistake on my part.

After transporting me to the hospital I was placed in a wheelchair, wheeled into the emergency room and moved to a stretcher. Doctors came to check on me and everything seemed fine. But as I lay on the stretcher in the emergency room, all my problems began to seep back into my mind. I began to cry, feeling helpless and alone again.

Suddenly, my estranged wife appeared and she too was crying. I did not understand why she was there. When I asked, she said the hospital had called her. Though I had not seen her in weeks, she took my hand and stroked my forehead. Watching her as she cried about me, I began to think that maybe she still loved me. But what she said next obliterated that hope.

"I thought you were much stronger than this," she said with pity in her voice. I did not know how to respond. I said nothing, still waiting for her to say something that might indicate to me that she still cared. But those were her only and final words to me.

Suddenly, we were interrupted by a nurse who had something for my estranged wife to sign. She signed the paper and then left as quickly as she had appeared. I lay there in a daze, not knowing what to make of the surprising and brief display of sympathy. But soon two men came, put me back into a wheelchair, and took me back to the ambulance.

"Where are we going?" I asked them.

"Don't worry," they said to me. "You're going to a very good hospital."

"Why?" I asked. "What's wrong with this hospital?"

"You have been 'BAKER ACTED,'" they said. Then it hit me. My wife had signed papers putting me away in a psychiatric hospital. What other cruelties could fate possibly have in store for me?

Fortunately, the next day I was visited by a doctor who actually listened to me. He understood that although I had suffered from depression and had been down recently, I was not suicidal. I was so relieved to finally have someone believe I did not try to take my life. The doctor also agreed to call my employer and explain that I would not be able to work for a couple of days, but I was okay.

Nevertheless, I knew in my heart that this incident would probably give Roger the ammunition he needed to fire me. Of course, I can only blame myself for my actions and I understand how suspect they may have looked to others. But the way events soon spiraled out of control made me wonder if someone was out to get me.

The day I was released from the hospital I called Mark to see if he had received the doctor's phone call explaining my absence. He said that he had and understood what happened. He asked how I was and said he hoped I was doing better. But when I told him I would be ready to come back to work the next day, he told me, "I think you'd better call Roger first." I had a sinking feeling in the pit of my stomach. I was certain upon hearing Mark's words that my worst fears were about to be realized.

When I contacted Roger, he told me that I still needed to tell him where I had been and what I was doing during my vacation or I would be fired. I told him that his not knowing what I did on my vacation was not a legitimate reason for firing me and that it was not his business to know details about my private time. "If you fire me, I will certainly take you to court," I said angrily.

Roger replied, "I'll call you back next week to discuss the matter further." He added, "But you are suspended until further notice and you are not to return to work at the hospital."

During the next days I awaited Roger's call, but it never came.

At the end of the week, I received a letter from him telling me that I had been removed from my position at the hospital and that they had found a temporary replacement for my job. It went on to say that I had been placed "on the bench" until another job could be found for me.

I wrote back that I would not tolerate being fired in such an underhanded manner and that I had already hired a lawyer. Interestingly enough, immediately after receiving my letter, the contract company suddenly found a position for me at a hospital they service in Washington, D.C. As they told me, the hospital was "interested in hiring you."

When I checked it out, I realized that the company was giving me a chance to redeem myself at a facility where few wanted to work. It was located in a high crime area and so dangerous the hospital had to be surrounded by a fence topped in razor wire. Though it was an obvious slap in the face, I decided to look at the challenge as a new opportunity to revive my career and start a new life. I made plans to move to Washington.

And indeed my new position seemed to be going along well when a few months after arriving in Washington, I got a call from my estranged wife. She told me that she had not realized how much she cared about me until I had moved far away. Now, suddenly, she wanted to reconcile. She pleaded with me to come back home and try to start over again.

I was hesitant at first to leave this job so soon after all the trouble I'd had with my employer. I was also unsure whether I could trust in my wife's feelings. *What will prevent her from just leaving me again?* I thought. Yet I missed my son tremendously and I began to cling to the hope that his mother was sincere in wanting to work things out. I asked for a re-assignment with the company and left my new job, returning to Florida and my family with high hopes of my wife and I saving our marriage. Despite all that had happened with my employer, the last few months in Washington D.C. had been going very smoothly; so I hoped that my company would find me a job with another hospital in Florida. Whatever happened with my job, I decided that saving my marriage and family was worth the risk. However, not more than two weeks after I returned, not only hadn't I been offered a reassignment, but I was fired from my job because I left the Washington job of my own accord.

Soon after that, my wife announced that our marriage was over for good this time. After all the assurances she had given me that convinced me to return, I was shocked and angry. I had risked and lost my career, because I trusted too much. So there I was again, on the outside of a marriage looking in. In addition to child support, I was pressured to pay everything she and the lawyer she'd hired could come up with and now I did not even have a job.

For several months I tried getting new employment in the healthcare and hospitality fields for which I had so much experience. But a mysterious wall seemed to have arisen blocking my every effort. Perhaps the area hospitals and hotels simply were not interested or had plenty of applicants, but I suspected I had been blacklisted. There were many positions open and the job market was booming, yet somehow, despite my long and distinguished career, I could no longer get in the door.

I tried working other jobs, everything from selling sports memorabilia to telemarketing. No matter what I did, I still suffered from pain and weakness in my back and leg. At times I could hardly walk and limped noticeably. But I prayed for strength and kept pushing. I had to keep working for my children's sake.

By then I was barely getting by and had to move out of my one bedroom apartment. I took a room in someone else's apartment who would accept as roommates both me and the small dog I'd adopted. I kept selling my belongings to survive until I had nothing left but my car, a bed, television set and the computer I would need if I got a job. My circumstances continued to grow more and more desperate. During those terrible times, my church was the only thing that kept me from going crazy. I began going to services twice a week because it was the only place I could find support, comfort and peace.

Finally with my back against the wall economically, I swallowed my pride and began using the so-called "social safety net." I filed for unemployment benefits. It was a bitter pill to swallow, but I was in desperate financial straits, struggling to make even small payments of child support for my two children. And my body was giving out on me, leaving me with fewer and fewer options. Finally, I was told by my doctors that I was becoming severely disabled because of the damaged nerves in my back. Fighting depression, constant pain and weakness in my back and leg, my will to go on also was being destroyed.

One day, after spending most of the week in bed because of severe pain, I realized I had reached a point where I could no longer work the way I once had. Perhaps I would never be able to do it again. I was running out of money. I could no longer pay my doctors or buy medicine to treat my depression and injuries.

I could not sit for long periods of time; I could barely walk and could not even stand for long stretches of time either. And the nerve damage I had suffered was now affecting my internal organs causing increasing problems with bladder and bowel control.

Being in management for many years, I was vaguely aware that there were laws like the Americans with Disabilities Act and benefits that were supposed to protect those like me who'd been injured on the job. I finally decided to find a lawyer who might give me some guidance about what my rights were. After doing some quick research, I settled on one and we set a date to meet. And so began another chapter of frustration which only added to the stress that I was already enduring. I now had to expose myself to lawyers and doctors, some of whom treated me like I was a criminal and did their very best to prove that I was not suffering from the disabilities that I had. It was a humiliating and degrading process which ultimately went nowhere.

Meanwhile, I struggled to survive. Supplemented by unemployment benefits, I bounced from one part-time job to another having difficulty keeping steady employment for the first time in my life. My body and mind continued to deteriorate, leaving me only the shell of the man I used to be. Even working several temporary jobs, I was barely able to pay for living and car expenses, to feed myself and my little poodle, while attempting to give a consistent amount each month to my children. And soon I couldn't see a way to continue to do even that.

At this point, I felt nothing short of a miracle would save me from ending up on the streets. I finally decided I would have to swallow my pride and do the unthinkable: call my parents and ask them if I could come home to live until I could get back on my feet.

After all my success in life, the thought of having to beg to go to my childhood home in order to start over was almost too much to bear. What hurt me the most was I would have to give up living near my children and thereby give up any hope of seeing them on a regular basis. However, there was nothing left to do; I saw no other options.

So I made the call. I spoke to my dad and he told me he would have to talk it over with my mother. The next day he called me back. His voice trembled. "I can't allow you to come home. I'm sorry." It was the first time I had ever heard my father cry. He told me my mother simply did not believe that I was in that desperate a condition and she felt I had to stand on my own feet and handle my problems myself.

My heart sank. I could not believe that the only people left on whom I thought I could depend—my own parents—were now abandoning me also. I felt like I had been kicked in the stomach. Stunned and saddened, I put the phone down.

My life, which had been a mostly happy and fulfilling success story until the early 1990s, had now collapsed around me like a house of cards. How could so many terrible things happen to one person in the span of only five years? Why was all I'd created collapsing?

With no funds and nowhere to turn, I told my roommate I was going to have to leave soon and began making preparations to move out of the little room in which I had been staying. I put an advertisement in the local newspapers in an attempt to sell the few things of value I had left. I would only be able to keep what fit in my car where I would also have to sleep. And I did not know how long I would be able to keep my car either.

I walked around in a daze trying to figure out what in the world I would do next. Where would I go? How would I eat? A few nights later reaching the end of my strength, tossing and turning and unable to sleep, I broke down completely and cried uncontrollably. Then my cries turned to sobs. Unable to stop, I went into the bathroom to splash cold water on my face, but it did not help. "Why Lord?" I cried as stumbled back to me bedroom, closed the door and sank to the floor beside my bed, my fists pounding the mattress. On my knees, I prayed and cursed my bad luck begging the Lord to tell me why my life had fallen apart again.

It was during this most desperate of moments that I experienced a second vision.

> *Out of the yellow glow of the hallway light seeping under my door, I saw a figure emerge. It was the unmistakable outline of a man in a long,*

flowing robe. It was, I truly believe, the spiritual
embodiment of Jesus Christ.

"Open your heart to me and accept me as your
savior and your burdens will be lifted," he said. His
tone of voice was like that of a father comforting a
child.

Without uttering a word, I spoke to him in my
mind: I have always believed in you, *I thought,*
trying to assure him of my faith.

"You must release the false hopes of this
world." He went on, "Give up your life to me and
you will be lifted to a higher consciousness." And
suddenly I understood! His love shot through me
like a lightning bolt. I opened my heart and vowed
to give my life to Him.

Over the next week I sold everything I had left, parting
with the few things that I once thought were indispensable. One
task that was particularly hard to do was finding a home for my
beloved dog. My little poodle had been the only female in my
life that stuck with me through the good and the bad. She was
like a child to me and knowing I could no longer afford to take
care of her was heartbreaking.

Fortunately a pair of elderly sisters, who had come to
buy some items I had put up for sale, fell in love with my poodle and she with them. I saw immediately that she was very
comfortable with the two women, so I asked if they would like
to have her. They were momentarily shocked by the offer but
when I explained my predicament, they enthusiastically agreed

to adopt my dog. After being reassured that they would take excellent care of her, we made arrangements for them to pick up the little dog the next day. The brief peace I felt the night of my vision was challenged temporarily by this new loss. Giving away my dog was the final act in the tragedy which had become my life. I tried to comfort myself with the belief that even though only God, whom I was desperately trying to trust, knew what would become of me now, He would someday allow me to understand why all this happened to me.

I visited each of my sons to say good-bye telling them both that I would try to stay in touch with them. I had already asked my ex-wives to tell my children that their daddy was sick and had to move away to get better. When I returned home, I prayed that the women would do what was best for my children until I got back on my feet.

Having managed to whittle my belongings down to two suitcases, I placed them to the side of my room to take out to my car. There would be just enough space in the car for my few possessions and for me to sleep in the driver's seat.

The afternoon before I was to move out, I went to clear out my mailbox and found a notice about a function taking place at my church that night. Seeking solace from the only place I'd ever found it, I decided to go. As I sat there listening to the church leader's appeal for people to make their lives God's work, it suddenly dawned on me that this just might be my call-ing. Maybe this was why my life had been turned upside down. Maybe this was the very thing of which the vision had spoken: a new life dedicated to serving God. After the meeting that night, I gathered my courage and approached the pastor. I asked him about the opportunities that might be available for me in church ministries abroad. The pastor was enthused about my inquiry, telling me that among the many countries that had missions were Cuba and the Philippines. Since I spoke Spanish he suggested, "You would be valuable to the mission in Cuba." I shook my head firmly; having lived and worked among many Cubans in Miami, I knew of their fierce patriotic feelings and their hatred of Castro and what's he's done to ruin their homeland.

"I'm sorry, but I can't go to Cuba. I would feel like a traitor to friends and colleagues if I went there," I told the pastor.

The pastor nodded. "I understand. Perhaps you would prefer to do God's work in the Philippines. It was a Spanish colony at one time so much of their culture and language is affected by this Spanish heritage, but their second language is English."

I thought for a moment then slowly nodded my head in agreement. "I think that sounds like a very good opportunity," I said, my enthusiasm growing.

"Then it's settled. I'll have the church secretary prepare the paperwork." The pastor gave me a list of the things I should bring and all the tasks I should take care of to prepare for the trip.

That night when I returned home, I told my roommate about the church opportunity and asked him if, instead of leaving tomorrow, I could stay a few days longer. He was kind enough to agree and told me he was very happy for me. I slept soundly for the first time in weeks.

The next morning, I brought my resume to the church pastor. He sent it to the church's mission in Manila. Soon I was given telephone numbers and a fax number for the pastor in Manila and told to contact him. I quickly contacted his office and although they seemed hesitant about bringing on an American, the officials told me that I was welcome to come there. For the first time in months I felt I had a reason to live and a purpose to my life. This was the answer to my predicament, I thought. I would finally get to do God's work in its most pure and powerful form, helping the poor.

Information was sent to me about the location of the church in Manila, which was now under construction, and maps of the area to help me find my way. In addition, they sent me a credit slip for the Holiday Inn nearby at which I could stay. Having already packed to move out of the room I'd been renting, all I had left to dispose of was my car, so I decided to sell it. A friend of a friend quickly bought the car. With the money I received, I went to several travel agents trying to get the cheapest roundtrip ticket I could to Manila that would be good for one year. I knew that I would eventually want to return to the United States and I wanted to have the ticket prepaid in case I couldn't afford to buy one while I was overseas.

Once I had the airline tickets, I sent my ex-wives most of the money I had left, retaining only what little I thought would be necessary for my travels. It saddened me to think that my ex-wives, family and friends might believe I was just running away from my problems and responsibilities. And, in a way, I felt guilty of just that.

The shame of not being able to take care of myself let alone take care of my obligations to my children hurt my pride and obliterated my self-esteem. No one felt worse than I did about my impoverished circumstances and the fact that for the first time in my life, I could no longer be a good provider for the children I loved so much.

But out of the darkness of the shame and humiliation, rose a fire of faith. It was my faith in God that gave me the hope that I still could make something out of the shambles of my life. I truly felt that for reasons I did not yet understand, He had brought me to this point.

And so, in March of 1996, I boarded the airplane that would fly me to Manila. I resolved to believe in myself and have faith that God would help me find my destiny.

The words emblazoned across the walls of our church kept running through my mind: "When there is no way, God will find a way!" I resolved to move forward despite the obstacles of pain and paralysis, clinging to the belief that I was doing the right thing. I had to; I had nowhere else to go.

Chapter Four

Shades of Prophecies

Aboard the plane to the Philippines my nervousness alternated with excitement. I could hardly sit still as I tried to imagine the new life awaiting me. Looking around I saw a young Filipino man sitting to my right. He seemed to sense my agitation and began speaking quietly to me.

"Hello," he said giving me a warm smile. "Are you an American tourist?"

"I'm an American, but I'm going to the Philippines to work helping poor children with the pastor of a church."

"Ah," he said, "a missionary."

I shook my head, "No, I'll just be helping," I said, but his words gave me pause.

At the time, I did not think of myself as a missionary. I assumed that all missionaries were people with theological training and I had none.

I continued, "I am happy just to get the chance to assist the pastor with the charitable work he is doing."

The man nodded. "The woman sitting over there is a missionary," he said, pointing at her. "She is returning to the Philippines where she has quite a following. They call her 'The Blind Prophet.'"

His words intrigued me, but my mind was too preoccupied with my journey to pay much attention at the moment. However, some time later when I got out of my seat to go to the bathroom, the man I'd been talking to was standing next to another passenger's seat. He stopped me as I tried to pass and introduced me to the woman. I looked at her more closely, realizing she was the one he had pointed out earlier and called the Blind Prophet. She was a pleasant looking woman in her late thirties or early forties. The blank stare of her eyes was framed by chubby rose-colored cheeks and short, salt and pepper hair cut in bangs on her forehead. Her smile was constant and seemed to put everyone around her at ease. She looked and acted very much like a jovial, matronly schoolteacher.

"You are an American, my friend tells me," she said.

"Yes," I answered. "Are you?"

She nodded, "I am from Washington. What part of the United States are you from?"

"Illinois," I responded. "I grew up near Chicago and most recently I lived in Florida, but I've visited your lovely home state."

We spoke a bit about our Christian beliefs and her missionary work in the Philippines. I was struck by her easygoing nature. She did not act pushy or overly righteous about her spiritual beliefs. She did not act as if I were a stranger. She treated me more like someone about whom she had heard a lot and had been waiting to meet. I was a little taken aback.

As we discussed the poor conditions of the Filipinos she served, she said, "Why don't you come with us on our crusade?" I thought it odd that she would invite a total stranger to travel with her. But then again she was aware that I was going to the Philippines to assist a missionary.

I explained that I was going to be working with a pastor recommended by my church. "He's expecting me," I said. "I'm sorry, but I can't join you." Then I excused myself and moved down the aisle toward the back of the plane.

A few minutes later when I passed by the Blind Prophet again on the way back to my seat, she stopped me. "You will find out much about your past and future destiny on our journey in the Philippines." The words "our journey" sounded strangely prophetic as if I was already going with them. In fact, her words turned out to be truly prophetic. She handed me her card. "In case you decide to come with us," she said smiling cryptically.

Later, as the plane circled over Manila, I stared eagerly out the window and studied the landscape. The turquoise water and the varied ships of Manila Bay disappeared abruptly as we descended slowly over the scattered shantytowns surrounding the city itself.

The tropical scene was divided into two very different worlds. Directly below us were dirt roads lined with houses which appeared to be made of cardboard and scraps of tin. Narrow, straight canals seemed to run through the enormous mass of little shacks and homes squeezed together with no space between them. I was amazed that so many ramshackle homes were packed so close together and stretched for miles in every direction. Never had I seen living conditions so poor. I could not help but wonder how many people lived in the mass of humanity below me.

In stark contrast, the tall buildings of downtown Manila rose into the sky before us looking much like the New York City skyline towering over the thousands of little shacks, now lost in the shadow of big city edifices. Unlike the flat, tightly packed neighborhoods of the impoverished outskirts, the center of the city was an impressive, modern metropolis gleaming in the tropical sunshine. It was my first look at the dual realities of this exotic country called the Philippines. I had heard that it was a very poor country despite the modern amenities and luxuries existing in some areas. From the air, however, it was obvious that the city was an intriguing combination of old and new, elegant and meager.

The thrilling rush of my journey and the work ahead coursed through me as I smiled down at the new world I was about to enter. It had been such a long time since I felt excitement about anything. The anticipation of exploring this new culture and helping its people would be, I hoped, just the medicine I needed for my weary mind and aching body. For the first time in years, I was looking forward to my future rather than lamenting my past.

Upon landing I could see that the airport on the outskirts of Manila was not particularly big. Yet it seemed well organized for the amount of planes that were flying into and out of it. However, there were none of the modern conveniences like indoor gates leading up to the planes to which I was accustomed in the United States. Standing up in the aisle as we waited to disembark, I looked around for the Blind Prophet to say goodbye, but the stewardess came over and quickly escorted the woman off before I had the chance to say anything. So I slowly and carefully made my way through the aisle and down the steep metal staircase that had been wheeled up to the airplane. As I stepped from the plane onto the tarmac, I took a deep breath and found it actually felt refreshing to be enveloped in the hot, humid, tropical breeze that smelled like the nearby ocean.

I followed the group of people in front of me into the arrival area of the airport. We entered a hallway where the line of passengers passed through a checkpoint being manned by two military policemen wearing helmets and carrying assault rifles. One of the men sat at a desk checking passports and asking questions.

Looking around I was surprised to see military style guards posted throughout the airport, but I was not shaken as I had seen a similar sight when I had traveled for work to Bogotá, Colombia many years back. As we moved along slowly but steadily, sweat began to pour from my body due to the intense humidity. I rolled up my shirt sleeves and unfastened the top two buttons at my collar trying to cool down a little while shuffling along in the line. Finally I reached the simple wooden desk where an official looking Filipino man was examining passports and stamping them.

The man, dressed in a freshly pressed khaki uniform, had the look of a distinguished Latin diplomat. Standing next to him was a guard manning an automatic assault rifle, also dressed smartly in a beige uniform with a military helmet adorning his head.

As I approached the desk and presented my papers to him, the man smiled warmly, but I noticed his eyes were studying me intently. His curious, intense brown eyes did not leave

my face as he asked me question after question. I did not understand him at first and wondered if he was speaking a dialect,
though it was obviously English.

"I'm sorry?" I responded and he spoke to me again a little more slowly. Despite his heavy Filipino accent I finally made
out the meaning of his words. He was asking me why I was in
the Philippines. I told him, "I'm meeting someone in a church
in Manila."

He nodded approvingly and said, "Ah, you missionary?"

I smiled, struck again at the sound of the word, missionary. I was about to reveal I was just a volunteer, but I thought it
would be too hard to explain my role so I simply replied, "Yes."
He stamped my passport and waved me forward.

Following the other travelers down to a very large room
I saw baggage carousels that were beginning to deliver cardboard boxes and suitcases to waiting passengers. It was a well-
lit room that was not air-conditioned and there were armed
guards at every doorway.

I found a good spot close to the checkout stations and
waited for my luggage. As I stood there watching box after box
go by on the carousel, I wondered if anyone coming to the
Philippines used luggage at all. I guessed that there had to be
many modern conveniences and items unavailable in the country since it appeared everyone brought with them so many huge
boxes. I guessed the boxes were the bounty of many Filipinos'
shopping trips to the United States.

Standing there feeling out of place, I began to have some
doubts. *What am I doing here?* I wondered. I quickly answered
myself: *I have nowhere else to go.* As thoughts ricocheted through

my mind, I felt a familiar emptiness returning to my heart. The wounds of the past were still too fresh to forget the pain and loss that I had suffered over the last several years. It was still hard to believe that I now had no home.

Everything I owned was in my luggage. My back and left leg throbbed as the wait continued. But I realized that an even deeper pain was still aching inside my chest.

Meanwhile the carousel kept turning around and around in front of me, pushing my past life far away, literally a world away. "Excuse me," a man said as he pushed past me to reach for his luggage on the carousel. I stepped out of his way. I did not want to get knocked down by the large piece of luggage he was swinging to the floor from the carousel.

The crowd around me was thickening as more and more people peered down the line searching for their luggage. I decided to move to another spot where I could better see mine when it arrived.

Suddenly I caught a glimpse of my large black suitcase and moved closer to the carousel preparing myself to pull it quickly off the conveyer belt. Soon after that I spotted my smaller bag as well. With both pieces of luggage in hand, I maneuvered into a line forming at a table where Philippine authorities were opening luggage and inspecting the contents. I was not sure what they were looking for, but I assumed it must have been contraband like drugs, plants or weapons.

With my bags inspected and immigration approval complete, I looked for and found a money-changing booth where I could change my American dollars into Philippine pesos so I would be able to pay for the cab ride to the hotel among other things.

After that I made my way slowly out onto a sidewalk that was shaded by a large overhang. Barricades ran from one side of the driveway to the other and along the sidewalk that ran parallel to the street.

Looking up I was amazed to see hundreds of smiling Filipino faces calling out from behind the barricade. They all had the jet black hair and small builds characteristic of their race. Being only 5 feet 4 inches tall myself, I was not used to being among people as short or shorter than me. To my surprise some of them seemed to be waving at me and shouting out names. As I looked around trying to find a taxi, several young men with two-way radios approached me.

Suddenly a Filipino girl with long dark hair behind the barricade waved at me and shouted, "Are you John?" in a cute accent. I was surprised by the question. Then I looked around and realized most of the people waving and yelling behind the barricades were young women.

"No, I am not John," I shouted back to her. Her face saddened with disappointment and I felt sorry for her. I could not help but wonder if her friend really was on the plane with me. Then my attention was again grabbed by one of the men carrying a walkie-talkie.

I turned and started walking down the long driveway toward the small white cabs sitting along the curb. The young men with the walkie-talkies began following like a swarm of bees shouting at me. One of them grabbed my luggage out of my hands and started hauling it toward a car parked down the driveway.

"Where you go? I take you!" He said over his shoulder as he quickly trotted ahead of me.

"No, No, No, wait!" I yelled at him, remembering that I should be cautious about who I let take my luggage.

He turned smiling and said, "No problem, I take you!"

I hurried after him, reaching him just in time to grab my luggage back before he tossed into the trunk of his taxi. Catching my breath, I said, "No. Wait one minute!" He stopped and looked at me anxiously. I asked, "How many pesos to the Holiday Inn?"

He thought for a minute then said, "Cheap, I take you for 500 pesos only; I take your luggage." I hesitated, wondering if 500 pesos was good or bad. I really had no way of knowing if I was getting ripped off so I decided not to take his word for it.

However, before I could say no, two other men were in my face telling me they would take me. Taking advantage of this change in my predicament, I looked at all three of the men and asked, "Who can take me to the Holiday Inn?"

One skinny young man boldly replied, "I take you for 300 pesos!"

"No, I take you for two hundred seventy five," another piped up. *Wow*, I thought to myself, *I've got a bidding war going here.*

I looked at the third man to see what he might offer, but he just stood there grinning. I spoke up. "I will pay 200 pesos to the Holiday Inn." My offer got an immediate reaction from two of the men.

"No, cannot do!" said one.

The other looked at me and then said, "You pay 250 pesos to Holiday Inn."

I waited a moment to see if any of them would bring the price down further. Finally, realizing I'd gotten the best offer I

was going to get, I said, "Okay, I'll pay you 250 pesos to take me
to the Holiday Inn." And with that I shook the man's hand.

He smiled and said, "Okay, come" and began pulling
my luggage toward his car.

Good, I thought to myself, *I survived my first big test and
I was savvy enough not to get ripped off big time.* I felt comfortable
that I had negotiated a fair deal for both me and the cab driver.

After taking care of my luggage, the young man politely
opened my door and then jumped into his seat behind the
wheel. I made myself comfortable and was ready to enjoy the
scenery. However, the ride we took from the airport to the
Holiday Inn was quite an eye opener. It quickly became apparent to me that the traffic in Manila was terrible and that, unlike
American drivers who followed some order in the way they
drove down a street, the drivers here were very aggressive and
didn't follow any rules, if rules even existed. There seemed to be
no right lane or left lane, just organized chaos with cars darting
in, out and around each other.

Using their car horns to blast warnings as they pushed
their way in between other vehicles, the taxi drivers were very
daring. I found myself cringing and grabbing the armrest as my
driver pushed our cab within inches of other cars forcing them
to stop and allow his vehicle to slide into the thick traffic. It was
a wild ride and all I could do to keep from screaming was laugh
nervously as the cab driver, sometimes grinning at me, pushed
and prodded the automobile through traffic.

Looking out the window I saw that traffic in Manila
consisted of mostly small cars, a variety of motorcycles and
some other conveyances unfamiliar to me. As I looked closer I

saw the motorcycles were really small scooters. By the sheer number on the streets, they were apparently the favorite and most affordable means of personal transportation. But there were also three other kinds of transportation that I had never seen before. The driver told me their names.

The "tricycle" was a motorcycle with a cab fitted to it that provided room for two to three people. The cab was made of metal and aluminum that was welded into a covered box with a window and a bench seat to sit on. Little stools were provided on the floor of the cab between the bench seat and the window for use by a child or other small adults. At the back of this metal cab was a small open trunk for luggage or bags of rice or even animals that were tied or caged. Also, on the back of the motorcycle itself was an extended seat, providing two additional seats to the tricycle's capacity.

They were brightly painted and had beads, figurines and other colorful ornaments adorning them along with radios and sometimes blinking lights. I noticed that most tricycles had names of family, children, movie stars and religious figures displayed in large letters on their fronts and sides. My driver said that a ride in a tricycle usually only cost a few pesos depending on how far you were going. Plentiful and cheap, the tricycle also seemed to be a popular mode of transportation for most people, foreigners and Filipinos alike.

The "multicab" was an interesting version of a small Japanese pickup truck with a metal roof covering the back end. It could hold more than eight people in the back and maybe two more in the front pickup truck cabin. Often used as taxis, they were usually a white or plain color with the cab company's logo on it. It was really just like riding in a covered pickup truck and was a little cramped for space. But again this small version of a minibus was popular because it was cheap, only a few pesos more than taking a tricycle.

The "jeepney" was the Philippine version of a jeep, but made into a bus. These were mostly made of gleaming stainless steel and were breathtaking in their appearance. A jeepney consisted of a normal jeep cab with an attached, covered body the size of most school buses. They were bigger and more comfortable than the multicabs and had comfortable padded bench seats and plenty of room for head and feet. However, like the tricycles, the jeepneys had little stools for people to cram themselves in the middle of the cab when the surrounding bench seats were taken. Jeepneys were also very colorful and ornate and have become a symbol of Philippine transportation with its American-influenced jeep front and the unique bus-like body. The jeepney usually followed a route similar to a public bus and also was a little more expensive than the multicab.

I found out on this first trip that along with the terrible bumper-to-bumper traffic in Manila, there was also considerable air pollution due to the many vehicles spewing black smoke every time their drivers' stepped on the gas.

With no environmental controls on their vehicles, the air in the city of Manila, I decided, was as bad as some parts of Los Angeles. I was certain it would not be long before the polluted air started causing serious misery for my allergies and sinus condition.

Nevertheless, I watched with curiosity as we made our way through crowded and dusty side streets onto larger four-lane roads packed with even more vehicles. My cab driver seemed to know every shortcut and whenever he reached slow-moving traffic, he floored the gas pedal and somehow managed to find a way around it.

I gave a sigh of relief when we finally arrived in front of the Holiday Inn. It was a welcome sight with its large recognizable sign and familiar green colors. The hotel stood out as the most modern building on the street compared to its antiquated surroundings. After giving the cab driver a tip of 50 pesos, I slowly climbed the marble stairs to the classy-looking hotel entrance. As I reached the glass doors several uniformed doormen rushed forward to take my luggage to the front desk.

Looking around the large, spectacular marble and brass lobby, I made my way to the front desk. The Filipino hotel workers really kept the lobby looking sharp and their excellent service and courteous attitudes were extraordinary. But I had to remind myself that I had very little money, so I would have to be very prudent with my tipping.

I was delighted to find that the young woman at the front desk spoke very good English and there was no problem finding my reservation. I gave her the credit slip the pastor had sent me. A few minutes later I was escorted to my room which was carpeted, clean and had a fully marble bathroom. "Very nice," I murmured as I surveyed the splendor of having a remote controlled television, a dining table and a fully stocked refrigerator with bottled water and cans of soda pop. For now, at least, I could relax in my air-conditioned room and quench my thirst. I was tired, my body ached and I was in need of something sweet and cold.

I unpacked my things for the three days I would be staying in Manila until I was assigned by the Philippine church.

Then, putting my hot, sweaty feet up in front of me on the bed, I puffed up a couple of pillows, laid back and turned on the television. It felt good to be in a quiet, cool room by myself and to anticipate the start of my mission. Weary from the long trip, I soon fell asleep.

Chapter Five

The Island Nation

I awoke to the sounds of car horns and motorcycles and quickly climbed out of bed. The bright, early morning sun was burning through the mist of a fresh new Manila morning as I stood at the window staring out into the busy streets below me. Rubbing the sleep from my eyes, I stretched feeling rested and ready for this new challenge in my life. I was eager to begin my mission.

Digging through my luggage I found the map and phone numbers that had been provided to me by the pastor with whom I was to meet. I thought I had better let him know that I had arrived, so we could set a time for our meeting. I picked up the phone and dialed his number. Unfortunately, the woman who answered told me that he was not there, but she was kind enough to take a message.

After showering and getting dressed, I went to get some breakfast, bringing the map along with me so that I could try to identify the church, which I knew was only a few blocks from where I was staying. They were supposed to be erecting a new domed cathedral and thought that the construction would help me recognize the building. I hoped the pastor would be in his office by the time I finished breakfast and found my way to the cathedral.

The hotel lobby and restaurant were bustling with activity. Every employee I met was gracious and courteous, stopping to greet me with "Good Morning, sir." I was happy to find a nice buffet with Philippine and American breakfast foods and I was even happier, because of my limited funds, to find my breakfast would be free. After a refreshing tropical fruit punch and an omelette, I was ready to tackle the task of locating the church.

As I walked out the front door of the hotel that morning, a new excitement took hold of me. I was venturing out into a strange new world and experiencing the stimulating sensation of exploration and discovery, things I had not felt in a long time.

Stepping out onto the sidewalk in front of my hotel, the first thing I noticed was the uncomfortable humidity and the intense heat. Even though I had spent most of the last twenty years in Florida, I was surprised to find the Philippine climate to be even more oppressive. I only walked a few steps before I began sweating profusely. Still, the new sights and sounds around me were totally captivating; I was delighted to be there.

Following the map, I carefully found my way through the congested, noisy streets near my hotel. As I walked, I was taken aback by the amount of dirt and smoke churning in the air stirred up by motorcycles and fast moving cars belching smoke. I had to stop periodically to wipe dust and grit from my eyes.

Surrounding me were smiling, dark-haired Filipinos; walking, running, riding motorcycles and jeepneys. Unable to ignore the foreigner, most smiled or waved at me as they went by while others just stared.

After stopping a couple of times to get my bearings, I found myself strolling in the shade of an elevated subway track supported by tall cement columns rising from the street to the platform overhead.

I watched and learned as many Filipinos across the street from me waited for traffic to thin out and then quickly walked across the street. Following their example, I did the same, preferring to stay with the crowd, just to be safe.

After successfully navigating several very crowded intersections, I found myself near an open lot. Nearby I discovered a large domed building in the final stages of construction and was sure I had found the place for which I was looking.

I had to circle the building to find an entrance, because most of the area around it was littered with construction equipment and materials. Then I saw an area where two vehicles were parked in front of a large, unfinished doorway.

On entering the cathedral I was surprised to see that it was being used for church services, even though the facility had not been completed. Wooden benches and folding chairs were neatly arranged in rows surrounding a large, circular stage with a pulpit and microphones.

Looking around, I found a stairwell that seemed to lead to an office area, so I made my way slowly up the steps. At the top I found some offices, still under construction. A couple of desks were placed in one of them.

Walking inside, I couldn't see anyone, so I called out, "Anyone here?" There was no answer. I called out again but still there was no answer. I decided to go back down the stairs to see if I could find another office area, but I stopped at the top of the stairs when I heard footsteps coming toward me.

A young Filipina woman with short black hair was moving up the last few steps. She smiled but flashed me a quizzical look.

"Can I help you, sir?" she asked.

"I am supposed to meet the pastor here. I just arrived from the United States," I said, following her into the office where she sat down at a desk.

She put some papers down on the desktop and said, "Do you have an appointment with him?"

"No, but he is aware that I would be coming soon and I was hoping to catch him here today," I said, explaining my unannounced presence.

She smiled and asked me with a sweet, inquisitive voice, "You're an American?"

I nodded, "Yes, I am."

"I'm sorry you have come so far for nothing, but the pastor is not here today."

"Really?" I said with surprise. I was a bit disappointed to learn this so I asked when the pastor might be returning.

"He's away and I don't really know when he will be back."

Now I was really disappointed. I could not believe my bad luck! I traveled thousands of miles and the pastor went on vacation! Where would I go? What would I do? In a moment of sheer panic I blurted out, "I don't understand how that is possible. He was expecting me!"

Her eyes widened and she looked shocked by my sudden emotional outburst, but she quickly regained her composure and smiled sympathetically. "Sir, the pastor is recuperating from an unexpected injury to his foot that occurred a few days ago because of the construction debris around the cathedral." I stood there dumfounded. I felt bad for the man's injuries, but being a stranger in a foreign country, I was beginning to really worry.

"Now what do I do?" I murmured in a concerned voice. Before she could reply I added, "Is there any way I can get in contact with him?"

She shook her head and said gently, "I am sorry; I don't think so. He is taking a leave of absence and can't be disturbed."

As I turned to leave I stopped and appealed to her again. "Could you please find out how I can contact him? I've come a long way to work with him."

She looked at me sheepishly and said, "I will try." I told her the name of my hotel and gave her my room number, praying she would be able to find a way for me to get in touch with the pastor.

Walking back to the hotel I was filled with worry over this unlucky turn of events. I could only ask myself over and over, "What am I going to do now?" How could I wait for the pastor to return? It might be weeks or even months before he came back. Yet how could I not? Where else would I go? What would I do? My free room credit was only good for a few days and when it ran out, I would not have the money to stay in the Holiday Inn much longer. I had been under the impression that I would be given a more permanent place to stay within days after arriving in Manila.

Nervously looking around for someplace that I could get a cold drink and collect my thoughts, I headed straight for the McDonalds that I remembered seeing across the street from the hotel. Here I was in Manila on the first day of my new mission and I felt like I had been punched in the stomach. What in the world was I going to do?

I tried to calm myself as I ordered a cola, but a wave of panic rose deep inside me. I had to find someone who could help me. I could not go back to the United States now; I had nowhere to live there. While I debated what to do, I suddenly remembered that the blind lady I'd met on the airplane had given me a number in Manila where I could reach her. Maybe I should go with her and her missionaries after all! My spirits immediately began to lift.

If this was not fate, what was it? Yes, I felt suddenly that God had a hand in this strange turn of events. One door had closed but another might certainly be opening. Feeling better, I left the restaurant, quickly walked across the street to the hotel and headed up to my room to find the card with the telephone number of the Blind Prophet.

Opening the door of my hotel room I noticed a piece of green and white paper on the floor. *What is this?* I wondered. I turned the paper over in my hands to see the Holiday Inn logo and the heading A MESSAGE FOR YOU.

As I scanned the paper and read the faded computer printing on it I smiled. The message read, "Please call regarding your appointment with the Pastor." This must be a good omen, I thought. The woman I'd spoken to at the church probably had gotten in touch with the pastor since I left. I rushed to the phone. Maybe I would not have to abandon my original plans after all.

Quickly picking up the telephone, I called the church's number. Again I heard the sweet voice of the young Filipina woman answer the phone. When I explained to her that I was returning her call, however, she informed me, "The pastor definitely will be unable to see you due to a serious construction accident. He will be away indefinitely recuperating from his injuries." Thanking her, I swallowed hard as I hung up. She had left me a message only to confirm what I already knew. Now I had no choice but to pursue my only other option.

I searched among my airline tickets where I thought I had put the card with the phone number of the Blind Prophet. Finally finding it, I picked up the telephone and dialed. I felt embarrassed to be calling her, but I did not know where else to turn.

She answered after one ring. Strangely she did not seemed surprised at all to hear from me. In fact, she said, "I knew you would be joining us." Her words gave me an odd and eerie feeling.

Giving me an address, she told me to be there two evenings later at 5:00 P.M. She also informed me, "You will have to purchase a ticket right away on the same flight that I am taking to Cebu." She gave me the airline and flight number and told me that I could probably find the airline ticket office at the mall near my hotel.

After hanging up, I thanked the Lord for the hundred dollars of credit left on my credit card, as I retrieved the card from where I'd hidden it in my bag. Then I headed downstairs to find the mall. Using my credit card to buy the airline ticket would help me avoid spending what precious little cash I had left.

I have to find the mall fast, I thought, exiting the front door of my hotel.

I hailed a cab. Seated inside, I tried to take stock of this new turn in my search for my destiny. Yes, I was on my way again to the spiritual journey I'd undertaken, searching for my identity by doing God's work with the missionaries of the Philippines. And I felt this was my last chance. I asked myself again, *Am I running away?* But I did not feel that way. I really believed that I had found the path to seek out the answer to the riddle which was now my life: What did God have planned for me?

With the physical pain of a bad back and the emotional pain of being abandoned so completely, I desperately needed to cleanse my soul. What I needed was a new starting point in my life. So I smiled and asked for God's beneficant support, as I tried to become the kind and loving man I knew I could be.

I learned a lot that day in Manila as I ventured forth. After the cab dropped me off at the mall, every Filipino that I met and asked directions of wore a constant smile and was courteous beyond what I was used to. Most addressed me as "sir." I have to admit, it was a refreshing change from the rushed, often unhelpful attitudes of many people in the United States.

With their help I was able to find the airline offices and I bought my ticket for the flight on which I would be joining the Blind Prophet and her group. This small success made me feel a little more at ease about my situation. I would still be working with missionaries only in a different way now.

Later that afternoon and evening I set out to explore more of the area around the hotel. I brought along bottled water and some crackers to help keep my stomach settled. Although at first, I tried to stay within sight of the Holiday Inn, which rose above the other buildings around it, I was surprised as I continued my tour to find a very different world not far from where I was stay-ing. As I walked on, my curiosity increased.

The farther away that I roamed, the poorer the neigh-borhoods became. The streets were very dusty, strewn with garbage and had no curbs. Most shops along these streets were inhabited by Filipinos trying to eek out a living selling common, inexpensive items like sodas, candy, peanuts and combs. Some vendors were frying peanuts over a camping stove right on the sidewalk. The sights and smells of Manila were different from anything I'd experienced and very intriguing.

As I trod through those poorer areas I was greeted with smiles and sometimes a "Hey, Joe." When people in the shops saw me coming they rushed out onto the sidewalks pointing to their stores calling out, "Water? Beer? Soda?" Sometimes I was a bit frightened by the rush of people around me. Perhaps assuming I was a wealthy tourist, they all seemed to be drawn to me like a magnet.

Most of the streets had a variety of stores and home-made shops mingled together. There were little stores that were poor man's five and dimes called "Sari Sari" stores. You could walk by a "Sari Sari" store next to a restaurant that was not much different from one in the United States and then pass a wooden storefront covered with chicken wire. There would be people standing at the wood framed window beckoning you to come and try their products.

In most of these crude wooden storefronts I saw every-thing from magazines to candy to small packets of shampoo hanging from the chicken wire enclosure. There were usually dif-ferent empty cans and bottles sitting on a ledge behind the chicken wire demonstrating what kinds of beverages were inside.

I learned quickly to ask for a beverage *malamig* which meant cold. Some of these little family stores had small refrigerators and others did not. If you did not look for a refrigerator or did not specify that you wanted a beverage *malamig* you would be disappointed to get a warm drink. Of course you paid a little bit more for the cold one, just as we often do in the United States.

Another unique type of business I found on the streets of Manila was the small, cafeteria-like restaurants that served food being cooked right in front of you in pots and frying pans. They were set up like buffets, with lines in which you picked the foods you wanted and then sat down at a table in a small dining area. They were called *carenderias*, which was also a general term for small restaurants.

With some time on my hands and feeling relieved to be part of the Blind Prophet's group, I was able to relax and enjoy my new surroundings. The Filipino people, I was finding out, had a way of making you feel special. Once again, I was gladly soaking up this unusual attention which helped boost my sagging self-esteem.

After eating, I walked on, making a few small purchases. I learned the different denominations of the Philippine peso and wrote them down on a little sheet of paper that I kept in my pocket. It was then that I began to understand the benefits of being an American visiting the Philippines. It was definitely an advantage that I welcomed when I found that I could get thirty-eight pesos to one dollar.

During my journey as I got a distance from the hotel, I was solicited by different men and women for a variety of things. Sometimes they simply put their hands out asking for money; other times they produced watches or similar items pitching me to buy their wares.

During the heat of the afternoon as I walked by several Sari-Sari stores, a woman at least in her fifties, stuck her head out of one of the wooden doorways and shocked me with a proposition for a sexual favor. She opened her mouth as if she was sucking on a banana and called out, "Blow job? Only twenty dollar!" Then she motioned for me to come into her little store.

I was shocked that a woman, let alone an older woman, would be so bold as to loudly make that kind of proposition in broad daylight. Politely as I could, I said, "No," and quickly walked on. However, when I recovered from the initial shock, I could not help but chuckle at the boldness of the act, my own embarrassment and the fact that a woman trying to lure men with offers of sexual favors had no teeth.

But as I walked further, and had a few minutes to reflect on what happened, I felt sadness about what had taken place. The incident only served to underscore the desperate poverty these people had to endure. For the first time I understood and saw firsthand why some women were reduced to using their bodies to survive. Who was I to judge them?

It was getting late and I decided to return to my lodgings. However, on my way back to the hotel I passed a combination bar/restaurant where there were several people singing along with a videotape on television. Curious, I went inside. This was my first exposure to the popular phenomenon called Karaoke.

A video monitor displayed either a romantic background or a setting appropriate to the song playing and had lyrics scrolling across the television screen. The person watched the video and sang along into a microphone that was being amplified from a speaker system connected to the video system.

A small crowd of people were in the Karaoke bar/restaurant eating, singing and having a great time. Mostly they were ordering Tanduay rum and San Miguel beer, which I found out were the favorite alcoholic beverages among the locals. At times they smiled and waved for me to join them, but I shyly said, "No, thank you." After watching people sing a few songs and enjoying a cold soda, I made a quick getaway.

As I walked on, I was approached by more pretty Filipina ladies, one of whom asked me, "Do you want a companion?" I was not exactly sure what she meant by "companion" but I had a pretty good guess and I was not going to take any chances. Again, I politely refused the invitation.

Suddenly, feeling very tired, I decided to take a cab the rest of the way back to my hotel. When I finally flagged one and climbed in, I was surprised to hear the driver ask me, "Would you like girl?"

"What do you mean?" I asked.

"You know, a companion," he explained to me.

I thought that a companion might be nice, especially in guiding me around.

Then the cab driver said, "You can keep her all night! She gives good service." I quickly realized the "companion" he offered was more than just a friendly guide. It dawned on me that these girls were rentals in every sense of the word.

I was more and more shocked to see how openly sex was offered and sold on the streets of Manila. It was another insight into the desperation that existed for the poor of the Philippines. A unique and accepted part of their society, prostitution in the Philippines was a blend of companionship, tour guide and casual sex.

As we drove, we also passed many street vendors on the sidewalks selling everything from beverages to fresh fruits. Even inside the cab, I seemed to attract them like a magnet, because, I guess, they saw any white foreigner as someone with money. At each stop along the way I was constantly bombarded with "Pssst, here!" or "Hey, Joe!"

I decided to get out of the cab a few yards away from the hotel where there were a couple of air-conditioned stores that were open twenty-four hours. I bought some more bottled water, soda and snacks. I learned a little more about the different denominations of Philippine currency every time I purchased something.

Looking around, I had another pleasant surprise. Not only was there the McDonalds at which I'd eaten, but a number of other American fast food restaurants nearby. I discovered a Dunkin Donuts and a Kentucky Fried Chicken located very near the Holiday Inn. Although Manila had a good mix of traditional and modern places to eat, because of my meager funds, I had to stick to the exceptionally inexpensive American-style fast food spots. The menus of these places were much more limited than their counterparts in the United States, but they always included rice and spaghetti, as well as some traditional Philippine foods. And just as I found with everything else in

Manila, the price in pesos for a hamburger or fried chicken was much cheaper than in the United States. There were precautions, however, that I had to remind myself to take. To avoid a bad case of stomach or intestinal problems one had to be on guard at all times to stay away from tap water, ice and other unprocessed things to eat and drink.

In addition to the bottled water I kept in my room, I developed the habit of always ordering bottles or cans of sodas to drink rather than fountain beverages. I had learned the hard way what happens when you drink soda with ice.

The more Filipinos I met, the more I was impressed by their friendly and easygoing manner. I also liked their kindness and sense of humor. It was refreshing to be addressed as "sir" and to always be treated with the utmost courtesy.

I decided to have a late dinner at the Kentucky Fried Chicken. I sat down to eat the savory fried chicken just as I would in the United States. One thing that struck me was the very efficient way in which the employees served customers. After the cashier said the customary, "Good evening, sir. Welcome to Kentucky Fried Chicken; can I help you?", she did something else which I thought was unique.

She repeated my order to me and then when she took my money she said, "I receive one hundred pesos from you and give you twenty-three pesos in change." I thought it was a very nice touch and a good sound business practice in making sure that there was good communication between the customer and the cashier.

As I sat there eating my dinner, I noticed two young women sitting together nearby, staring at me and giggling. I smiled politely and tried to keep my focus on my food. The chicken and fries were very crispy and except for the lump of rice that came with my meal, it felt like I was back home.

However, I could not help but be distracted by the giggling women and the way they were eyeing me. A young Filipino man was sitting to my left and he too was watching the commotion with amusement. I smiled sheepishly at him wondering what he must be thinking. Surely there must be some Filipinos that were angered by the excessive attention a foreigner received from the many beautiful young women.

About halfway through my meal one of the young women looked directly into my eyes, leaned over and asked, "Where are you from?"

"I'm an American," I said, and she smiled with satisfaction.

When I turned away, partly out of embarrassment, the dark haired man who had been watching looked curiously at me and asked, "Where from in the United States?"

"I grew up near Chicago," I replied.

"My name is Andy. I have a friend in Chicago." He paused then added, "Do you know Michael Jordan?"

I tried not to chuckle at the question and told him, "No, I have never met him in person."

At that point the two women giggled again and one of them said, "What is your name?" I told them and they politely introduced themselves to me. The woman who had spoken first said, "I hope you excuse my English, it's not good."

I smiled and told her, "Your English sounds very good to me."

They giggled again and I went back to finishing off my chicken and fries. Andy smiled at me and said something that I did not quite hear.

"I'm sorry?" I said to him.

"They have a crush on you," he said, referring to the two girls.

I was surprised at the observation and said "On me? Really?"

Andy nodded approvingly and said, "Yes, they like you!" To that the women erupted in laughter. I could only sit there blushing, not knowing what to say. I was not used to women in their twenties acting this way.

What followed were questions about where I was staying, why I was there and how long I would be in Manila. Andy gave me a look that said, *Go for it!* He was obviously amused by the situation but also seemed genuinely interested in helping me to get to know them.

Finally, one of the women produced a piece of paper, wrote a phone number down on it and handed it to me. "My name is Ricca. I would like to know you," she said sweetly. The other woman giggled and said, "My name is Maria and Ricca has crush on you!" At her words, Ricca smacked her friend gently on the arm in mock anger.

I looked over at Andy who seemed to be guiding me through this encounter. He moved his eyebrows up and down, indicating to me that I should take the number. I took the paper and somehow murmured "Thank you."

As I sat there frozen with embarrassment, the women got up and walked by me, Ricca saying sweetly, "Happy to meet you! Call me!" I told them that I would try.

Andy finished his meal and got up to leave soon after that. He winked at me, looking satisfied, and said, "You should call her, she likes you."

I smiled and said, "Thanks, I appreciate your help."

My encounter left me puzzled as to how these beautiful young women could be so bold and open, yet seemingly so innocent in their behavior. I was also surprised at Andy's role in the encounter. I wondered if one of the real industries in the Philippines, formal or not, was the introduction of young Filipina women to foreigners for the purpose of marriage.

Feeling vulnerable and lonely, I was flattered, but I was not interested in romance and even if I had been, I did not want to begin a relationship with a woman who was probably only interested in me as a ticket out of the poverty in which she lived. But I could not help but be touched by the innocence, beauty and gentle natures of the young women.

I also noticed another aspect of behavior that seemed a part of the culture. Filipinos spoke more with their eyes than with their mouths. When a Filipino, male or female looked at you and raised his or her eyebrows, he or she was saying *Hello!* Once I realized this, I reminded myself often that this was one way they communicated and tried hard not to ignore these non-verbal messages so as not to offend.

As I walked back to my hotel, temptation seemed to be everywhere I looked. But I kept moving and was determined even though extremely lonely not to get involved in a situation that later I might regret. I soon found out it was good to be careful.

The next morning I read in a newspaper provided by the hotel that there were groups of Filipino men and women who entice foreigners away from their hotels with offers of "companionship" and then drug them, taking their money and valuables.

In fact, that very day I was approached on the street in front of my hotel by a woman and a man who greeted me warmly and asked me where I was from. They were very friendly and both of them shook my hand and put their arms around me as if I were a long lost relative. I tried to be polite, but after having read the newspaper article I was wary. When they invited me back to their place for a drink, I politely but firmly refused. They persisted, the man telling me that the woman, his sister, was in love with me. Finally giving up on trying to get me to join them at their place, the man suddenly motioned toward the hotel and asked what room I was staying in. He said adamantly, "My sister wants to get to know you." I could see the only way I was going to break away from the conversation without making a scene was to tell them something, so I finally gave them a fake room number and left them smiling and waving at me. As I walked through the lobby of the hotel and headed toward the elevator, I felt relieved and blessed to have read the newspaper article that very morning.

Back in my room I reflected that in just a few days, I had experienced the many wonders and also the darker side of the big city of Manila. But I felt so grateful to be experiencing this adventure and for the opportunity to help others. Besides, I was learning to really admire the beauty and strength of the Filipino people.

Another impressive aspect of Philippine life I found out about was the people's strong religious convictions. I soon discovered that the depth of their faith was truly inspiring. Religious objects were sold in abundance near churches and most vehicles had some kind of religious adornment. There were even times during the day when everything and everyone stopped for prayer.

I was amazed that a whole nation of people ceased everything they were doing at an appointed time just to pray together. This prayer was a traditional, daily event that stopped all activities in their tracks.

I first witnessed this phenomenon while purchasing groceries. As the cashier checked out the items I had brought to the counter, a bell began ringing over the radio broadcast piped into the store. The cashier stopped immediately and kneeled behind her register as all of the people around me bowed their heads in prayer. I could not help but think that I indeed had come to the right place to improve my relationship with God.

I also found that there were some areas of Manila that were very sad to see. Whether I was walking or taking a cab, there were areas where I was mobbed by dirty, sickly, thin little children begging for pesos or food. One even pointed to the can of soda I had in my hand, while I was sitting in a cab, entreating me to give it to him. I did.

It broke my heart to see so many homeless, malnourished little children and I prayed that I would be able to help some of them. The children and sometimes even adults looked emaciated and often had rags to wear if any clothes at all. In some areas boys, men, girls and women begged in traffic and on the sidewalks.

One haunting sight was a woman in her thirties, totally naked, squatting to urinate next to a tree in full view of every car going by. As the taxi I was in drew close to her I saw her entire body was covered in dirt and her eyes had the look of a ghost. "God help her," I murmured as the cab drove by. What terrible life had the woman endured? I knew that the Philippines was not as developed as some countries, but I was shocked to see the level of poverty.

The sorrow I felt for those street people reminded me that I was not the only one who was down on his luck. My father used to tell me, "There are always people who are worse off than you." And here on the streets of Manila was a vivid demonstration of that very fact. It reminded me of why I was there and how I could be of help.

After a few hours in the heat I was happy to get back to my air-conditioned room. In the short time that I had been in Manila I found myself troubled by sinus infections from the pollution caused by the thick blanket of car exhaust that perpetually hung over Manila. I took my allergy medicine and rested, staying in my hotel room the rest of that last day in the city.

Feeling better that evening, I decided to check out the music of the band playing in the lounge of the hotel. The music was quite lively. The all-Filipino group performed with energy and enthusiasm even though the crowd was a small one. And surprisingly, most of the music was sung in English.

Looking around I realized that this only made sense, because most of the people staying at the Holiday Inn were tourists from Europe, Australia and the United States. I enjoyed a tasty fruit beverage and the music for about an hour or so and then headed upstairs to my room. I was tired and needed to pack my things.

Back in my room, while preparing for the trip I would be taking the next day, I began to again think about the Blind Prophet and the conversation we had days before on the plane which brought me to the Philippines. How did she know that first time we met that I would be joining her? And how would our sojourn turn out?

I felt more and more confident that I was called to this country to do God's work and find myself. A saying I often heard from my church friends came back to me: *When one door closes another door or window will open.* Yes, God's hand was surely in this turn of events.

And so the next day, I began my spiritual journey in the strange and awesome island nation of the Philippines. The experience, I hoped, would be a transformative one.

Chapter Six

Cebu

Early that morning, I checked out of my hotel and found a cab driver who knew how to get to the hotel address the Prophet had given me. After a short drive, we arrived. In the lobby, I met the Blind Prophet and her entourage. We all rode together in a jeepney to the airport.

Our flight, in a small prop-driven plane, took only about an hour and passed over many of the more than 7000 islands that make up the country of the Philippines.

I was lucky to get a window seat and was amazed at the number of lush, dark green islands we flew over. Some were mountainous while others were flat and some appeared inhabited while others seemed totally deserted.

As we neared our destination, the plane descended slowly over a large island with peaks at one end. Then the plane flew in over the mountains and suddenly I saw Cebu on the other side, nestled between the hills and a large seaport. At that moment, an extraordinary feeling of wonder, excitement and trepidation filled me. After circling once the plane landed at a small airport on an island called Mactan that was connected by a long bridge to Cebu.

After emerging from the airport and finding three cabs to accommodate our large group, we headed across Mactan Island and were soon crossing the bridge into Cebu. From the bridge we could see many ships anchored in Cebu harbor. They ranged in size from small wooden fishing boats to large ferries, which looked like cruise ships from a distance.

I was in a cab with the Blind Prophet. While discussing the different types of ships using the port, the Blind Prophet told me about a unique and modern way in which the Filipinos traveled from one island to the next. "Because there are so many islands and people to transport between them, the Philippines has a very unique transportation system. There are numerous ferries, which carry people, vehicles and goods from island to island. And for transportation to and from cities like Cebu there are also ships they call 'Super Cats.'

"A Super Cat is a very large enclosed catamaran that is powered by jet-like propulsion engines. They are modern, fast ships that have all of the latest electronics and computerized navigation equipment. The interiors are impressive also, providing seats as comfortable as an airliner and with much more foot room."

The prophet became animated as she continued describing the luxurious Super Cats. "They are roomy and modern and have at least sixteen rows of seats across, bigger than two jumbo jets. There are refreshment counters where meals and drinks are served, just like any good airline. They also show movies and have several restrooms."

Another member of the group added, "These wonderful ships are very quick and comfortable and run regular routes between major cities in the southern Philippines."

As we came off the bridge and headed into the city of Cebu, I was amazed at how this poor country was able to develop and use a state of the art transportation system like the Super Cat to link its people from island to island. The contrast of their simple lifestyle with their utilization of some of the most modern conveniences on earth was incredible. *What an interesting society this is! What a beautiful and intriguing country this is!* I thought.

We traveled most of the distance between Mactan and Cebu on a modern four-lane highway, but then we found ourselves funneled down into the congested two-lane traffic leading into and out of Cebu.

"The city of Cebu is about half the size of Manila and its suburbs but almost as modern," one of the prophet's followers explained. "An even bigger tourist destination, Cebu is a bustling seaport city much like Manila, except for the beautiful mountains and beaches that surround it."

We arrived in Cebu late in the morning and the drastic change in heat and humidity was immediately evident. I could tell we were even closer to the equator because of the muggy, tropical atmosphere. The people in Cebu were different too, much darker in skin tone and more indigenous in their features. They also spoke a different language. Just when I thought I was becoming familiar with Tagalog, the Philippine national language, I found out that I would have to learn Cebuano and Visayan.

But the beauty of this island was breathtaking. *Tahiti must be like this,* I thought as I looked around the city of Cebu.

Majestic mountains loomed in the distance. I was awestruck by the panorama and the many happy island people I observed.

The women here were even more beautiful than those in Manila! They didn't wear makeup, nor did they need it; they were naturally beautiful, dark skinned women with jet-black hair that hung down to their waists. Here, just as in Manila, the women vastly outnumbered the men.

And just as in Manila, these women, most of them in their late teens and early twenties, stared as if they hoped I would take them away from their difficult lives right then and there. The look in their eyes was truly wanting and yet innocent and childlike. I felt badly for them, knowing that many men would seize the opportunity to take advantage of the women's hope, trust and desperation. This was clearly a place that not only attracted tourists and missionaries, but unsavory men, intent on sexual pleasure and conquest and unconcerned with the feelings, dreams or sad existences of these women. *It is no wonder the sex and prostitution trades flourish in this part of the world,* I thought sadly, as I witnessed many women call out to men on the street. My heart went out to them and their plight.

Yet our mission was not to save the women of the Philippines; it was to help the many homeless and helpless children who roamed the streets of Cebu. Much as in Manila, they ran naked in the streets and banged on the windows of cars begging for pesos or food. Most were not more than six or seven years old.

Again I saw heart wrenching scenes, especially the emaciated children who had no energy left to beg and lay withering in the dirt under trees and bushes along the roadside. Not only deprivation but starvation existed here in Cebu, where I first really saw its face. Tears came to my eyes as I watched the passing poverty and despair of the local people through the windows of our cab.

We settled into a pension, which by American terms was a boarding house, not a hotel. Very spartan in its features, the rooms had cement floors with a bed or beds, plus a table, stool and mirror. Most of us were placed together in a room with six beds. We all shared a common bathroom where a pipe sticking out of the wall served as a shower. The water faucet, about two feet off the floor, was used to fill a bucket with a ladle. When washing, you filled the bucket with water, soaped yourself, and then used the large ladle to rinse yourself.

The toilet consisted of a mushroom-like stump sticking up from the floor with no tank or flush handle. It was hard on your rump to sit upon. To flush the toilet, you would use the same bucket used to wash your body. You had to fill it up and pour the water into the toilet to flush your waste down the drain. I did not mind that there was no hot water, because you really did not need it. Washing with cool water was one way of beating the heat. Even at night the air stayed hot, humid and stagnant, especially inside any building.

It was a simple way of life, but it really was not that difficult to adapt as you learn some common sense habits very quickly. For example, I immediately found out the value of wearing slippers or thong sandals (flip-flops) in the shower and bathroom, because, except for soap, shoes were the only protection against bacteria.

My towel and slippers fast became my second and third most valuable items, right after the most important item, toilet paper. I soon learned to carry toilet paper with me wherever I went, because it was not provided in most of the bathrooms, public or private, in the Philippines.

Since they are so easily stolen, there were not even toilet tissue holders located near the toilets. Only the best public restrooms provided a vending machine where you could purchase tissue.

Despite the lack of what we Americans think of as essentials, I was enchanted by the exotic beauty of Cebu and its people. The city spread out from the base of a lush green mountain range fanning into a sprawling port complex on the ocean. It was beautifully located and it was easy to see why it had become a historical port of call. The harbor was full of neatly docked ships with many other ships anchored farther out, waiting their turn to reach port. Although it was nowhere near the size of Manila, Cebu had the same "mix of the old and the new" quality to it. There was a small city center, a business hub, consisting of a few tall buildings. Most of the tall buildings in Cebu were hotels.

When I accompanied some friends of the Blind Prophet on their rounds, I met a personable young man named Remy. A Cebuano, Remy would be using his knowledge of the island and its surroundings to assist the Blind Prophet and her team. I liked him immediately. I was also befriended by Ronnie and Teresa, a Filipino couple, who had a daughter who was married to an American. They were part of the Blind Prophet's network and immediately took a liking to me, because I was American. In fact, most Filipinos that I met liked Americans, especially the older ones. I learned that alot of the older males had fought alongside Americans in freeing their country from the Japanese in World War II.

Of course, there were a few who only remembered the excesses and abuses of the American military during the Vietnam War. But many of the very young Filipinos admired Americans and everything American. I was constantly mobbed and bombarded with the same questions like, "Do you know Michael Jordan?" And occasionally they would tell me that I looked like Chuck Norris. Some of them even called me "Chuck," which became comical at times.

It soon became obvious to me that watching basketball was a favorite pastime among the Filipino people. They loved the Chicago Bulls even though they were no longer NBA champions. In addition to watching basketball, the men loved to watch and talk about boxing.

The southern Filipinos from Cebu were even more friendly and easygoing than the people I met in Manila. Always smiling and joking, they made me feel at ease and welcomed me to their island paradise. This experience was turning out to be everything I needed and more.

With Ronnie and Teresa as guides we traveled in and out of the Cebu city limits running errands. The couple was always friendly and polite, introducing me to every person or group with which we came in contact. Cebu was not as flat and spread out as Manila. There were many very colorful sounding communities like Lahug, Banawa and Guadalupe bunched around Cebu. The people of those suburbs were very poor but friendly and courteous.

After completing some errands we headed to downtown Cebu. I was surprised by the amount of movie theaters. The theaters normally played Tagalog movies but usually had at least one American feature in English. Going to the movies here was a good, inexpensive form of entertainment. I made a mental note to make an effort to see a Tagalog movie before I left the city.

Then we visited some department stores and walked through some of the downtown streets, checking out shops as we went. Cebu, much like Manila, had new, modern-looking shops alongside wooden, makeshift booths with wood and chicken wire storefronts. And even Cebu had a Dunkin' Donuts and a McDonalds.

At one of the many small downtown *carenderias*, I was able to taste some of the local foods. The typical fare was chicken or pork barbecued on a stick. And, of course, this was always accompanied by rice, usually packed in a tidy little ball inside neatly woven green leaves.

I also noticed that there were many pawn shops. Most of them were really jewelry stores where you could also pawn jewelry and cameras. In fact, everything from sunglasses to radios could be pawned in most of the shops along the streets.

Downtown Cebu, like Manila, had pollution, with tricycles, motorcycles and cabs making up most of the traffic. The streets were covered with an ever-present layer of dirt and dust. Although the traffic was not quite the bumper-to-bumper kind that I had seen in Manila, the roadways were crammed with fast moving vehicles always jockeying for a better lane.

Hailing a cab always entailed the same kind of wild ride that I had experienced in Manila. Cab drivers quickly got frustrated with the heavy traffic and twisted and turned their vehicles using every short cut, side street and alley at their disposal. Again I was amazed that there were not more fights or accidents between these intensely competitive drivers. However, soon I decided it was just their nature to drive aggressively, honking their horns in order to let the people around them know that they were coming through.

Just as in Manila, the people of Cebu were gentle and outgoing. Even when I was riding in air-conditioned taxis, the people on the streets who caught glimpses of me waved and smiled. At times, it was as if I were a celebrity.

In fact, when I walked the street, whether I was going to a store or returning to the pension, I was overwhelmed with attention from children, teenagers, women and even men. I felt conspicuous being so pale-skinned and I could not help but be the tiniest bit envious of the natural, tawny beauty of the native people.

Another thing that I noticed was the local style of dress for most of the Cebuanos was very conservative. They wore subdued colors like white, black, gray and brown, not the bright colors, pastels and flashy, sometimes garish, clothing I had been used to seeing worn in Florida. But this old-fashioned way of dressing only made the men and women look more polished and seem highly genteel. Men often wore dress pants and button-down shirts or suits while most of the girls and women wore skirts and dresses with old fashioned shoes or sandals. Both genders took great care in grooming their hair and skin and many smelled like fresh soap when they passed by.

One morning shortly after I'd arrived in Cebu, I passed three young women on the sidewalk, maybe eighteen or nineteen years old, who stopped and began talking to me. They asked the usual questions—where are you from, what is America like, do you know Michael Jordan, etc. I was getting used to the fascination with my "American-ness" but what surprised me this time was how the girls couldn't seem to hear enough about my life in the United States. The girls began following me, asking if they could come along wherever I was headed so they could learn more about my country.

I was amazed at the unusual combination of both assertiveness and shyness they exhibited. The young people normally traveled in groups of three to five and the girls, in particular, always held hands or wrapped their arms around each other. They did this even while walking. It was the picture of innocent, carefree youth. Cebu was a truly a remarkable place.

That evening, Ronnie and Teresa took me to a place high up on a mountain that overlooked the city. They brought along a young woman who they introduced as their niece, Clarissa. It was obvious that they were hoping to match me up with her, and they kept talking about their daughter who was also married to an American. I gently reminded them I was in the country to do God's work, and I had to stay focused on that goal. However, not wanting to seem impolite, I gave the young woman my full attention.

Their niece was shy but curious and did not seem as comfortable speaking English as they did. So I tried to utilize as much Cebuano as I could that evening just to keep a conversation going.

The Filipino couple took every opportunity during the evening to push us together. I got the feeling that Clarissa was no more inclined to be matched up than I was. She was only eighteen and as far as I was concerned, she was way too young for me. But I did my best to seem attentive out of courtesy to her even though both of us knew that it was just to please her aunt and uncle.

When we reached the mountain top, we found a little restaurant where we ate dinner and enjoyed the view. Cebu at night was a beautiful sight. We were high enough on the mountain to enjoy the clear, starry sky while looking down onto the city lights twinkling below us. The tropical surroundings and the ocean background made the view that evening absolutely awesome.

I could not believe my good fortune to be on a spiritual mission in this beautiful tropical paradise. As we sat at the mountain top café eating barbecued pork and enjoying the breathtaking view, I said a silent prayer of thanks to God for leading me to this wonderful place and its kind and loving people.

After only a few days there, the Blind Prophet told me that she needed to make a short trip to another island just south of Cebu and wanted me to come with her. "You will help me to serve the children there." Anxious to begin my missionary duties, I made plans to leave with her the next day.

The Prophet explained, "My purpose in going there, just as it was in Cebu, is to raise money and find ways to provide food, clothing and housing to homeless and disabled children." She went on to say that we would hold revivals, fundraising drives and build shelters as well as also provide some much needed medical assistance for impoverished children. I was looking forward to finally getting the chance to actively help others who were so much more unfortunate than I.

That night, Remy, whom I had met when we first arrived in Cebu, proudly took me to a large, indoor mall. It was very similar to malls in the United States; in fact it was nicer than some I had frequented at home.

Stepping through the doors of the shopping center, we left the hot, dusty streets of Cebu and entered a totally new and modern world. The mall was about one mile square and had every kind of shop, restaurant and institution that you could want. There were two different amusement areas at each end which featured the latest in video gaming and rides.

American restaurants from Pizza Hut to Subway were in abundance. Banks, music stores, toy stores and department stores filled the mall along with six movie theaters.

Inside this air-conditioned, clean city-within-a-city, I was able to see the more affluent side of Philippine life. Most of the people in the mall were wearing expensive clothes and jewelry, and looked much like Americans do. Some were even talking on cell phones as they walked by. It amazed me that in the middle of this impoverished city with its dirt roads, street people and traffic congested with motorcycles and jeepneys, there was this high tech mall, like a sparkling oasis in the middle of a desert of heat, dust and poverty. It was very much a contrast between two different worlds.

Remy also took me to find a "Money Changer" and I changed some more of the little money I now had left into pesos. The rate was thirty-nine pesos to the dollar, even better than in Manila. The American dollar took you a long way here and I again was grateful because my funds were so meager.

After eating dinner at the mall, I suggested we head back to the pension, because it was getting late. Remy said, "You must sample Cebu's nightlife before you go off."

"I don't know. I can't spend very much," I said uncertainly.

"I will pay," he offered and so I cautiously followed him.

Remy took me to a different kind of Karaoke bar. This one was filled with beautiful, scantily clad young girls who were doing the singing and were also dancing on a large stage. Remy smiled and laughed when my jaw dropped upon seeing the many raven-haired, tropical beauties offering me a chance to sing. They all stared and pointed at me when we walked in and flirted shamelessly with us the whole time we where there.

Remy found us a table where we sat and ordered two sodas. After the drinks came, an older woman approached smiling and shook my hand. "Welcome, welcome," she said as she sat down next to me. "Where you from?" she asked politely.

"U.S.A.," I responded.

"Many pretty girl here," she said. "You choose one, yes?"

My face flushed red and I was speechless. I smiled shyly and blurted out, "Too many pretty girls. I cannot pick one."

Remy and the woman laughed at me and she insisted again, "We find nice girl for you!"

Remy told me that the girls earned only what tips they might get from the customers for their dancing and that it was also expected to buy the girls drinks. "Well, you pick one that you like and then I will pick one," I challenged.

Remy smiled, "No, I have wife, but you don't!"

I surveyed the many girls who all seemed to be staring right back at me. I felt guilty just looking at them; it did not feel right. However, I couldn't help but look into a pair of eyes and feel the eagerness and admiration pulling me toward them.

Remy laughed again at me as I just sat there speechless staring at the twenty or so beautiful young women. "No, I cannot do it," I finally said to Remy. I looked him right in the eye and told him, "I cannot choose one over another, it's just not fair. If I bought one a drink, I should buy all of them a drink!"

Remy looked surprised by my sudden burst of logic. But he shook his head in agreement with me. "You are right," he responded. I could not help thinking that he was testing me. I was being tested for sure, but by whom?

We left soon after and I found out from Remy that the place we had gone into was very common in Cebu. He told me, "There are many of those places, because there are many families whose only income comes from their sisters or daughters who work there." Once again, it made me sad to think that the women of this country had to use their youth and beauty in that way.

Remy also told me one other shocking aspect about the many Karaoke bars in Cebu. "Men who go into these places can negotiate a deal with the boss woman, or mama-son, to take a girl home with them. It's called a 'Bar Fine.'" I asked Remy if he had ever done it. He told me no, that even before he met his wife he never had the money it would require.

I felt a little upset that Remy would take me to a place like that, but at the same time it was another eye-opening experience that educated me further about the poverty of the Philippines. It reinforced what I had already come to suspect: there was a sleazy underside to this beautiful country, one born out of desperation.

Before we returned to the pension that evening, Remy and I went to a store where we could buy some cold sodas and water. On our way back we passed in front of one of the bigger hotels in the city center. As we walked by, first one and then two Filipino boys came up to us. They approached me and said, "You want girl?" and "You want companion?" I was shocked, because they were so young themselves. I felt a little sick seeing these teenagers acting as pimps, selling young girls to foreigners for sex.

When I said no thank you they still persisted, saying, "I have young girl, pretty girl, you like to see; I show you many girls, you pick." I was astounded. Remy just looked at me, watching my reaction.

"Look here, I have three girl here," another young man said, pointing to a car parked near by. "There, you choose one you like," he continued. I peered over at the car and sure enough, there were three young girls inside, not more than seventeen years old, waving and smiling at me. "Girls give good service," the young man said.

I shook my head in disgust. "No thanks, no thanks," I said as I turned and tried to escape the situation.

A different man jumped in front of me and said, "You want virgin?"

"No!" I practically shouted. "No, no need!" I quickly walked away from them, not caring if Remy was coming with me or not. I just had to get away from there as fast as possible.

As I turned a corner, I looked back and saw Remy say something to one of the guys. Then he followed me around the corner of the building. I was appalled at the casual way in which these people were peddling sex. At the same time I was reminded of my own loneliness. I missed being in a loving relationship with a woman. Yet, there was nothing appealing about the degradation I was seeing on the streets of Cebu.

Sure, there were many beautiful young women in this country. And now some were being offered to me like pieces of candy in a candy store. But the sad truth behind these offers, the poverty and desperation, turned what would be considered sexy or alluring by some, into something I saw as sad and depressing.

When I returned to my room at the pension, I prayed for strength and enlightenment. I asked that despite any hardships, I would do God's work here in the Philippines. I asked to make a difference. I needed that to feel whole again.

I did not sleep well that night in the hot, humid air of the large sleeping room. Every sound made by the other five sleeping people seemed magnified in the quiet darkness. The bed was hard and uncomfortable and my bad back was aching with pain as hour followed hour. As the first daylight broke through the windows, I hurried to become one of the first into the bathroom for a cold shower.

Tired but clean, I felt refreshed and ready for the coming boat trip. I thanked God for this opportunity to renew my spirit through Him. And most of all, to make something meaningful of my life again by giving what little I had to help the people here who had nothing.

As we emerged into the bright sunlight of the early morning, the streets were again busy with motorcycle traffic, noisy and spewing fumes of exhaust up and down the dusty streets.

The Blind Prophet and her entourage entered two cabs while Remy and I waited for another. "You know the way to the ferry, right?" I asked him.

"Yes, yes," he assured me. It took another five minutes for us to find an empty cab willing to take us to the port. Fortunately, we had paid for our rooms at the pension and had left most of our luggage, locked and guarded there while we traveled to this other island. I had one small carry-on bag with me and Remy had a small duffle bag with him.

As we drove, I reflected on how quickly Remy had grown fond of me and I of him. He was a pleasant young Filipino man in his early twenties, married with a two-year-old child at home. Trim and muscular, he had the appearance of a handsome, well-conditioned boxer and I wondered if he had played sports in school as I had.

After about fifteen minutes of maneuvering through heavy traffic we approached an area clogged with cardboard and wooden shacks. Toward the end of this shantytown, in the blue morning sky above the rooftops, we could see the top of masts and communication antennae from ships in the port ahead of us. The driver, like most cab drivers, seemed to have his own little short cuts around traffic to get us where we needed to go. At each impasse he pulled out of traffic. Now he turned right, driving down a long row of boxcar type containers that a freighter would carry. The driver slowed the cab down to a crawl and peered through the rows of containers looking for a quick path between them.

Remy and I were talking about what time the ship was supposed to leave when suddenly the cab came to a lurching halt. Both he and I were thrown forward bumping our heads on the seats in front of us. The driver let out a strange sounding yelp as Remy and I looked with astonishment out through the front window of the cab. Quickly surrounding us were a dirty looking bunch of men, some wearing bandanas across their face, others wearing black ski masks, waving assault rifles at us. We froze, not knowing what to do. "Are they the Port police?" I whispered to Remy.

It was then that he said quietly, "I think they are bandits." I looked in horror as the men yanked open the doors of the cab.

This can't be happening, I kept thinking. *Are we being robbed?* The cab driver was yanked violently from his seat and pushed spread-eagle against one of the shipping containers. Another man reached in and pulled Remy out. For some reason the man on my side did not reach in and grab me; instead, screaming loudly and waving his AK47 rifle at me, he motioned me out. As I stood up outside the cab I lost sight of what was happening on the other side of the car, but I could hear men screaming at Remy and the cab driver.

In front of me the man raised his rifle and pointed it right between my eyes, only inches from my face. The blood drained from my head to my feet in an instant and I thought I would urinate in my pants. It was like a scene from a bad dream, but I was frozen in fear knowing that this was real. Someone on the other side of the cab yelled in pain as I heard something hit with a loud thud. But I could not move, staring at the rifle pointed at my head, praying that he was not going to pull the trigger.

Then everything went black. I fell to my knees and my hands instinctively reached out in front of me to break my fall. I felt a sharp pain in the back of my head and realized I had been hit from behind. Suddenly I was aware of some kind of cloth or hood being pulled over my head. I could not see. *My God,* I thought, *Are they going to hang me?*

I gasped for air through the cloth. Then I felt a rope dropped over my shoulders and pulled down tightly over my chest and arms. Someone pulled me to my feet then tightened the rope, pinning my arms against my sides. At almost the same instant someone grabbed my hands and tied them together in front of me. Both the ropes around my hands and around my waist were pulled tighter and tighter until all I could do was yell in pain. "Ahhhhhhhh!" I protested loudly, just before the hood was raised up to my nose and a roll of cloth was shoved roughly into my mouth, abruptly silencing my cries of pain. I choked and gagged on the cloth in my mouth as the hood was tied tightly around the back of my head.

Then I became aware of the anguished cries coming from Remy and the cab driver. There was more yelling and then loud thuds. I assumed they were being beaten and tied up also. But the cries turned to muffled moans as I heard the pounding sound of fists or guns against their bodies. Were they now gagged too or unconscious? For a brief moment I wondered why I was not being beaten like them.

I could not breathe and I was struggling to take in air through my nose. It was then that a voice yelled into my right ear. In a heavy Filipino accent he spoke broken English, "YOU, YO FOLA ROP! NOW! EY YO PATAY!" My mind raced, trying to figure out what he was saying to me.

My heart froze, and for a moment my legs turned to jelly. I could not move, I was shaking. "NOW!" He yelled louder. "EY YO PATAY! Or you will die!" I didn't understand the words, but his threat was clear and shook me to the bone. I felt the rope pulling me and began to take small uncertain steps forward.

God help me, I thought, and stumbled forward amidst the yelling and muffled moans of pain.

Part Two

Chapter Seven

A Trip to Nowhere

In those first few moments after we were kidnapped, I was too stunned to think. Then the horror of the event hit me. Never had I felt so helpless. Still struggling for breath and essentially blind because of the hood over my head, I was dragged along by the tight rope around my waist. I had no idea how far or how long we traveled. It felt like an eternity, but the muffled sounds of the city and ships told me we weren't very far from the spot where we'd been forced from the cab at gunpoint. All the while my captors yelled and kicked me in the legs and hit me from behind with rifle barrels.

Between the pain and noxious smell of the old, dirty fabric covering my head, I nearly passed out. I felt like vomiting, but the cloth gag in my mouth seemed to hold this impulse in check. Nevertheless, my body was a mass of nausea and misery as I stumbled along, almost falling to the ground several times. That was when they screamed and cursed at me the most in a language I did not understand. They continued kicking and prodding me to stay on my feet and keep going. I was aware that somewhere in front of me several people were crying out with pain from being taunted and kicked. I assumed among them were Remy and the cab driver.

I could not help but think how terrible the news of our being taken hostage would be for Remy's wife and child. But I wondered if anyone would even miss me at all. Maybe this was my fate. Maybe this was to be my punishment for all the mistakes I had made in my life. Fear fogged my mind. I felt utterly bereft.

Finally, we stopped. The yelling turned to whispering. I could not understand anything that was being said. My captors spoke in fast, guttural grunts. Suddenly the strong smell of salty ocean air penetrated the stinking cloth covering my head. *We must be on a pier at the port,* I thought to myself. A second later I was yanked forward again by the rope and pushed up a ramp onto something that was bobbing up and down. I could feel us rocking backing and forth and hear the roar of water breaking against the shoreline. *They're forcing me onto a boat. Where are they taking me?*

I was guided a few feet then forcefully shoved forward; I stumbled down some steps into a room, barely managing to remain standing. Suddenly, what felt like a gun barrel smacked me across the chest sending me backwards onto a bench or seat of some kind. Hands grabbed my feet and I felt more rope being tied around my ankles. I struggled to keep my balance and sit upright without toppling over on my side. I was growing more and more fearful by the minute.

I kept asking myself why they were doing this to me. And then I remembered some of the stories I had heard and read about Christian missionaries being abducted and killed in places with political turmoil. Some were held for ransom. Some were tortured. One news report said a man was decapitated and his skull cooked like an egg; the rebels then ate his brains from a hole smashed in the top of his skull. I shivered. Is this what was going to happen to me? What possible interest could they have in me? I wasn't a priest or pastor and I had no money.

My dark thoughts were interrupted by the loud grinding sound of an engine starting. Soon the grinding turned to a roar as at least two engines were brought to life. After I heard them gunning the engines several times, the boat leapt forward. I was thrown sideways off the bench smashing my head into a wall. I tried to sit up again but, dizziness overcame me and I passed out.

I don't know how long I was unconscious; it might have been hours. When I awoke, all I heard was the sound of the boat pounding the sea as it jumped from wave to wave, banging my head against the floor. It throbbed with pain as I tried to focus on where I was, what was happening. At one point I used all my strength to twist my body up against the side of the boat trying to get into a sitting position. The stench of gasoline and oil hung in the hot, humid air around my covered head. I squinted trying to see through the cloth covering my face. I could not. And there was no other sound except for the engines and the thumping of the waves as they hit the hull. *Thump, ka-thump, thump, ka-thump*, the severe jolts threatened to turn me over on my side again and again.

As the voyage went on I listened for other sounds, human or otherwise. The boat seemed to be traveling very fast. But to where? Where were these guys taking us? I wondered if Remy was on the boat and, if he was in the same area as I was, unable to see or speak just like me. "Ooonnie." I tried pitifully to call Remy's name through the gag in my mouth. I paused hoping to hear him moan back at me. But there was not a sound, only the ferocious beating of my own heart.

My thoughts traveled back to Cebu and the Blind Prophet. Did she know what had happened to us? Would she send someone to search for us? She must have realized by now that we were missing. The anxiety I was feeling made my body sweat profusely. My clothes clung to me and my mouth was dry and crusting. *I have never been so thirsty.*

My mind wandered, thinking about the vast ocean around us. *My God,* I thought, *no one will ever find us.* Again came the incessant question. *Where are they taking us?* Suddenly the boat veered to the right throwing me down again, face first onto the floor. Then the boat made a turn, straightened out and picked up speed again. *Thump, ka-thump,* the pounding started again.

By that time I was too exhausted to move; I just lay there on my side, my head banging against the hull in time to the rhythmic crashing of the waves. *All I can do is pray,* I told myself. *Dear God help me.* I tried to mouth the words and soon fell into unconsciousness, rocked to sleep by the rhythm of the sea around me.

I don't know how long I was out when suddenly, searing pain lurched me into consciousness. "Ouuwwwwwww!" I tried to scream, the pain in my ribs burning me as a boot kicked my chest again and again. "Ahhhhhhhhh!" I moaned angrily through the gag. The kicking stopped. Someone grabbed me by the rope around my waist, yanking me to my feet. Then I heard the unmistakable sound of a knife cutting through the rope around my ankles and I was able to move my feet again.

I was attempting to find some balance when I realized that the boat had stopped and the engines were off. As the boat rocked slowly back and forth I tried to remain upright. I felt someone pulling the rope around my waist, leading me up some stairs and into the fresh salty air above. Ahhhh, fresh air, it smelled so good even through the hood I still wore.

A moment or two later a man's voice yelled something into my ear, but I did not understand what he was saying. Then two sets of hands grabbed and held me still as the rope around my neck was loosened. The cloth covering my head was pulled violently backwards and off, creating a sting like a rug burn on my nose and forehead. The gag was ripped from my mouth. My body felt like jelly and I squinted. I tried to focus my eyes, but I could hardly stand straight and could not see. My eyes were watering as they tried to adjust to the sunlight reflecting brightly off the water around us. But the men gave me no chance to pull myself together. They began dragging me stumbling off the boat and onto an old, wooden dock.

Reaching the end of the dock, we stepped onto land and I looked up to see thick foliage ahead of us. Turning to my left, I could see the curve of the shoreline winding its way along the turquoise water, the mid afternoon sun shining down. How I wished that I were on this island under much different circumstances, but my wistful hoping was quickly cut short as the precariousness of my predicament flooded back.

POW! I went crashing to the ground head first. I felt my jaw start to swell from the impact of being hit by the rifle butt. My mouth was filling with blood and something else, hard and gritty. Using my tongue, I searched the inside of my mouth and sure enough, felt first an empty space and then, one large lower tooth. I wanted to reach up and get it, but my arms were still pinned to my side by the rope around my waist so I spit it out.

The pain of the blow made me dizzy as I tried to stand up on the muddy shore. I couldn't get off my knees.

The kidnapper closest to me yelled angrily in my face; again I did not recognize the language. Another man strode towards me and pulled me up by the rope. "Go! Go!" he yelled, pointing his rifle into the jungle in front of me.

I looked in that direction. It was then that I caught a glimpse of Remy and the cab driver several yards ahead of me. There were a number of other men tied together with them. I wondered why the kidnappers were keeping me separate from the others, but had little time to consider it as I felt myself being dragged by the rope up a path and into the cool, dark cover of the jungle.

I staggered and fell several times, my left leg growing weak from the constant pain in my back. At the same time I was swallowing my own blood as it continued to fill up my mouth. Each time I fell I was abruptly kicked and pulled to my feet amidst angry screams from the armed men around me.

Every time I tried to look around or at them they raised their rifle butts to my head, threatening to strike me again if I did not keep my eyes fixed on the trail in front of me. I obeyed, but tried to concentrate on remembering the landmarks we passed as I used the little energy left in my body to keep my legs moving forward. I feared what the consequences would be if I fell again.

Deeper into the jungle we went. And as the brush and tropical plants got thicker and thicker, the ground itself began to rise slowly but steadily upward. Even the men in front of me were slipping and sometimes falling as they tried to climb their way up the arduous path in front of us. Chunks of coral rock as well as the thick underbrush jutted up and out as we moved forward. As we continued farther into the jungle, the thick canopy of trees, vines and bushes created a spooky darkness.

It was as if we were moving slowly through a tunnel so dark that you could not see except for the small shafts of sunlight shining through tiny open spaces. Steeper and steeper the muddy path rose before us; the angle of the hill we were climbing was becoming more difficult to navigate.

Coral rock and mud cut at our feet with every step. I could not help slipping and then stumbling from one muddy slope to jagged pieces of rock, which stuck out of the ground. In the semi-darkness, I tried to concentrate on finding safe places to step.

Finally, the man behind me stopped and loosened the rope pinning my arms to my body. He knew I would have to use my hands on the next part of the climb. Now, even with my hands still tied together, I was able to move my arms enough to reach out and grasp the rope in front of me that the captors had used to bind us all together. This gave me better control over my own balance and direction.

After a moment of adjusting to this newfound freedom, I glanced back at the man who had freed my arms. But before I could get a good look at his face, he raised his rifle to my head, threatening to strike me with it. I flinched and ducked my head anticipating the blow. He barked out some words to me. Then he motioned me up the path swinging the barrel of his rifle in front of my face. I obeyed his silent command. Turning quickly and moving forward, I kept my eyes and my hands on the rope in front of me.

My mouth still ached because of the tooth they had knocked out. I felt around with my tongue. I was surprised to find that a metal post, as thin as a needle, was still sticking straight up from the hole where my tooth used to be. *Amazing,* I thought to myself. The steel post from the root canal had survived the blow and was still imbedded deeply and securely into my lower jaw.

As the day wore on the air was becoming more humid and the pungent smells of rotting vegetation on the jungle floor replaced the fresh ocean air of the shoreline. Deeper and higher we went, like a trail of ants all tied to each other, some pulling and others struggling to keep their balance. Small flies began to stick to my sweaty face and I could not move my hands to swat them away. Soon I felt the sharp, prickling sensations of mosquitoes taking their time feeding on my blood. Looking down I saw the big, black mosquitoes, larger than houseflies, biting on my arms and legs. I could also feel them assaulting my face and neck. My legs were muddy and stinging from the small slashing cuts I received from plants and outcrops of coral that scraped and cut me as I pulled myself upward.

The silence of the jungle was broken occasionally by the sharp grunts and loud screaming of our captors prodding us on. I felt relieved that the steepness of our climb had now limited their ability to torment us with kicks and blows.

As the air thinned I had to breathe through my mouth, my lips and throat now parched except for occasional drops of sweat coming from my mustache. Even my own sweat tasted good, momentarily easing my thirst as I struggled to stay focused on the line in front of me and tried to keep my legs moving forward. Then as the climb got steeper, our pace slowed even further. Each person helped pull the next up, slowing our line to a crawl as we went from one coral outcrop to another.

By then my eyes stung from the salty sweat dripping into them. The muscles in my arms and legs burned with the effort of struggling upwards and the strain of trying to keep my balance. Yet there was nothing I could do but follow my captors' commands, moving forward like an animal, harnessed and tethered by the rope. The pulling, grunting and straining upwards on the jungle hillside seemed to go on forever.

My left leg continued to weaken as both it and my back burned and throbbed from the difficult climb. In the several years since my back surgery, I had learned to live with almost constant pain radiating from my back down into my left leg. Lately, however, I had been experiencing a gradual paralysis of my left leg. I attributed it to nerve damage in my back.

I had also been noticing a lack of control of my bladder and bowels. Now the feeling returned with a vengeance. I knew what was happening; yet, I tried to pretend it did not exist. I was too proud to think any other way.

After what seemed like hours, I saw that the group of kidnappers in front of us was moving toward a small clearing ahead. As a wide beam of late day sunlight lit up the center of the clearing, I saw old trunks from dead trees laid across a patch of grass. It was like an oasis in the middle of the dense, dark jungle. Once we reached it, we were finally allowed to sit and catch our breath in this surreal setting.

As we rested on the fallen tree trunks in a circle around the shaft of waning sunlight, I had a quick vision of my days as a boy scout, sitting at a campfire. Now the last flickering rays of sunlight lit the jungle earth in front of us. It was one of those strange but beautiful scenes etched in my memory forever. I looked around and suddenly reality returned. I was at the mercy of armed bandits with whom I could not even communicate. I asked myself again, *What could they possibly want from me?*

My own helplessness washed over me as I realized that I could no longer hold my bladder. I did not dare request a private moment to relieve myself; I was too afraid of their reaction. So I just sat there, frightened, sweaty and exhausted and urinated down my leg, hoping that no one around me would notice. In a day filled with degradation and cruelty, it was a moment of hopeless humiliation that I would never forget.

As I sat there having reached this low point, I prayed for God to give me the strength to survive this horror. I prayed for Him to help me find a way to escape from my captivity. I prayed for Him to spare Remy, the cab driver and me, so that someday we would all see our children again. Tears filled my eyes and I fell forward on my knees as I realized that only God could help me now. I was powerless.

"Utt! Utt!" A man in front of me waved his rifle at me, motioning me to get up and start moving again. The brief rest had brought life back to my legs. I thought of trying to run away but realized that I didn't know the terrain and would be caught immediately. I thought to myself, *Don't do anything stupid!* My lips started to curl into a smile as I realized how funny it was that I was silently coaching myself. I tried to stop, knowing that grinning would only get me in more trouble. I put on my best poker face and trudged on behind the line of men in front of me.

With the daylight now fading into murky shadows, I looked for something, anything, which would help me remember our path and surroundings. I knew I had to learn all I could about this place and keep my wits about me if I was to survive here.

I realized I now had work to do. It no longer mattered why they had me as their captive. I could not waste time obsessing about why they had captured me. Nor was there time for grief and pity. It was time to be alert, smart and aware, if I wanted to survive. I began to focus again in a subtle way, on the smallest details of my surroundings and my captors. I knew I had to start laying the groundwork for my own escape and stay levelheaded enough to help Remy and the others who were captives like me.

As if in answer to my earlier prayer, a rush of resolve shot up my spine, straightening my body as my courage began to return to me. It brought a newfound confidence that soon turned into a silent anger I felt building inside me. *Who are these people? How dare they think they can abuse us this way!* Angry thoughts shot through my mind. But the voice of reason intervened. *Store it,* I said to myself. *Don't waste that energy on hate. Use it to power your legs; use it to power your thinking. Use it as fuel to make you stronger!*

Suddenly, I realized that my steps had quickened and I was climbing faster. I looked around and saw the dim form of a man behind me. The shadowy outline of the assault rifle in his hands reminded me to be careful. I was beginning to outpace him. *Slow down,* I said to myself, *don't give away your new found strength.* The pattern of pulling and tugging resumed as our rope line stretched out single file again to climb up a steep, bushy slope. Vines and plants whipped my face as I was pulled from one muddy foothold to another.

Then I did something that surprised both me and the kidnapper who followed me. After being pulled to the next ledge, by the rope still around my waist, I turned around and reached out my hands, still tied together, to assist the armed man behind me. He slung his rifle over his shoulder and, almost instinctively started to reach his hand toward mine. I stared first at my hands and then at his in disbelief. Then his eyes met mine. The determined look on his face changed suddenly to a look of shock and disdain. Stopping he waved his hand angrily at me, yelling "No! No no!" Quickly I withdrew my hand and turned around, feeling stupid and embarrassed.

"You idiot!" I murmured to myself. *What if my offer of help angered him?* I could be beaten or even shot for such an act. I tried to compose myself as I pulled upward on the rope in front of me.

Now we were climbing almost straight up a cliff of coral rock, still sheltered by the heavy overgrowth of trees above us. I did not dare look back at the kidnapper with the gun. "Don't give him more reasons to beat you," I muttered to myself. So I kept my eyes straight ahead and pulled myself from ledge to ledge like the men in front of me were doing.

As we pulled ourselves up the mountain, I could not help but wonder how my offer of help was perceived by the man? Did it make him angry? Or would it be a moment of kindness he might remember in the future? One thing seemed clear: he was as startled and embarrassed as I was by that awkward moment. I could only hope that I had not made him hate me more.

It must have been an hour or so that we continued our slow, painful climb up the mountainside. Blisters, which had formed earlier on my hands, were now torn open creating raw and bleeding creases in my palms. When we finally emerged from the thick jungle into a rocky ravine that ran sideways around the side of the mountain, a blanket of darkness lit by stars had fallen. Everyone, including our captors, stood still for a few moments to catch their breath.

Above us the stars twinkled in the now clear, cool evening air. The mountainside was brightly lit by a full moon looming large overhead. Below us, the ocean danced with the sparkling lights from the evening sky. Not a man-made light could be seen, only the contours of the island bathed in moonlight, as it sloped downward into the sea around us.

Once again I saw awesome natural beauty that moved me, yet my feelings about the setting were out of place considering the dire circumstances. As I looked around at our captors, they too seemed transfixed by the sight of our beautiful surroundings. "What are they thinking?" I murmured quietly. How could such hatred and brutality exist in this God given scene? Perhaps these men did not believe in His goodness and love? *In what, then, do they believe?* I wondered.

Would I ever know human love again? I could not help thinking that maybe this beauty before me was one last gift from God before my life ended. I stood there in the moonlight soaking up the pleasure of the night, knowing that, like many of life's pleasures, it was fleeting and would not last long.

The bliss of the moment was abruptly broken by loud voices coming from behind us. Turning around I saw the figures of several men coming toward us, greeting our captors. Then the newcomers walked up and inspected me carefully, checking me up and down in the moonlight like some new prized horse.

Some of them wore gloating smiles as they stared at me. It was the first time I had actually had a chance to look at the faces of the men who had captured us. Perhaps they felt less conspicuous in this isolated place, because all of them circled around me, openly facing me, as they talked and laughed. This time there were no rifle butts raised in anger at my face as I looked them straight in the eyes.

Studying their features in the moonlight, I was astonished to see that many of the gang appeared to be teenage boys. They had military assault rifles and grenade launchers. One carried what appeared to be a bazooka and most of them wore military vests with ammunition in them.

In addition to the boys were older men who had faces that were creased with deep wrinkles. I thought they must be younger than they looked but weather-beaten from the tropical climate. I could also see, when they opened their mouths, that a lot of them were missing several teeth. Most of them had black, cotton masks that they had used earlier to disguise their faces now rolled up above their foreheads. Others wore colored scarves wrapped around their heads. A few of them wore baseball caps from which I could see long, dark stringy hair either hanging down to their shoulders or tied in ponytails.

Most of the young boys had bandoliers of ammunition criss-crossing their chests and appeared to be wearing military-style camouflage pants. One of the newcomers, a short man with a black mustache, moved closer to me trying to look into my eyes. Then he smacked me hard on the cheek. It startled me, but I tried to look unfazed.

Suddenly from behind me came the surprising sound of words spoken in English. "You Mercano?" I turned and searched for the source of the words. A middle-aged man with short hair waved his hand at me and asked again "You Mercano?" He looked intently into my eyes.

"I am American, yes." I said quietly in reply.

"You missionary?" he questioned.

"No, I am not a missionary," I responded. He laughed disdainfully and the others standing nearby watching began laughing also. I gathered my courage. "Why are you doing this?" I asked. "What do you want from me?" The man turned and said something that sounded sarcastic and the others all erupted in laughter again.

A younger man, with a bandana wrapped around his head, came forward sneering at me. He said, "Aha, you missionary," taunting me as though I was lying to them. Then he whirled around and waved to my captors pointing up at the ridge. He barked out some words in their language and motioned that we were to follow him up a very narrow path.

Our group once again fell in line, single file, and we were pulled along by the rope that still tied us together. Like a chain gang, we moved slowly and deliberately along the path as it wound its way up and around the mountainside. My burst of energy was ebbing. I was beginning to feel weak, hungry and very thirsty. I tried to keep my eyes on the path at my feet. My legs had begun to feel weighted down and heavier than lead with every step. Only the bright moonlight and the constant pull of the rope around my waist kept me on course.

Suddenly, I stumbled and went down on one knee. Unable to catch my breath, I stayed gasping for a moment until I felt the rope yanking me forward. A moment later someone kicked me in the side. I struggled to my feet trying to regain my balance as the rope pulled me.

Then, just as I got on my feet, steadied my legs and took a few faltering steps, a rifle butt suddenly dug into my back. The blow knocked me forward. I stumbled but tried to stay standing up as pain shot through the muscles in my lower back. The blow generated within me a strange kind of energy and I moved forward. The rifle butt dug into my back again, pushing me forward as the man behind me yelled angrily. Quickening my pace, I tried to look both in front of me and down to make sure I would not trip again as the rope pulled me along.

As I walked the pain in my back throbbed. Then slowly it started to fade. I did not look back, for I did not want to see the face of the man who had struck me. The fear, rage and pain I felt served as my motivation to keep moving. I was not going to give this man the satisfaction of seeing me grovel or beg. I focused on the moonlit path in front of me. *Think of something pleasant*, I thought to myself. My mind searched the past for memories that would take me away far from the fatigue, pain and hunger threatening to overwhelm me.

My thoughts immediately turned to my children—the two good things that I had left in my life. Visions of happy times only a few years earlier, when I still lived with them, came to me. Even though I could no longer live with the boys, they gave me a reason for living. My eyes swelled with tears as I thought of my two sons. Would I ever see them again? Would they grow up knowing how much their father loved them?

They were only the tender ages of six and ten; would they remember the things we had done together? I tried not to let the sadness of losing those days take control of me. Surely, I told myself, my boys were all the inspiration I needed to give me the strength to survive this ordeal. The very thought of my sons helped me hold on, though exhausted, and push forward.

My love for them and my desire to see them again was a motivation that I knew I could draw on. How I loved them; how I missed them at this moment. The sound of their laughter echoing in my thoughts buoyed my spirits as I struggled up the dark, steep mountain path. *I have to hope that I will see them again,* I thought. "No, I have to believe that I will see them again!" I whispered, trying to reassure myself that I would come out of this nightmare alive.

Up ahead I saw the flickering light of a fire. *Ah, finally, maybe we will stop and sleep.* My body and mind ached with weariness. The hunger and thirst I had been feeling was replaced by the overwhelming urge to just lie down and sleep. After a few more faltering steps down the ravine, we came into a clearing where several small huts surrounded a campfire. Shadows moved toward us from the clearing around the fire. I could hear loud voices greeting our captors and then shouts and laughter.

Suddenly, the rope around my waist tightened as two men pulled me to them. Each grabbed one of my arms and yanked me forward to face a stocky, round-faced man whose face was illuminated by firelight. Glaring at me with a menacing stare, he grunted a command to the two men holding me. Violently the men dragged me to the trunk of a large, leaning palm tree facing the fire.

Then they cut the rope around my wrists, pulled both of my arms behind me. I yelped in pain as they yanked my arms back and began tying them together behind the trunk of the tree. My right shoulder, which had been surgically reconstructed while I was in high school, twisted and popped from the awkward position it was in. Searing pain tore through my shoulder joint. I screamed as I felt tissue and cartilage tearing. The men smiled and drew the rope tying my hands behind me tighter until it cut into the skin on my wrists.

Almost immediately another man was at my feet, tying my ankles together with another piece of rope and then tightening it to the tree. Once again I cried out in pain as his comrade continued to pull my bound hands upward behind me, hooking the rope on something, suspending my upper body outward on the already leaning tree and forcing my head down. My heart pounded, my mind raced; *What are they going to do to me next?* I asked myself as fear knotted my stomach. With my head bowed downward and my arms pulled behind me, my shoulder, neck and back writhed with pain. "Ahhhhhhhhhhhh, no no don't!" I heard myself cry out, pleading with them to stop the agony.

Before I could utter another sound a hand grabbed my forehead, pulling my head sharply back. Someone moved forward in front of me and stuffed a rag into my mouth, muffling my cries of pain. Then another rope, holding the gag in my mouth was tied tightly around my head. "Agghhhhh. Oommffffffff."

My muffled screams were met with laughter. Struggling for breath and moaning in pain, I searched the darkness in front of me. Against the flickering light of the campfire, dozens of shadows moved about in front of me, laughing, pointing, taunting.

Desperately, I looked for a kind face, someone to come to my rescue. But there were only the laughing, cruel silhouettes in front of me, faceless in the darkness, the orange glow of the campfire lighting the jungle behind them. *Please God, help me!* I silently prayed. I had entered a living nightmare where unbearable pain came with every breath. *Why are they doing this to me? What have I done to deserve this hell?*

I hyperventilated gasping for air. I screamed in vain and felt a blizzard of whiteness fill my sight. Then there was nothing but the dark void of unconsciousness.

Chapter Eight

Living With Fear

In the soft bliss of unconsciousness I began to dream.

Out of the fog in my mind I emerged into a warm sunny morning on the beach. As I walked along the shore, the ocean was calm, dark blue and smooth as glass. Ah, just the way I love it when I go snorkeling! The sand felt good between my toes as I walked down the beach holding the soft little hand of my youngest son. I stooped down to wipe away the sand he was trying to put in his mouth.

"Yucky," I said to him as I brushed the sand from his tiny lips and hand.

"Daddy, let's go swimming!" a sunburned, blonde haired boy called out running toward me. "Let's go swimming," he repeated, smiling at both me and the toddler by my side.

"Look!" I said to my younger son, "It's your
brother! He wants us to go in the water with him!"
My younger son giggled and jumped up and
down. He loved his big brother.

My older son was bounding into the ocean
surf. "Careful!" I yelled to him, "Don't go in too
deep!" My younger son began to run into the ocean
after him, but I held him back so that we waded
together in the shallow water. Suddenly, the ocean
spray hit my face as my older son splashed play-
fully in front of me. The salt water stung my eyes,
"Stop it, it stings," I told him.

"Stoofffffffiiiiit," the strange, muffled sound of my own
voice abruptly woke me as a barrage of water hit my face. I tried
to rub my eyes; I couldn't. My hands were tied behind me. I
squinted, trying to focus. Then, I realized that the scene with my
sons was just a dream and this living nightmare was reality.

My heart sank as I apprehended the cruel truth of my
situation and fear once again took hold of me.

In front of me a man holding a blue, plastic bucket in his
hand was admiring the job he had done. To my right and left I
could make out several sets of legs, some in camouflage pants
with boots and others clad in different colored blue jeans with
sandals on their feet.

I struggled to lift my head and realized that I was still
hanging face down from a tree trunk. In front of me whispers
turned to louder words and sentences. I tried to make out the
faces of my guards, but I could not keep my head up long enough
to study them. Each time I lifted my head, dizziness set in.

Finally, I gave up and let my head hang down. Staring at the ground below me, I looked around. To my left was a dirt path leading to the front of a bamboo hut. The bamboo stalks that made up the walls had just enough space between each stalk for me to partially see inside. The door appeared to be made of plywood hinged on a wooden frame. The floor of the hut was reddish, packed dried mud, just like the ground outside of it.

For the first time I noticed that the mud was similar to the reddish brown clay of Georgia. Several small clumps of tall green grass lined the outside walls of the hut. I could also see a worn mud path surrounding two large outcroppings of coral rock.

To my right the mud path curved away from me into a large open area, dotted with wooden benches and tables. One table had a worn red and white plastic covering hanging in tatters almost to the ground. In the soft early morning light, the dark shadows of the jungle around me were beginning to brighten with small beams of sunlight dancing on the dried mud.

To my surprise, I spotted two small purple flowers jutting from a clump of brown grass at the base of the tree to which I was tied. Feeling dizzy again, I closed my eyes and took a deep breath trying to calm myself as best I could.

When I opened my eyes again the haziness in my mind cleared and I realized my guards were young boys. As they continued to mumble, I looked back at the small purple flowers and wondered what would happen to me. In the distance I heard more voices and also the sound of a spoon being banged against the outer rim of a metal pot.

The smell of wood burning told me that someone was cooking food. But what were they cooking? I could smell nothing familiar in the smoke. Still, something in the fragrance of the burning wood fire stirred my stomach and made it gurgle with hunger.

I had never been so hungry and thirsty. I tried to think of the last time I had eaten. It was the dinner I had in Cebu, the night before we left. No wonder I was starved, that meal surely had been more than a day ago.

My right shoulder began throbbing again. I winced in pain as I tried to move my arms still bound and stretched behind me. Trying to move only made my shoulder worse. I was better off just staying still and hanging there motionless.

SMACK! My head twisted violently to the side as a hand roughly slapped the side of my face. The renewed feeling of terror which accosted me removed all thoughts of hunger.

SMACK! This time the other side of my face burned from a second sharp slap. Then there was silence. I waited for the usual yelling, but there was only a palpable stillness. I hung there face down afraid to look up. Then I heard the shuffling of footsteps coming closer to me. *Now what?* I asked myself.

Suddenly I felt rough, calloused hands grabbing my chin and pulling my head up, bringing me eye to eye with a man still wiping his breakfast from his mouth. His face was worn and unshaven, covered with a salt and pepper mix of black and silver whiskers. He muttered something that I did not understand. Someone else moved to my side. Then the gag was yanked from my mouth. I tried to muster some spit to clean my mouth from the dirty rag that I had been choking on.

A moment later the same rough hand pulled my chin up again, this time holding a cup of cool water to my lips. His face was blank as he tipped the cup into my mouth, almost drowning me with a deluge of water which ran down my throat. I coughed, gagged and then coughed again. Several of the boys standing around us erupted in laughter. But the man pouring the water into my mouth stayed expressionless, tipping the tin cup higher and higher, dumping all of its contents into my mouth.

Despite the force of it choking me, I swallowed the cool water gratefully and looked into the eyes of this man with the rough hands. His brown eyes showed only the concentration of a person completing a task. I eked out, "Thank you." He just nodded and walked away.

Then someone held a wooden spoon up to my mouth. There was something white on the spoon, rice I guessed, peppered with small black dots. Before I could get a good look at it, the spoon was thrust into my mouth. Momentary relief at being fed was immediately replaced by horror as I felt the food moving inside my mouth. I quickly spit it out, coughing and gagging. The men exploded in laughter. When I peered down at the ground, I saw a pile of small white worms squirming among black ants. My stomach turned and I fought back a wretch. I let my head hang down, hoping that if I looked as beaten and disgusted as a felt, they might leave me alone. I don't know if my appearance did it or they just got bored, but I heard them slowly shuffle away.

Soon there were no more voices, no more slapping, no more insect meals, just the sound of my own breathing. For the moment the delicious cup of cold water had cooled my mouth and filled my stomach. For a moment I did not even care that I had been hung face down from a tree. No one was beating or berating me. I was learning to cherish such brief moments of peace.

As the day wore on the sun grew hotter, the jungle grew noisier and the pain in my shoulder returned with a vengeance. Occasionally I looked up to see several sets of feet milling about.

Sometimes pointing and laughing, they inched up to me and poked me to see if I was awake or just to antagonize me. I tried talking to them, asking "Where am I? Why am I here?" But they only replied with mumbled words that I could not understand.

By midday I realized that I had not seen or heard Remy or the cab driver. Why were they being kept separate from me? Were they here in this same camp? What did our captors want with me or with them?

The afternoon sun beat down on me. With not a whisper of wind to cool me, I soon sweated out all the water they gave me that morning. The palm tree to which I was tied had no branches so there was no shade to shield me. I could see and almost feel the cooling cover of the jungle, but I was exposed to the merciless sun. I felt like I was burning up. Flies and other insects buzzed around my head perching on my ears and forcing me to close my eyes for fear of the insects getting into them. I waited and prayed for the man with the water to come again. But he did not. My only companions were fear and thirst.

Time passed. As shadows of darkness began to creep across the path in front of me, I could stand it no longer and begged for a drink. "Please, water, Please! *Tubig*, please!" *Tubig* was the Tagalog word for water. I could only hope that they understood my pronunciation. But if they did, there was no reaction to my pleas, and the more I spoke the drier my mouth became. I soon gave up. I gave in to the exhaustion I felt and, despite my position, fell asleep as the night sounds of the jungle creatures, high-pitched and constant, overcame the silence of the day.

SMACK! Again I was awakened from my sleep by a violent slap. This time a man with a dark moustache was yelling in my face. Again I heard shouts and yelling coming from one person or more walking quickly down the path toward me.

Suddenly, two men were behind me and at my feet, untying the ropes that bound my wrists and ankles. As my legs and arms came free I attempted to stand upright but fell flat on my face. Several men surrounded me as I tried in vain to get up. With each attempt my legs crumbled and I fell drunkenly to the ground, my arms flailing in the air. Suddenly I felt very sick, very weak.

I looked up at the guerrillas surrounding me trying to see their faces, but they separated, scattering as a short wiry man strode through them yelling and screaming. He sounded very angry as he yelled at the men behind me. In an instant, two hands on each side of me brought me to my feet, holding me under my armpits on either side. The angry man continued to chew out the others. They scattered like a bunch of schoolboys caught doing mischief. Then the angry man turned to the two men holding me up and gestured to them with his hands to follow him and bring me along.

They dragged me as I tried desperately to walk under my own power. But my legs crumpled under me and I could not take more than two steps on my own before they dragged me forward. The yelling continued while two other men came up behind us, muttering apologetically to the angry man.

Soon we came upon the campfire, surrounded by several chairs. The two men holding me abruptly threw me into one of them. I squirmed as I hit the seat while the angry man continued his tirade.

As I tried to adjust myself in the chair I noticed, through a small gap in the trees, I could see the ocean and the full moon in the distance. At that moment, I realized just how far away from civilization I was. I felt alone and afraid.

The angry man now seemed to be barking out orders. Immediately, several men with rifles in their hands scurried to carry them out. I turned and tried to get a good look at their leader. His eyes were ablaze like the campfire in front of us. Highlighted by the flames, I could now see his face with his thin mustache. I realized he was the same man who had slapped me the night before. He spit out his words in sharp, grunting segments, his high-pitched voice raging. The others called him Andong.

Then out of the darkness a man jumped to my side. I recoiled in fear, thinking I was going to be hit again. But he insistently thrust a wooden bowl at my face, picking up a glinting spoon in the bowl and then dropping it again.

I reached eagerly for the bowl with both hands and weakly brought the vessel down to my lap. However, before I could lift the spoon to search for bugs in the liquid another hand came out of the darkness thrusting a plastic cup into my face. Because I was trembling, I cradled the bowl in my lap and reached again with both hands to grasp the cup. The commotion around me began to die down and many of the shadowy figures around me moved away and disappeared into the darkness of night.

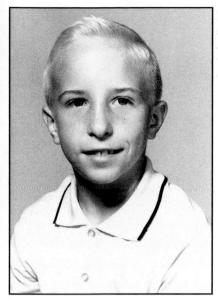

Despite suffering from serious allergies and asthma as a child, Greg was a good athlete and enjoyed games.

When serious injuries ended his future dreams of being an athletic star, Greg developed a new passion: music. Touring with a rock and roll band was exciting and brought him success, but Greg soon realized it did not provide the spiritually fulfilling lifestyle he sought.

Following a new professional path, Greg moved to Florida to pursue a career in hospital management and became a successful businessman.

Despite previous success, Greg's health and mobility deteriorated and he lost both his job and family. Turning to God, Greg heeded a spiritual call to help those in need in the Philippines. The hardest part was saying goodbye to his two beloved sons.

Within days of arriving in the Philippines, Greg was kidnapped and taken hostage by the Abu Sayyaf, a Muslim guerrilla group which demanded a high ransom and threatened to kill him as it had others.

AP/ Wide World Photos

Former Abu Sayyaf leader, Abu Sabaya, was one of many who interrogated, humiliated and tortured Greg. Sabaya is believed to have been killed in a battle with Philippine authorities in June 2002.

AP/ Wide World Photos

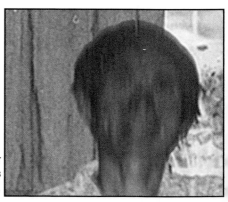

Joseph acted as translator for Abu Sabaya and others who interrogated Greg.

After a miraculous escape from his captors, Greg met Nheni, who was studying to become a pastor in the Philippines. After he left the country, they corresponded and fell in love.

Any past rifts were laid to rest as Greg's joyous and relieved family welcomed him home.

Greg returned to the Philippines to marry Nheni, a union he felt God had blessed.

Greg and Nheni's marriage ceremony was followed by a large celebration with her friends and family.

With his new family and working to help others at Nheni's church, Greg finally found happiness but was stricken with cancer for which he underwent surgery and chemotherapy.

Celebrating Nheni's daughter's graduation from grammar school was a bittersweet moment for Greg, who missed his own sons living thousands of miles away.

Despite serious health problems, his desire to be part of his sons' lives and see his family was very strong. Greg moved his new wife to the United States where she met his parents.

When they moved to America, Greg and Nheni became active, devoted members of their new church pastored by David Lyon.

Adjusting myself as best I could in the rickety wooden chair, I put the cup between my legs and lifted the bowl closer to my face to inspect it. Using the spoon, I picked at the food that was in the bowl, hoping to identify what it was. On closer inspection I could see that it wasn't moving and appeared to be some kind of soup with a grass-like substance floating in it.

Having already been fed worms and ants, I knew I should be careful. I was weak and hungry. I began scooping the liquid into my mouth. It tasted like a diluted broth of some kind with green leaves and grass in it. Whatever it was, I gratefully slurped it down.

Before long nothing was left but the bowl. I drank down the cup of water also. It was my first meal in two days and I was thankful, very thankful. I could not help but stop for a moment after I had finished to say a prayer. I thanked God for looking after me despite my hostile surroundings. "Please," I prayed quietly, "please, Lord, don't desert me. Please be with me in my time of suffering."

After only one day of suffering the torment of being hung from the palm tree, the strength I'd momentarily felt earlier was ebbing. Still, I knew I could not give in to my desperation. I had to stay alert or I would go mad.

Thus began the rituals of my days in the guerrillas' camp. In my mind I attempted to keep a calendar of time and events, using the hours of pain, fear and hunger to review my perceptions of each day. Over and over in my thoughts, I reviewed the details I'd scrutinized hoping to remember more accurately what I'd seen so that I could mark the time that was passing.

In addition, maybe, somehow, I could find a weakness or pattern to the behavior of my captors that might give me information on how to get away from them. I tried to encourage my mind's activity so that I would be distracted from the constant fear that haunted me every waking moment.

Escape—the very word tantalized me—became my mantra. I began to look for a method while I had a chance to sit and survey the area around me at my one meal each day. In the evening while sitting by the fire eating, I studied the set up of the camp and where the armed men were usually posted.

Each day that followed the same routine was repeated. In the morning they hung me from a tree, unprotected, to endure the intense sun and humidity; I was released from the tree only when the sun went down, given a chair to sit in while I ate and then allowed to sleep.

During the hours the sun shone there was seldom anyone in sight. The men who were holding me captive apparently stayed in the shade of the jungle's foliage or under the roof of the only thing other than the hut that was near me in the clearing. It was really just a shelter with a roof that served as a kitchen and dining area next to the campfire.

While I baked in the sun I sometimes heard the men and boys around me in the shadows of the large trees lining the clearing. Their camp, the buildings and the campfire were all located on the jungle's edge around me. At first, it was hard to keep track of how many men were occupying the camp. But after a couple of days I had counted about twenty different ones who came and went during the day and night.

Several times I asked, "Why am I here?" No one ever answered. None of these men seemed to understand English or, if they did, they did not want me to know. No matter how many different men I asked, none of them ever responded to my questions.

All the men and boys had guns and there were never less than ten armed guards in the area near me. The only time that they seemed to relax and put their weapons down was when I was fed.

But I could not summon the courage to make a break for it during those brief periods I was not tied up. For one thing, my legs were so weak that I doubted I would get far. Compounding the numbness in my left leg due to my bad back, was the loss of confidence in my ability to move quickly even if the chance presented itself. I felt a constant dread of being shot in the back by one of the armed men. And if I did get away into the jungle, where would I go? I had no idea where I was.

There seemed to be a method to their madness in the way I was being treated. It was as if they knew that tying me to the tree during the day and feeding me only once would keep me alive but keep my legs weak and my body drained of energy.

At that one meal of the day I was given the same watery, grass soup to drink. Sometimes they gave me a few small pieces of dried fish to eat. It smelled horrible, but I ate the solid food just the same. Grass and fish became my daily ration, but it was better than nothing.

From sunrise to sunset ants and bugs crawled over my body. I worried there might be deadly snakes or scorpions around me also. Flies circled my head sometimes landing and sticking to my face and hair.

I dreaded the evening when mosquitoes came out to feast on my blood. Still clad in shorts, I was covered from head to toe with large red bites.

Each morning I was visited by groups of young men with guns who mumbled and laughed as they poked and taunted me. Most days there were at least a dozen of these visitors and on a few mornings I was relieved when there was only four or five. Some of them seemed as young as twelve years old, but the majority appeared to be from the ages of sixteen to thirty, although there were a small number of men even older than that.

Some wore military-style camouflage pants while others wore camouflage vests and belts with hand grenades and ammunition hanging from them. In contrast, most of the younger-looking boys had on average dime store T-shirts, some with popular sports logos. A lot of the guards had on military-style boots, although others in the group wore only sandals.

Wrapped around most of their heads were cloths that looked somewhat like tablecloths. Others wore baseball caps or round caps that appeared to be a traditional Muslim adornment. And they all carried some kind of military assault rifle, brandishing them like their most prize possessions.

I saw everything from old AK-47s to modern-looking M-16 automatic assault rifles with grenade launchers. Many of my kidnappers had bandoliers of ammunition strung across their chests. Yet despite their bravado, these smiling young boys, proudly showing off their impressive firepower, were a motley crew. I asked myself what group or gang they belonged to and tried to listen to their conversations for a clue. But only rarely was I able to understand a few words here and there.

I was soon able to identify who was around me by their sandals, shoes or bare feet which I could see from my painfully uncomfortable position hanging on the tree. But it was during my brief periods of rest at sunset when I received my scant rations that I got a better look at this grubby group of characters who were my captors.

Tinoy, at least that is what the others called him, was my keeper. He was older than the rest and tall for a Filipino. His somewhat bony face was sunken, dark and wrinkled like an old seaman and always expressionless. His wavy black hair was just long enough to cover his ears. When, on occasion, he would come to me with fresh cool water, I would feel his rough, calloused fingers on my chin. Tinoy smelled like smoke and half-cooked food and usually had food and grease spattered all over him. His dark brown eyes always gazed upon me as if disinterested and uncaring. But to me he was the kindest of them all.

I nicknamed another guard *Bucktooth* for obvious reasons. He appeared to be in his late teens and had one large upper tooth that jutted from the top of his mouth. His straight black hair was shiny and shaped like a bowl. He never wore a cap. His wide, almond-shaped eyes gave a hint of his Asian background. Bucktooth was a follower. He was one of the many who just hung around doing nothing except taunting me and laughing. He was never without a mean smile on his face. Bucktooth wore loose cotton pants that looked like old brown sweat pants and his shirts always had some kind of logo on them. I knew when Bucktooth was around because of the ragged, old brown sandals that he constantly wore.

Pops had graying hair and a beard. He was an older man, thin and weather-beaten in appearance. Pops had a soft-looking face, a kind-looking face, but his eyes were always scowling and you could never tell what he was thinking. He had yellow teeth which indicated to me that he was a smoker. Pops appeared to be the oldest in the group, maybe around fifty, and he always wore long sleeve shirts with loose old-fashioned pants. I knew Pops by his bony, bare feet clad only in flip-flop sandals.

Berto was a handsome but cruel-looking young man, maybe twenty years of age, whose most distinguishing feature was the small chin beard that accented his lower lip. In addition to this tuft of hair below his lower lip, a thin line of black hair ran along his jaw line. His skin was light brown and very smooth with a youthful glow. He always wore a headdress which varied in color but looked like a checkered tablecloth wrapped around his head. He had I think some interest in fashion because the T-shirts that he wore always matched the color of his headdress. Berto wore camouflage pants with military-style boots and always walked as if at attention. He was one of the meanest ones who delighted in badgering and scaring me constantly.

Greasy was thin and scrawny and looked to be in his twenties. The long, greasy hair that he constantly played with hung down to his shoulders. On his head he wore an old black baseball cap. Surprisingly, Greasy always seemed to have on a clean pair of jeans which was in stark contrast to his dirty, long sleeved shirts and his overall grubby appearance. Even his old worn-out sandals looked like they were coming apart. He partook in the taunting and particularly enjoyed threatening me with his knife.

Andong, as he was called by the others, seemed to be one of the leaders of the group. A wiry little man in his thirties, he had curly black hair and pointy ears. His face was always intense and sweaty and he had a sparse, black mustache that accented an Anglo-looking nose. His eyes always glowed with diabolical sharpness and, unlike some of the others, he hardly ever smiled. He dressed the part of a pseudo military leader always wearing military pants, shirts and boots. Quite often he wore a checkered cloth around his neck instead of on his head. Andong spoke in shrill, commanding tones, and when he was around, everyone dropped what they were doing and listened out of what I suspected was both respect and fear.

And then there was the man they called *Abu*. Abu also seemed to be in charge, although I could never tell whether he and Andong were equal in rank. Abu was tall and stocky. Unlike the others, who were typically small-framed Filipinos, he stood out because of his size.

Abu appeared to be younger than Andong but must have been in his late twenties. Dressed in military fatigues and boots, he wore dark shirts and wrapped his head in dark scarves. Altogether, with the dark sunglasses he frequently wore, Abu projected a sinister presence. Yet despite that, his skin was flawless and smooth and he had a round, baby-faced countenance. In the center of his face was a large flattened nose underlined by the wide full lips of his mouth. Most of the time, Abu maintained a silent, seething exterior. When I looked into his eyes, there was an unsettling cold darkness that chilled me to the bone. I had no doubt that I was looking into the face of pure evil.

But one question kept nagging me. Who were these men? Was this a gang or an army? No one would talk to me. Even when my gag was removed and I could get someone's attention, they never responded to me. Was it because they did not know English? Or were they just trying to keep me in the dark?

I was aware that there were communist rebels and
Islamic rebels who were supposedly fighting the government in
parts of the Philippines. I could only assume that I had been
captured by one of these groups and they somehow saw me as
an object of value.

During the first days of my captivity these armed men
and boys took turns provoking me just to watch my face contort
with fear or pain. Sometimes they slapped me, other times they
poked me as hard as they could with the barrels of their guns.
And I was always the butt of their mumbled, unintelligible jokes.

I also had to endure venomous tirades of unfamiliar
words directed at me like sharp arrows with poisoned tips. I
could not understand why these people seemed to hate and
despise me so. I only knew by the tones of their voices that they
seemed to think themselves superior to me.

In addition to my guards, there were many other young
men and boys who came and went. Most were dressed in
fatigues and had weapons, others appeared to be just followers
who were curious. The camp was quite busy during the morning hours and the evening hours. It seemed that most of their
activities revolved around the cooler times of the day. During
midday, when the sun and heat was at its peak, most everyone
either stayed in the shade or took naps while I sizzled in the hot
sun.

During those hours when I was tied to the tree, the men
around me did everything they could to intimidate and humili-
ate me. There was a certain psychological warfare element to
their actions. I kept wishing that I could have understood what
they were saying. But it was probably best that I didn't.

Late one afternoon, Berto, Pops and Bucktooth approached me while Greasy pulled my head up by my hair. Berto first looked me in the eyes disdainfully and then spit in my face. I blinked and closed my eyes in attempt to keep the saliva away. They all sneered and erupted in laughter, then began talking very fast in their language.

When I opened my eyes again Bucktooth grinned, and leaning towards me, he spit in my face. They all erupted in laughter again as Pops stepped up for his turn. This time I flinched and closed my eyes before Pops could do anything and they all laughed even harder.

Suddenly, Berto jumped forward and slapped me hard across the face. He said something to Greasy, who let go of my hair dropping my head back down. Greasy walked around in front of me and lifted my face by my chin until I was eyeball to eyeball with him.

I could see his yellow teeth and smell his foul breath. I looked back into his bloodshot brown eyes trying to figure out what he would do next. Suddenly, Greasy dug a fist into my stomach, knocking the wind out of me. The sudden pain of the blow was replaced quickly by dizziness. Before I could catch my breath he stepped back and kicked me low in the stomach, apparently trying to kick me in my genitals. But thanks to the angle at which I was hanging and the fact that my legs were tied together, he could not penetrate the area between my legs. However, the pain of his foot digging into my bladder was still sufficient to make me scream with pain into the rag stuffed in my mouth.

Then Berto walked up, and taking a wide swing, punched me in the jaw swinging my head to one side violently.

Within seconds after the blow Berto also attempted to kick me in the groin, missing just as Greasy had and hitting me hard in my bladder area again.

This game went on for about an hour with each man, except Pops, trying to provoke the loudest response from me with his kick or punch. As I looked from one to the other it became obvious that they were betting on who could inflict the most pain on me.

I was being used as a human punching bag just for their own amusement. However, because of my position on the tree, I was fortunate in that they could not inflict really serious damage to my body. But I was soon bruised and bloodied. Flies, ants and mosquitoes, who showed up immediately when fresh blood presented itself, quickly covered me.

This little game became a favorite source of amusement for Berto, Greasy, Bucktooth and Pops during my first days of captivity. That is until they found different and more threatening ways to terrorize me.

On the morning of my second day in the camp the four of them arrived to confront me again. I thought I knew what was coming. But that day they had devised a new game. Stick him until he screams or bleeds was the name of the game. And it was Greasy who became the main antagonist in their newfound entertainment.

Producing a large military style hunting knife, Greasy proceeded to poke and prod my skin starting at my ears and throat. It felt like he was carving me up little by little and leaving small cuts everywhere on my body.

I knew that they would probably not kill me, but I was still terrified at each cut the cold blade inflicted as it pressed relentlessly into my skin. Then the knife blade came painfully close to cutting deep into my throat as I resisted, screaming into the rag in my mouth. I winced as I felt blood accumulate there and later run downward from this deepest cut.

Almost immediately small flying bugs began feasting on the fresh blood trickling down my throat. Was this part of their plan? Cut me open and let the insects torture me? It was maddening to feel the bloodthirsty creatures crawling all over my skin dining on every cut they could find.

I prayed that there were no vultures or other creatures being attracted to my misery. Nevertheless, the images of birds of prey and wild animals feeding on me while I was still alive accosted me. I tried to stop the grotesque pictures filling my mind by praying. *Lord, don't forsake me now. Don't leave me here.*

At one point Berto took the knife and proceeded to make small indentations around the nipples on my chest. Pretending to be surgically removing my nipples, he soon had the group laughing uproariously. Then Greasy pulled my head back while Berto traced the knife under my nose and around my eyes, again pretending that he would be removing them.

I could only whimper as the knife Berto used put dreadful thoughts in my head while he inflicted small cuts in my face.

Finally they finished their day's amusement, but on the next and subsequent days this group of four—Berto, Greasy, Bucktooth and Pops—snuck up and terrified me in other ways. Sometimes they just surprised me, hitting me in the back of the head while I was dozing off. They did everything they could to keep me on edge and in constant fear of what might come next.

Early one damp morning as I hung on the tree, I heard a hissing sound coming from behind me and thought for sure it was a poisonous snake. But it was only Bucktooth trying to scare me. He had played upon one fear that never left me, even during peaceful hours: the fear that a snake would find me an inviting target hanging there.

I could only imagine the number of poisonous tropical snakes and other creatures that might call the island their home. And how many insects were there in the jungle around me that might possibly be toxic?

With my serious allergies I knew that I would not survive even a tiny bite which proved venomous. A simple bee sting could send me into respiratory arrest. I prayed that I would somehow not become the victim of such a bite before I even had a chance to try and escape my captors.

All day and night I had to be vigilant. Every time I relaxed even a little bit, someone found a way to heighten my fears again. The games of intimidation that they enjoyed playing, using me as their victim, were endless. And as time passed, the extent of their viciousness took on new dimensions.

Even as the energy was being drained from my body and mind from the heat and lack of food, I continued to experience sudden rushes of adrenaline brought on by the constant hit-and-run attacks from these four men. It did not take long for their tactics to wear me down emotionally and physically.

In the late afternoon of my third day tied to the tree, as the sun was going down, the four of them, Berto, Pops, Bucktooth and Greasy, came strolling out of the jungle with Andong leading the way. They looked as if they had been drinking and they were talking loudly, almost jovially. But as they approached me their eyes narrowed with looks of evil intent and I felt myself shiver despite the heat.

Andong suddenly raised his assault rife and fired it in an automatic burst hitting the tree trunk right above my head. I flinched as the sudden, loud burst of gunfire peeled pieces off the tree trunk which rained down onto my head and shoulders.

In the next instant Berto raised his AK-47 and sprayed bullets at my feet and the ground around me. I began to shake uncontrollably hanging there unable to flee. *How much closer can they get without actually hitting me?* I asked myself. I squirmed against the ropes holding me, trying to make myself a smaller target.

Seeing me do this, Andong casually walked up to me and poked the muzzle of his gun between my legs. I winced as the hard tip of his rifle barrel found its mark, sending shockwaves of pain outward from my groin.

The others gathered around egging him on. I felt like a wounded animal on the verge of being finished off by a pack of wild dogs. In my mind I silently begged, *God, please give me strength. God, save me from this cruelty!*

Andong raised his rife and pointed it between my eyes, holding the cold steel there for what seemed like an eternity. Then he stepped back slowly and with eyes full of purpose he aimed the gun again at my genitals. "Bang!" a voice shouted to the side of me as I jumped and strained against the ropes holding me. "Bang! Bang!" shouted Berto, making me flinch again. I almost fainted from the shock.

The group erupted in laughter again as they stood there admiring the way in which they had humiliated me. *Why do they enjoy terrorizing me?* I asked myself. But as they began walking away from me with an air of superiority, I realized why.

To them I was weak, someone they had no respect for because of my religion and because of my nationality. And they believed themselves to be strong because they had guns and knives.

I was a great source of amusement for these young men who delighted in terrorizing me. Anger and shame filled me and I began to cry. Was I really that weak and pathetic? Was this merely an exaggerated form of the disdain that my family and friends felt for me because of past failures? Was it a punishment I deserved? The humiliation I now was experiencing on a daily basis was even more crushing than the pain.

At this point I could not help thinking maybe I really was better off dead. I did not want to live anymore in a constant state of fear and terror. But unfortunately, there was no way to escape from the horror I was experiencing.

Every day I learned to live with fear. Not knowing what was going to happen next kept my fear fueled with an ongoing anxiety.

By the fourth day of my captivity I had become very weak and began to lose track of time. Now the days were running together as the predictable routine of terror and starvation wore down my body and my spirit.

I had begun to realize that my captors' treatment of me was probably a calculated plan to break me down physically and emotionally, because the weaker I became the more they tortured me. At this low ebb another man, Joseph, showed up in the company of Andong and Abu.

A clean-cut man of about forty, Joseph was thin and had the look of a rugged farmer. Unlike the others, he dressed neatly and never wore any sort of a hat. His hair was short and his face was very dark from a lifetime in the sun.

Joseph always wore old-fashioned slacks as well as conscrvative-looking casual shirts. But his feet were always clean and clad in black sandals. Joseph seldom smiled but his eyes were inquisitive and he seemed educated.

When the men first approached me, Joseph came up close to me as I hung from the tree trunk. Andong pulled the gag from my mouth and then surprised me by giving me a sip of water. Abu said something to Joseph and he stepped forward and began to interrogate me in English. "My name Joseph. Your name?" he said as he eyed me carefully.

I was momentarily shocked to be spoken to in English, but not wanting to anger Abu and Andong, I quickly answered. "My name is Greg."

"You Mercano?" he asked.

"Yes," I replied. "Why am I here?" I blurted out.

Joseph looked at me and then, in his language, asked Abu and Andong a question. The three of them grinned for moment and then Joseph said to me, "You missionary?"

"No," I replied. "I have no training."

Joseph's face screwed up angrily. "Yes! You missionary!" he said loudly.

"No! I am not a missionary!" I replied emphatically. Andong jumped up and slapped me hard across the face as if to punish me for a wrong answer. I glared back at both Joseph and Andong but said nothing. Abu barked out something to Joseph and Andong and they began arguing.

After several exchanges between them, Joseph stepped forward again and looked intently into my eyes. "Where are your missionaries?" he asked firmly.

I was not sure what he meant so I just responded, "I don't know." Then I quickly asked, "Where is Remy!" I received no answer to my plea for information about my friend. This time Abu jumped forward and drove his fist into my chest. The punch knocked the air out of me and I hung there gasping.

"No! I ask questions! You no!" Joseph yelled angrily. "Now, where your missionaries? Where your friends?" Joseph went on asking, his voice rising.

"I don't know, I think...." Before I could finish my sentence Abu yelled something to Joseph.

Joseph's face suddenly turned soft and understanding. "You can go home soon: tell us where your missionary friends." I was surprised by the sudden change of his tone, but suspicious also.

I soon saw that the new game seemed to be "Good Cop, Bad Cop." Abu was the bad cop and Joseph was playing the role of the good one. I knew I should formulate an answer, but my honesty got the best of me as I replied to his question. "I am not really sure where they are."

"Yes, you know" Joseph said with a sarcastic smile. "Tell me now and you can go home." My mind searched for the name and location of the island where the prophet had told me we were going so that I could send them to another one.

"It's close to Cebu" I said. "I think just south of Cebu." Joseph looked at me suspiciously, then turned and walked over to Abu and Andong.

The three of them conferred for a moment and then walked away. Just like that the interrogation was over. I was surprised at how quickly it ended, but I knew they were not through with me. This was just a moment without torture. I tried to appreciate it as such and not think about the next one.

Joseph returned the next day and came almost every day after to question to me. He always left for the evening, apparently to return to his home. When he arrived during the late afternoon he was always with Abu or Andong. It was hard for me to tell if he was a close friend of theirs or if he was just recruited to help with the interrogations.

The more Joseph returned to our camp the less time the younger boys spent harassing me. I began to think that I might actually have some peace because of this but instead, it was Abu and Andong who now made threatening gestures and terrorized me psychologically.

Andong seemed the more humane of the two while Abu always exuded that evil which permeated the very air around him. In his dark garb with the sinister-looking sunglasses, he had the demeanor of a mad scientist in fatigues. He looked the part that he played, that of a deranged demon leader.

Andong visited me to grin intimidatingly at me, but Abu visited me to threaten me. Using his military knife he gave me a sinister grin while making a slicing motion near my head as if he was planning to cut it off.

Sometimes Abu and Joseph asked me if I needed water or food and promised to bring them to me. But they never returned with what they promised. With Joseph interpreting, Abu told me several times that I would be let go soon so that I could return to Cebu. But, of course, they were lying, playing cruel psychological mind games with me. I learned not to trust anything they said.

Then Abu and Andong began staying day and night at the camp. With their presence my endless hours of being tied to the tree finally ended. Instead, I was now shackled by a chain and metal handcuffs around one wrist and one ankle to another tree outside the bamboo hut. The chain was just long enough for me to be able to sit or lie down inside the crude little hut. But, at least, I had some shelter instead of being left hanging in the burning sun.

Finally I was able to lie down on the ground. Even the packed, hard mud that composed the floor of the bamboo hut was a welcome change from hanging on the tree.

But sleeping on the ground also had its drawbacks as I was constantly fending off ants and other critters throughout the night. As I lay there listening to the strange sounds of the jungle, I again feared being attacked by wild animals. One night I heard a strange moaning sound coming from the jungle that I had never heard before. I learned later that this sound was that of a very large lizard or iguana of some kind.

Most nights I was easily spooked and woke to the slightest of noises. My soundest sleep seemed to come in the semi-conscious sweat of afternoon naps.

There were always at least one or two armed guards posted outside the hut. These guards usually were teenagers with AK-47s. I could not believe how young these kids were and repeatedly I wondered why they were with this gang of thugs.

I took every opportunity that I had with Joseph to talk to him and get information since he was the only one who spoke English. But since he was almost always with Abu or Andong, there were only a few occasions to speak to him alone.

On both these occasions he wandered over with Berto and some of the boys, who gawked at me while they waited for Abu and Andong to finish eating.

Little by little I learned from Joseph that the men who held me captive were an Islamic group fighting a Jihad, a Holy war, against infidels. Or at least that is what they claimed. When I asked Joseph what the name of this Islamic group was he told me, "Bearer of the Sword." Later I overheard them using the words *Abu Sayyaf* and still later I heard the term *al Qaeda*, but neither meant anything to me at that time. I still did not understand how I was at all involved in attaining their goals. Later Joseph claimed that the group was at war with Westerners and Christians and I was led to believe that I was some kind of prisoner of war.

However, Joseph and my captors never told me clearly why they had abducted me. If I was a prisoner of war, were they trying to use me as a bargaining chip? Did they plan to swap me for someone who belonged to their group? Or did they plan to ask for money for my release? They never said. With no political connections and no money, I was mystified as to why I was of any importance to them.

Once when I remarked about the youth of some of those guarding me, Joseph told me that it was easy for this gang to recruit young boys, because they paid them well. Since most Filipinos dwelled in relative poverty, the young Muslim gang members could help their families who depended on the money.

As I listened to Joseph I thought about how poverty spawned the existence of many evils. In the Philippines, prostitution, drugs and gangs were some of the by-products of this societal plague. And one of the country's most successful industries had become the export of women.

I was learning firsthand about the third world and how fortunate I had been to grow up in a free and prosperous society despite the hard times which had befallen me before I'd come to the Philippines. Now I also was beginning to understand the desperation that drove many poor people to extremes in order to just exist.

Sitting on the cool, dried mud of my shelter I pondered the hardships that these young boys and their families had to face. I felt sorry for them and began to see how they could be driven to such extremes that they would embrace any leader who promised survival. I understood how easy it would be for them to be misled by others who offered a little money or hope.

I looked into the young weary faces of these boys with AK-47s and was saddened by the irony of their existence. Few understood the significance of their acts or cared who they harmed or killed as long as their families could eat and survive.

I surveyed the scene around me. A table and chairs had been set up in the comfortable shade of the trees surrounding my shelter. They always seemed to have plenty of water and food and made sure that they taunted me with it. Having been hungry most of their lives, they knew the value of food and water. They knew how to use them as instruments of torture.

Sometimes they drank beer and smoked some kind of rolled cigarette. The cigarettes which gave off a musty odor, appeared to be filled with some kind of drug, because after smoking them they were much more rowdy and aggressive.

In only a couple of days I adjusted to curling up on the ground and no longer cared about the insects crawling on me. By that time my condition, dulled by starvation and dehydration, had weakened even further.

I had reached a point where fear and hunger dominated my being most hours of the day and night.

However, having a shelter to lie down in was a definite improvement from hanging on the tree. The heat and the harassment from the armed men was no longer my biggest concern.

Now that I had a cool and less stressful place to stay during the day, I began to ponder again how I could get away from my captors. I tried to save the little energy I had and searched for ways I could unlock my handcuffs and chains.

It was during this change in my environment that Abu and Andong began spending more time drinking and shooting their weapons. While I cowered in my hut they played war games, sometimes shooting at faces painted on trees and pieces of wood.

They formed groups and stalked each other, sometimes throwing bottles or cans into the air at which to shoot. It was a wonder that they did not shoot each other during this so-called training. Quite often I noticed some of them looking in my direction as if trying to impress upon me the might of their military prowess.

By what I judged to be around the fifth day of my captivity, more and more food and beer was being brought to the camp. I actually enjoyed having some cooked rice for the first time since I had been taken there. And they also gave me some kind of root occasionally. Although it was hard, it was the only really solid food I was allowed to eat besides the occasional scraps of dried fish I was given.

Every night they set the garbage, which piled up during the day, on fire filling the camp with a smoky, foul-smelling haze. This seemed to be the only way that they could dispose of it.

The afternoon that I was given the rice, I watched as the men, following some target practice, put down their weapons and crowded around a table. At first I could not make out what they were doing. But as the group of men began to slowly disperse I realized what was going on.

One by one they were taking turns sniffing something into their noses. Licking their fingers, they returned again and again to the table to repeat the act. They also were rolling cigarettes and filling them with what looked to be the same powder. I found out later that the substance was the Philippine equivalent of cocaine. They referred to it as *shabu*.

When they were not target shooting they were drinking. When they were not drinking, they were smoking and doing drugs. The full extent of their depravity began to unfold before my eyes.

After the alcohol and drug binges, they invariably got into fights and threatened each other with their weapons. Sometimes they had arm wrestling contests that turned into large, violent brawls. It was frightening to see how human beings, in the blink of an eye, could become absolute savages.

One evening, after much alcohol and drugs were consumed, two teenage girls were brought to the camp. As the evening wore on, I witnessed a group of the drunken fiends gang rape the two Filipino girls. They had lured the girls to the camp then tied their hands and ripped off their clothes.

At least ten different boys and men took their turns. The girls could not have been more than fourteen or fifteen at the most. I felt physically ill and enraged as I listened helplessly to the boys beating and raping them over and over again. I was sure that they would kill them. And I could do nothing.

Then I had another horrible realization. Part of me was relieved that I was not the subject of the gang's abuse for once. I covered my ears the best I could and tried to sleep for I knew these villains were not through with me and I needed my strength to endure. The girls' screams eventually stopped. But I had no idea what happened to them.

Chapter Nine

Every Day a Gift from God

Having watched and heard the rapes and feeling that tiny kernel of relief that it was not me being tortured, I kept asking myself, *What is happening to me, to every value I once held dear?* I knew it was a terrible thing to feel relieved and safe while others were suffering brutality. I felt ashamed and guilty that I could feel that way just because their abuse of the girls was keeping the violence away from me. But it was true. I did feel a kind of relief that as long as these demons had others to terrorize they would leave me alone.

I prayed for forgiveness for feeling this way. I prayed for the girls and for the strength to survive this ordeal. And I prayed God would not allow me to become callous and unfeeling of the suffering of others. I clung to my faith to keep from drowning in the insanity around me.

And I also asked God not to let me be transformed from a frightened, cowering captive to a hardened, calculating predator of the jungle. As I accustomed myself to living with the threats and deprivation, my instinct for survival began to assert itself even amid the fear and confusion I was feeling.

Despite hunger and the ever present fear of physical harm, I was realizing I had to cultivate the one thing they had difficulty injuring, my spirit.

Nevertheless I also had to acknowledge they were weakening my body. It seemed like an eternity since I last felt clean. My lips were cracked and bleeding from the heat and I had rashes all over my body. Still wearing the same shirt and shorts in which I had been taken hostage, my clothes were rank with the smell of sweat and urine.

Only after I was released for my one daily meal in the late afternoon was I allowed to relieve myself. I was led to a smelly latrine dug in the mud where I had to squat like an animal.

There was no tissue of any kind and most days I simply looked for the softest leaves I could find to wipe myself. Then I attempted to wash myself from a small bucket of water, starting first with my face and then moving downward.

When I asked them where my clothes were, they just laughed. I had the feeling that I would never see the small bag of my belongings again. And I was never given time to wash the clothes I was wearing. So I learned to savor washing myself with the small bucket of water. After a while I even got used to the bad odor emanating from my clothes and my body.

By then I had developed the habit of praying every morning when I awoke. I told myself again that every day I stayed alive was a gift from God. It was another day that I survived and another day that brought me hope that I would go on and escape.

To my surprise, I was not the only one praying. I observed that my captors grouped together at least three times each day to pray. They did this at dawn, midday and sunset. I could not help but wonder what kind of God they were praying to. What kind of God would want human beings to use and abuse others the way these people did? What kind of God required the killing and torture of others and demanded his followers to kidnap?

It did not appear to me that these boys and men could be true believers. How could they be? They all drank and did drugs as well as behaved like animals. As I pondered these inconsistencies, I came to believe that this group of thugs misused their religion to justify their violent actions. They defiled their religion using their corrupt beliefs as a reason to justify terrorism against others.

They were not the "Holy Warriors" they professed to be. Nor did I believe them to accurately reflect the Muslim faith. Although I had never met any Muslims, deep in my heart I knew that the true followers of this religion were nothing like the band of outlaws holding me hostage.

During this period I spent a lot of time praying and contemplating our existence as human beings on this earth. Then suddenly, as if light dawned, I saw that no matter the time or contest or dilemma one had to face, it all came down to the struggle of good versus evil.

For all the horror I was being put through, I also was being given the opportunity to appreciate the wonder of the universe.

Each hour seemed to bring another event that made me think. I tried to make sense of what was going on around me and to understand what was going through the minds of my captors. But I also kept asking myself why I had been placed in this situation. What was God asking of me? At the same time, I could not rid myself of nagging fears which stayed clenched in my stomach day after day. What did they plan to do with me?

On the morning of my sixth day of captivity, after a tumultuous downfall of rain, the skies cleared and the sun again began to bake the mud into hardened clay. Tinoy had just brought me some water and rice and I was eating slowly appreciating each morsel. Suddenly the quiet was pierced by the screams of a man in the distance. They were blood-curdling screams that made my heart pound. What was happening to him?

Suddenly the screams ended and it was quiet again. I said a prayer for the unknown man, thinking that he was probably dead but feeling no more pain. I prayed that God would somehow purge this jungle of the insanity around me.

Some time passed and then I saw Berto and Greasy dragging a body into the camp. My heart sank and my stomach knotted as I watched them bring it to a clearing directly in front of me. The body had no head.

A group of about six men congregated around it. The body was naked and appeared to be a Filipino male around the age of thirty. As I sat there in the shade I wondered why they had killed him.

I had seen pictures before of dead and mutilated bodies, but seeing one up close and still bleeding was a shock. I wanted to turn away, but I could not for I knew my captors were giving me a message.

They wanted to either scare me or impress me. I bit my lip. How could any normal human being be impressed with anything other than revulsion at the sight of this poor man's headless form? What kind of evil possessed these people to do this?

Just then I saw Joseph walking with Abu across the camp toward me. They both stopped and stood for a few minutes looking at the body. Then Abu strode over to Berto and pulled a machete out of his belt. Abu walked slowly up to the body, bent over and using the machete, made two quick chops to the man's groin. Then Abu knelt down and, taking the genitals in one hand, he cut away the remaining skin and flesh connecting them to the body.

Then Abu raised the genitals high above his head like a trophy and waving the machete in the air eliciting a shout of triumph from the crowd of men. They all cheered and raised their arms as if celebrating some kind of bizarre victory.

Only Joseph stood there grimly looking on like a spectator, choosing not to participate in the perverse celebration. *Maybe Joseph, unlike the others, has some decency,* I thought. Although he was usually in the company of Abu and Andong when he was in camp, I had never seen him participating in any of the cruel jokes and brutality that I had endured from the others.

But all thoughts of his decency soon evaporated after Joseph walked towards me accompanying Abu and Andong while two other men carried the beheaded body away. That day Joseph's demeanor was as malicious and aggressive as Abu's. He became the inquisitor, warning me that what had happened to the farmer would happen to me and assaulting me with a barrage of questions. There was now no doubt, I thought despondently, that he was a willing participant in the conspiracy to hold me captive and make me suffer.

I lowered my head and stared at the ground trying to avert my eyes as these human vultures began playing with the farmer's dead body. I could not believe what I was witnessing. These men and boys were acting just like jungle savages I had seen in the movies. But this was real and they had made me part of it. A buzzing numbness swept through my body as I sat there in shock.

Then, as one grabbed my head so I could not look away, the butchering of this man's body continued. Greasy eagerly took the machete from Abu's hands and positioned himself to carve off a trophy of his own. Then he hacked two or three times through the wrist of one hand finally severing it. Greasy grabbed the hand and raised it in the air obviously thrilled to have a trophy of his own. And as the group of men around him shouted and fed off the bloodthirsty frenzy that Abu had started, two more men who had come over to watch took the machete and choose their targets.

Retching with nausea I tried not to vomit as my fear and disgust rose. Trying to calm myself I began to pray the words of Isaiah,

> *Fear not, for I am with you,*
> *Be not dismayed,*
> *For I am your God;*
> *I will strengthen you, I will help you,*

I will uphold you
With my victorious right hand.

Over and over in my mind I repeated those words, trying to summon the strength for which I had prayed to quell the fear overtaking me. However, before I could revive myself a foot viciously kicked me in the head and I went toppling backwards onto my back. As I reached up to rub my aching, swelling forehead I squinted in the fierce sunlight trying to see who had attacked me.

All I could make out was the dark outline of a man in front of me, but I recognized the belly and scarf-covered head of Abu. He yelled something at me and then I heard Joseph's voice from behind him, translating so I would understand.

"This is what we do to Christians!" Joseph said. "You are a Christian?" The question taunted me, daring me to put myself at risk of the same fate as the body before me. I said nothing, feeling like a coward for not standing up for my faith. I wanted so badly to say proudly that I was. But something inside me warned, *Live to fight another day.* In Abu's current mood I knew it would require little for him to kill me as he had the farmer, especially if I were to challenge him there in front of his men whom he clearly wanted to impress.

Abu and Joseph then launched into another tirade taunting my religious beliefs and hurling insults about my weakness intermingled with questions. This had become the standard procedure of interrogation for them: questions mixed with insults intended to provoke a reaction from me laced with hate.

Abu shouted to Joseph who began to translate what Abu had said. "Your faith is false and you are a weakling! Unlike us you are not willing to die for your beliefs." Then, looking at me as if I were the enemy, Joseph warned, "Your friends will be beheaded if you do not talk."

Stalling for time to pull myself together, I asked Joseph, "What do you want to know?" And then I blurted out, "Are you talking about Remy and the cab driver?"

Joseph took a step toward me, bent down and yelled, "Where are your missionaries? Where is your money?" That was when it dawned on me that they were holding me for ransom. But why were they keeping the three of us apart? Were the others still alive?

"I don't know where the missionaries are," I told Joseph.

"You lie, not so!" Joseph said in an accusing tone of voice. "Give us number, telephone number!" My mind raced trying to think of a telephone number that I could give them. Somewhere inside of me rose the false hope that maybe they would let me go if I did what they said.

But no number which would have fooled them came to mind. Finally raising my arms in a show of innocence, I said, "I cannot remember!" Joseph scowled at me and began to turn to leave. "Joseph," I called out trying to delay him. He turned and looked at me curiously. "Who is that?" I asked him, pointing in the direction of the headless body, hoping that it was not Remy or the cab driver.

"That man?" Joseph asked me pointing in the same direction.

"Yes, do I know him?" I asked.

Joseph turned towards me and said sternly "No. I told you he was a farmer. But he was friendly with Christians. Christians corrupt our land, corrupt our women," Joseph spat out.

I was speechless. I simply did not know what else to say. On the one hand, I was relieved to know that the headless body was not that of Remy or the cab driver. But on the other, I could not believe they would kill one of their own, a Muslim, just for associating with or befriending a Christian.

Joseph suddenly turned and walked away leaving me sitting on the ground bewildered and amazed. How could it be that, in our modern world, people could be this brutal and vengeful when it came to others who were different from them?

The lesson I learned that day was not just one of intimidation, but one of reality. For the first time in my life, I came face to face with people who would kill for the sake of their religious beliefs. The real world was much more treacherous than I had ever imagined and I was learning about it the hard way.

That afternoon I watched as Abu and Berto played with the farmer's headless corpse. They laughed and joked and seemed to be enjoying the desecration of another human's body. *What kind of animals are these people?* I wondered. The cold and senseless brutality of their actions was chilling and unbelievable. I could not help but ask myself. *Am I in hell?*

The next day the body was taken away, because it was drawing insects and birds and animals out of the jungle around us. Moreover, the foul odor of decaying flesh began permeating the air.

Now I knew a little bit about what soldiers had to deal with during war: the insanity, the brutality, the sights and the smells of death. I could only be thankful that I was still alive and pray and hope that I would not end up the same way as the poor farmer. The thought of my body being toyed with by these human animals was too grotesque to dwell on. I began making a conscious effort to think of other things. Once again, I invoked the memories of happy times with my children to provide the best escape for my frightened and weary mind. Whenever the horror of reality intruded, I replayed times of laughter and love with my two boys over and over again.

I tried to reconstruct in detail the last time I saw each of them. Conversations with my children were the music that I played constantly in my head to ease my pain.

Remembering holding them soothed and calmed me. I loved them so much. I missed them so much. The sounds of their voices echoed in my mind even at the most terrifying of times. I wanted to see them both so terribly. But sometimes when fear engulfed me I wept for hours simply because I thought I would never see them again. When that happened the only thing which revived me was to remember particularly wonderful days like my sons' birthdays. No matter how busy I was at work, I always made sure that I was there to celebrate with them. Those were very special times and regardless of what was going on in my life, I didn't miss them.

On their birthdays I always enjoyed planning little surprises for them. One thing I enjoyed, something I learned from the Spanish community which enriched Florida, was filling a brightly colored paper piñata with candy and toys. It always brought so much life and excitement to the children's birthday parties when we placed the blindfold on them and gave them a chance to break the piñata.

Once it broke there was always a mad scramble for the toys and candy. And we always made sure that we had games that everyone could play. I remembered watching with satisfaction as my two sons laughed and played. I enjoyed the party as much as they did.

I always took many pictures and videotaped several of their parties. But those pictures and videos were as far away as my sons were. Only my memories of their love and laughter were still with me. I replayed those sweet memories in my mind to keep me going.

To retain their pictures in my mind, I drew their faces on the bamboo that made up the wall of the hut. Everyday, no matter how tired and sick I was, I used my fingernails to carve or refresh the images of my two sons on the bamboo.

In that way they kept me company in my jungle prison. Seeing their little faces in the morning and again at night before I went to sleep kept me sane.

Sometimes, when I was lucky, I caught crickets or cockroaches and created activities for them. I felt like a child again, playing with toy soldiers. Only now I was using the living creatures around me to provide relief from the frightening reality of my own captivity.

One evening as the sun was going down I captured two crickets, using a piece of hollowed out palm tree bark as a holding pen for them. I put a leaf over the hole in the top of the bark and kept them inside it feeding them morsels of my food.

The childish delight that my insect friends brought me was amazing. I took one cricket and set him at a starting line and watched how far he could jump from it. I called it cricket

Olympics. I kept track of how far up the wall the crickets would jump and pretended I was giving the winners gold medals.

The games brought me a much-needed distraction and had me giggling like a schoolboy for the first time since I had been captured. The joy of having fun was a terrific morale boost for me. And I kept looking out of the shelter hoping that no one would see me and take my new friends away from me.

The crickets, the ants and an occasional moth all were my only friends. And when the sun went down and I lay on my cool clay floor to sleep, I looked forward to my moments with them as if they were more than silent creatures.

In those difficult days I learned to appreciate every little visitor that entered the small world of my hut. They kept me company almost all of the time. I only needed to be alert and aware of them.

And then I found a special friend who also kept me company. Moe became the only warm-blooded friend that I had during those dark days and he was my most frequent visitor. Moe was a small, black mole who began to come each morning when I woke up.

At first he scared me, because I thought he was a rat and I was afraid of what he would do to me as I slept. But I noticed right away that he did not have the shape, tail or nose of a rat. Being a mole he was blind and had a long narrow snout that guided him wherever he wanted to go.

I began to save him a few pieces of rice just so he would keep coming back to visit me. It was comforting to have a friendly visitor. He was someone who did not care if I was Muslim or Christian, Filipino or American.

Moe visited me via a hole that was located at the edge of the jungle underbrush behind my hut. It did not take long before Moe realized that I wouldn't hurt him and we began to get acquainted.

I never did find out if Moe was a boy or a girl and I really did not care. I was not about to traumatize the creature by grabbing it and turning it over to check its sex. I simply decided Moe was a boy. His company meant too much to me to risk losing him.

One afternoon I was lying on the clay floor of the shelter trying to keep cool and felt something soft rubbing up against the back of my leg. Startled, I looked to see what it was that was making itself comfortable in the space behind my knee. I almost burst out laughing when I discovered that it was Moe. He was taking a nap along side of me curled up in the crook of my bent leg.

For the first time since I had been taken captive I felt the warm feeling of affection. In some strange way, I loved Moe and he loved me. We had formed a bond and it was the companionship of this little rodent that reminded me again that there was good in the world.

That was the only time Moe and I took a nap together although he came every morning to be fed his rice. But the feeling of that little animal's warmth and trust touched me and rekindled my admiration for all God's creatures.

Through Moe I reconnected again to life. I was part of the living world again. He and the other creatures taught me that like all of God's creatures on the earth I was just one of many who lived with life and death situations each day. My perspective from the little world of my bamboo hut was changed as I realized that like this tiny rodent, I was only a small part of a much bigger picture.

Instead of feeling alone and pitted against evil creatures in the world I realized that God's creations still surrounded me. Through Moe and the others God had once again reached out and reassured me that I was not alone in this battle for survival against my enemies.

After that, whenever I felt myself slipping into the abyss of depression and despair, I consciously tried to appreciate the small comforts and living wonders I still enjoyed. Nevertheless, there were many lonely, suffocatingly hot and humid evenings when the desperation of my circumstances threatened to overwhelm me and suicidal thoughts crept up on me.

But I always thought of my children when I began to think about killing myself. *I have to stay alive for them,* I kept telling myself. Despite the hard times and things I had done in the past, I knew now I could not leave them that way.

I felt so many different emotions during that first week of captivity. But oddly enough instead of feeling angry with my captors, I found that most of the time I felt sorry for them. Though I was hardly the rich American they thought they had captured, in my worst days I had never lived as these poor young boys lived. Poverty was not their fault. How could I blame them for doing what they could to change their circumstances? With the hunger of a large family hanging in the balance, wouldn't I do anything to survive? These and many other realizations kept me from truly hating my captors.

The child-like faces of the boys with guns belied their taunts and cruelty. Instead of hating them I felt sad that they had fallen under the spell of people like Abu and Andong who had lured them with promises of a better life by doing their bidding and hating.

Instead of dwelling on my torment each day I tried to find different ways to keep my mind busy and away from hate. I spent many hours simply lying there in my hut playing music in my head. I selected my favorite albums and tried to remember the exact order of each song. Acting like a silent disc jockey, I played my favorite songs and whole albums by my favorite artists.

I kept a secret vault of music albums and videotapes stored in my head, often pulling one off the shelf in my mind to play and enjoy. This was one very important way that I worked to keep my mind alert.

But could I keep myself sane? Was I still a normal human being? After my first week in captivity my mind began to play tricks on me. Maybe it was the lack of food and water or the jungle heat, but several times I thought I heard voices from the past. Those were the moments when I felt my sanity might be slipping away.

And the weaker I became in body and spirit the more I heard voices in the wind and jungle noise around me. Was I losing my mind? Or was my mind just trying to create a friendlier environment for my desperate heart? After about seven days of begin held captive, I often was confused and doubted my own thoughts. It became a constant battle to keep my mind from slipping into a numb, coma-like state.

Despite my resolve I realized that I was in danger of losing touch with reality. I was increasingly drifting into a dreamlike state to escape the brutal, cruel conditions of my captivity.

I had to do something. I forced myself to move around my little hut. *Get up, get going,* I told myself. *You have to create more activities to keep yourself occupied and physically moving.*

To do so I began playing a game I had learned as a child. Digging tiny, shallow holes at each end of the hut I used small, round seeds that the wind had blown on the ground near me to play a game of marbles. I made a contest of how many seeds I could roll into a hole from about three feet away.

This activity, my memories and my friend, Moe, may have helped turn the tide against the fog filling my mind. And during one of my marble games my mind again began to think of ways that I might escape my jungle prison. Meanwhile, though physically I was still weak, I tried to improve my condition and even found a way to wash myself and my clothes at the same time.

I had observed that Tinoy occasionally took a shower with his clothes on. Although it seemed a bit odd to me, it began to make sense. He was able to keep himself and his clothes clean by soaping himself underneath his clothes and then rinsing himself with a ladle from a bucket of water. I noticed that he then soaped up his clothes while they were still on his body and rinsed them the same way.

I was inspired by this and got the idea in my head to try his method out myself during my daily break for food. I waited until one evening when most of the gang was not in the camp. Then, I asked Tinoy for some soap before I went to the latrine. He was not happy that I was asking to use something so precious. But I pointed to the rash between my legs and he grudgingly gave me a small piece.

In the Philippines most people wash their clothes by hand using soap bars. These bars are about a foot long, two inches wide and an inch thick. The women break off a small portion of the bar and then simply rub it into clothes that are already wet. Of course, the women usually have a tub or bucket that they use to wash their clothes in this primitive way. I had no such luxury.

The prospect of washing my body with the harshness of laundry soap made me wince at first, but I figured that it was better than nothing. So, after I had done my business, I proceeded to get my bucket of water and ladle. Then I washed myself and my clothes at the same time.

As the ever-present guards looked on grinning, I gasped as the soap washed away the grime and sweat from the sore rashes I had. The soap stung my flesh with its caustic ingredients. But the feeling I had after rinsing the soap off was one of liberation. I was clean and for a moment, triumphant.

However, all was not success. Shortly after my breakthrough in personal hygiene I had a frightening experience with a snake that decided to visit my hut. After a good night's sleep I opened my eyes to see something move in the corner. I assumed it was Moe making his usual morning visit. So I did not move, hoping he'd come over.

I closed my eyes and prayed my morning prayer as I normally did when I woke up. After I had finished I looked out into the clearing in front of the hut to see what was going on. I was happy to see that it was quiet and sunny. Only the dampness of the morning dew stuck to my grimy skin.

As I pulled myself to a sitting position something caught my eye. It was a dark brown circular object between the corner and the doorway that seemed to be moving. As I looked closer I saw it was a snake now coiled and staring ominously. Its head slightly raised, its tongue flicked in and out of its mouth. I froze, holding my breath for a second, wondering if the snake was about to strike. I told myself to try to keep still, something I had learned in the boy scouts when I was a child. But unlike when I was in the scouts, I could not slowly back away in order to escape. I was trapped, handcuffed. And I knew any movement of mine would surely trigger the snake's attack.

Long minutes passed. I continued to tell myself to be still, praying the snake would not move closer to me.

I tried to calm my fears by telling myself that maybe it was not a poisonous reptile. Even so, I was so allergic to animal and insect bites, I feared one strike by the snake would be fatal for me. I continued to pray for survival.

Finally, as I sat there frozen in a sitting position, the snake uncoiled and moved suddenly. For a moment I thought it was coming towards me. Then the snake slithered around the corner of the doorway and outside. As I watched the long, dark tail disappear, I breathed a seep sigh of relief. I had dodged another threat, but the encounter had shaken me. My heart pounded with fear.

In the hut I had become accustomed to having insects, friendly and vicious, crawling on my legs, arms and even my face. But I had learned not to react too quickly by brushing something from my skin before I slowly looked and identified it. Because the thing could be a scorpion or other venomous insect that might bite me in self-defense.

Weak and feeling ill most of the time, I learned to calm myself and just let the insects crawl across me. Most of the time

I found out they were only trying to get from one place to another. And if I waited long enough, these intruders which ventured onto my skin eventually left and went away.

This became true even of the flies and mosquitoes which infested the hut. After a while since my skin was always covered with grimy sweat, even flies began to avoid me, not stopping to land and check me out. It seemed humorous that the one advantage to being smelly and dirty was that I became a human insect repellent.

Heat, discomfort and other little things that might have bothered me before I became a hostage now became trivial in the overall scope of things. And when I prayed before going to sleep each night I thanked God for the gift of one more day.

Of course, as the interminable hours passed I could not help but agonize as to how long this ordeal would last. I didn't dare consider that I might never get out. I secretly had begun keeping a calendar by distinguishing light from darkness using my fingernail to mark each day on one of the bamboo slats of the lean to. I now approximated that I had been in captivity around seven or eight days. And I could not shake the terrible fear deep down inside me that my circumstances might get worse instead of better.

The same day as my encounter with the snake, I experienced more harassment from Berto, Greasy and Bucktooth. I had not seen Pops in several days, but the rest of the bunch returned to stir up trouble again.

Around noon Greasy brought an old metal pot over to the hut. There was rice in it and I wondered why they were suddenly bringing me an extra meal. It was not in their nature to be kind, so I became immediately suspicious.

As Greasy set the pot in front of me, he and Bucktooth motioned to me with their hands to eat. I was skeptical and hesitated wondering what they were up to. But they smiled and said "MMMMMMmmmmmmmmmm," encouraging me to eat the rice.

I peered into the bowl to see if it was indeed rice. Except for the usual burned moss around the edges of the pot, I thought it looked safe. Berto, Greasy and Bucktooth motioned again for me to eat and I tentatively reached into the pot bringing out a small clump of the rice.

Once again I looked at the rice now in my hands. It seemed to be fine though I had a fear that maybe the men were trying to poison me. But after inspecting the rice again, hunger got the better of my fear, I told myself I was getting paranoid.

I put a few pieces of the rice into my mouth tasting it to make sure there wasn't some other foreign substance mixed in. Another dark thought crossed my mind. *They may have treated the food in some way.* But the rice tasted okay, and with my stomach growling for the badly needed food, I swallowed and reached for another handful.

My three visitors were watching me intently and began grinning wickedly. Something was not right but I wasn't sure what it was.

Then as I reached for the second handful of rice to my mouth I noticed that the rice seemed to be moving. At that moment all three men burst out laughing.

I stared at the sticky white substance in my hand. Yes, the rice was moving now. What was this? As I squinted and blinked trying to see the handful of rice more clearly I saw the rice was filled with ants. I dropped the stuff immediately and began brushing the ants from my hand and arm. Unfortunately, I had momentarily forgotten about that first day tied to the tree when I was fed a spoonful of insects. Now that memory flooded back.

Berto, Greasy and Bucktooth laughed uproariously as I tried in vain to rid myself of the biting little pests. Unlike the relatively innocuous insects I was fed when I first came to the camp, I could not get the bugs away. They were infesting my mustache and beard, crawling into my mouth also. I summoned as much spit as I could and forcibly blew the foreign objects left in my mouth onto the ground.

As I frantically tried to brush away the rest, the guys in front of me laughed louder and began to boisterously pound each other on the back. Like a hurt animal I crawled away from them and into the back of the hut to get away from their cruel joke. With that they grabbed the pot of rice and ran back to the cooking area, jabbering like schoolboys about the success of their prank.

It wasn't long until their next nasty prank surfaced. This time they tried to feed me fish that had some worms in it. However, by then I knew better and carefully scanned every morsel they tried to feed me. Nevertheless, as the hours and days dragged on, my hunger grew and despite my apprehension, I became less picky.

Around my eighth day there, I noticed a change in the camp. Early that morning my teenage guards disappeared and a tall, muscular man named Eddy replaced them. While the two teenagers had been guarding me I had begun to think of ways I could deceive them and get away. They were just kids and I felt I could come up with some kind of plan to manipulate them.

I had been planning to talk—mostly using hand gestures and the few words of their language I had picked up—one of them into bringing me a reed mat to sleep on like the ones I had seen Tinoy use. I felt sure they would take pity on me and bring one. I thought that once I got the reed mat into my shelter I could devise a couple of hard, sharp reed sticks to use in picking and opening my handcuffs. But just when I had been able to establish some basic communication with them they were gone.

Eddy seemed more threatening. He had a military style crew cut and the hardened look of a well-trained guerrilla. And I wondered what the change meant. Was I now in the hands of a different, more militant group?

The only familiar faces I saw after that were those of Tinoy, Berto, Greasy, Andong and Abu. The camp became more silent and ominous. Where had everyone else gone? I kept asking myself, *What is next?*

When Abu and Andong had been at the camp, most of the time I had been left alone in relative peace. Even the surprise attacks by Berto and Greasy occurred less and less. But now a new threat emerged. Abu introduced a new and more terrifying weapon with which to intimidate me, a machete which they called a bolo. I recognized it as the same one he had used to mutilate the farmer's headless body, but after that horrifying day, he had taken the weapon away and not brought it back…until now.

The machete was old with a worn wooden handle and a long, curved, rusty blade on it. Only one edge of it was sharpened, but I was sure it had the frightening potential to do more harm.

Later that day, another interrogation took place. The machete took on a much more menacing dimension as Abu began waving it at me in a threatening manner when they grew frustrated with the same answers I gave them over and over.

Images of the headless farmer I'd heard executed kept flashing in my mind. Would they behead me? Or would they slowly cut different body parts from me in an effort to extract information? A new kind of terror was born in my mind. The very sight of the machete tied my stomach in knots of fear.

With Joseph translating, they continued to press me concerning the whereabouts of my ministry. As before, I continued to tell them, "I'm not a missionary; I'm not affiliated with any organization."

"Not so!" Joseph shouted angrily at me. "You missionary! Where mission's money?" Joseph's tone of voice grew louder showing his frustration.

"No, I am not..." I insisted. Suddenly I had a frightening thought. If they found out that indeed I was not a real missionary, would they rid themselves of me? The very possibility of that froze me in mid-sentence and I shut my mouth. A chill ran down my spine. If I were no longer of any value to them, they would have no reason to keep me alive. I doubted that they would just let me go. I knew that they would probably kill me.

From that point on I stopped protesting their assertions and began to just shake my head and play dumb, giving very general answers. As they worked me over I asked myself what they had done with Remy. Where was he and why had I not seen him or the cab driver? Had Remy given them information about the Blind Prophet or about his own position with her group?

As they continued to interrogate me it became clear that Abu and Andong had not been able to make a ransom demand, because they did not know whom to contact. From the angry, prodding questions they now asked and Joseph translated, it became apparent that they were growing frustrated and impatient. But even with the machete held close to my neck I knew that I had to quiet my fear and choose my words very carefully.

Obviously, they were still under the impression that Remy and I were missionaries with the Blind Prophet's crusade and that the Blind Prophet's group would pay a ransom to save our lives.

Of course, I knew we weren't ordained ministers since neither one of us had any theological training. But, of course, that did not matter to my captors. They were sure that we were both important members of a mission group and that they could obtain a lot of money for us.

Meanwhile my situation was growing more precarious with each passing hour. I began to wonder what torture Remy was receiving. Was he, like me, not telling them the things they wanted to know?

I was torn between saying nothing, which might lead my captors to kill me out of frustration, or telling them something, which might lead them to find out that I was not a missionary after all. Either way, I knew time was running out for me.

They continued to press me about the whereabouts of the Prophet. I finally decided to give them some kind of answer. "They went to an island south of Cebu," I said, repeating the only thing I had told them earlier.

"Name island!" Joseph demanded.

"I am not sure," I replied. It was true, I was not sure of the name of the island or the city the Prophet's group was going to.

Abu suddenly barked something to Joseph and he asked me, "What ferry name?"

"Super cat," I tried to sound confident. It was a name that I remembered, but whether it was helpful to the guerrillas I did not know.

"What Super cat?" Joseph demanded raising the machete again.

I tried to speak calmly. "Super Cat South?" I added the word south to the name hoping it wasn't true but would satisfy them.

The answer seemed to do the trick. Joseph passed the information to Abu. They conferred for a moment and Abu stepped away from me lowering his arm and the machete. But Joseph stepped close to me, looked me in the eyes and delivered a threat. "If not true, you die!" His words shook me just as I was feeling good about the harmless answer I had given them. As they walked away I wondered how long my reprieve would last.

Afterward I lay down on the dirt floor in the hut and could not help crying. In this hour of agony I felt doomed and sentenced to remain here with these vicious people until they killed me. Did anyone know that I was missing? I doubted it. Moreover, I could think of no one who would be trying to locate me. Even I did not know where I was and who these people were.

That night I could not stop myself from wallowing in self-pity. All hopes of escaping my captivity seemed to have vanished. But the next day when, to my surprise, I awoke, I watched a golden sun rising in the dawn sky. Again I said a prayer of thanks. After all, I had been given another day of life, another gift from God.

Chapter Ten

The Gates of Hell

As the next morning inched on I prayed for a miracle. I knew that was my only chance. In fact, it was the only chance for all three of us. I had not seen Remy in so long that I could not help wondering if he might be dead, suffering the same fate as the farmer. I resigned myself to the fact that I might never see him again, that I was on my own. Suddenly, I felt a new urgency to escape. In my mind, I began to devise an elaborate plan.

I decided that as stern and tough as Eddy looked I had to try to build a rapport with him and then attempt my escape. And so I began a slow and careful series of maneuvers designed to increase our communication and win his trust.

Over the next hours I requested things such as water, gum and a piece of cloth from Eddy. Surprisingly, he brought me all of them. Unlike the younger boys who seemed to enjoy teasing me, Eddy was turning out to be a man who was very business-like in nature and somewhat empathetic.

I made a great display of showing him how sleeping on the ground was harming me and pointed out that if something happened to me, their efforts to collect money would fail. I showed him how dirt was working its way into the cuts and bites of my skin. I had been using spit to clean my cuts. Now I quietly asked Eddy, who was intently watching me, for water to clean my wounds. Surprisingly, he brought it. In fact, I was even able to get enough water from him to rinse out the inside of my mouth which, because of the missing tooth, was now infected.

Then, giving Eddy my most pathetic look, I asked him if he could get a reed mat for me to lie on. At first he did not understand me, but I drew a picture of the mat in the dirt and demonstrated to him using grass as a prop until he understood what I wanted.

Later that afternoon, Eddy brought me a reed mat just like the one I had seen Tinoy use. I was astonished that this tough looking man seemed to have such a soft heart. And I was encouraged that just maybe through him my plans for escape could work.

From then on whenever Eddy, who was standing outside the entrance, wasn't watching, I worked on crafting two long hard reeds from the mat on which I was lying. When this was done I watched Eddy and when he wasn't looking into the hut, I used the two reeds to attempt to pick my cuffs open.

My heart pounded with excitement as I began to see movement in the part of the cuff that was secured to the lock. With every movement of the reed in the lock opening, I came closer to my goal and the lock began to release and loosen.

I can do this! I encouraged myself. It was working! But then one of the reeds broke, making a loud snapping sound. I immediately sat on the reeds to hide them as Eddy jumped up and peered into the hut. He had heard the noise and was looking to see what I was doing.

There was concern on his face as he entered the hut and I had to think fast. Luckily a subterfuge popped into my mind. Before Eddy could order me to move from my place on the floor, I raised one of my hands, grabbed one of my fingers and cracked a knuckle. There was a loud "POP" similar to the sound the reed had made when it broke. Without looking at Eddy I innocently took another finger and did the same thing. Again I was able to produce a loud "POP."

I did not even look at Eddy, pretending instead to be concentrating on my new exercise. My ploy worked and without saying a thing, Eddy walked back out of the hut apparently satisfied that what he had heard was just me popping my knuckles.

But the incident shook me. Although I was glad I had avoided being discovered, I realized that Eddy had extremely sensitive hearing and that in the future I would have to be very careful about making any noise. It was a close call and I scoured my mind for other ways to free myself.

I racked my brain to figure out how I could get the locks loosened. I wondered if Eddy carried the key to my cuffs and chains with him. I began discreetly spying on him to see if he had a key ring. I was disappointed when I did not see one on him and tried to think of other ways to gain my freedom.

One idea that came to my mind was to use some kind of sharp object like a rock to slowly bend one of the chain links and try to disconnect it. All I would need to do, I theorized, was to bend one link enough to disconnect it from the chain and I would be freed. Of course, I would have to do the same thing to

the chain holding my wrist cuffs also. I would have to open a
link on both chains for me to regain freedom of movement. I
began looking around for pieces of rock that I could use to do
this.

However, though I surveyed every inch of the hut there
was none of the coral rock that was so plentiful on the island.
There was nothing hard enough to use to attempt to bend a
chain link. I had nothing on me like a belt buckle or ring either.

Then I looked for screws or bolts that I might be able to
wiggle free, but there were only the hinges on the door. They
looked promising, but I would need something sturdy to pry
one of the hinge bolts out and I had nothing.

I searched and conspired to come up with something,
anything that I could use. I decided to take a chance and slip the
spoon for the soup they usually brought me into my pocket
hoping that it would not be missed. The metal spoon might be
just what I needed.

Finally, Tinoy brought my meal. I acted as normal as I
could and tried to finish the bowl of soup while Tinoy was not
looking. I was about to slip the spoon into my pocket when
Tinoy suddenly approached me, gesturing to some water in a
cup. He was asking me if I wanted more water. I nodded my
head yes and he handed it to me.

But as he handed me the cup of water he pulled the
spoon and bowl from my lap and took them away to be washed.
I bit my lip, feeling blood trickle as I watched him walk away
with what could have been the answer to my prayers. I had come
so close only to be disappointed.

The next evening, however, I got a break. When I sat
down in the rickety wooden chair to eat, I spied a bowl with two

spoons in it close to where I was sitting. Tinoy had evidently brought it for someone else. When Tinoy turned his back on me, I quickly reached over and grabbed one of the spoons from the bowl.

Now I had a spoon that probably would not be missed and I could leave mine in my bowl not arousing any suspicions. I could not believe my good luck! It had to be the hand of God again finding a way to assist me in my plan.

Later, in the dark I began using my new tool in an attempt to bend a link in the chain holding me. As I scanned the chain, I saw one link that appeared to be already bent and opening. I inserted the thin end of the handle of the spoon into the gap between the two apposing ends of the link and worked it in half way so that I could apply pressure on one side of the end link. Then applying all the pressure I could generate by using the underside of the other link as a fulcrum, I pressed down on the other end of the link. At first, there seemed to be no give at all. The spoon kept bending and I could not apply enough weight to budge the end of the link.

But I kept trying and after a long period of quiet exertion, the other end seemed to move so that the gap between the two had widened slightly.

However, the spoon was becoming mangled and unusable and the pressure that I had to exert in order to bend the link was exhausting. I decided to rest for a while rebuilding my energy so I could resume my work.

As the night went on, I began again to make progress in bending the link, but my strength was so minimal from lack of food and my weakened condition that I had to stop often. In addition to my physical limitations, my fear of being caught was mounting. Again I stopped for a while. Finally, after working on the gap at various times during the night I was close to slipping the link off the chain.

So far so good! I was on the verge of accomplishing the first part of my project. All I had to do now was work on a similar link in the other chain that bound my leg. A fresh infusion of hope was growing in my heart. "I can do this!" I kept telling myself.

While I began prying on the second link I began to formulate the rest of my escape plan in my head. I would wait until the first light of morning penetrated the darkness when I knew that Eddy would be asleep. Then I would slip the links off the chains, run toward the jungle and quickly disappear into the thick foliage.

In my mind I tried to estimate approximately where I was on the island and felt reasonably sure that I could track back the way from which I had come. I had made mental notes of some of the landmarks my captors had brought me past. Now I prayed I would get the chance to follow those landmarks back down the mountainside and hopefully to the docks where we had originally landed.

Once there my only chance would be to try and steal some kind of boat. If I could get my hands on one I could head for the nearest island. I could only pray that there would be friendly Filipinos there who would help me get back to Cebu.

Escaping at night, I figured, would give me some time periodically to stop and rest, which I knew I would have to do because of weakened condition. I had to hope that my body could make it down the mountainside fast enough to get away before anyone knew I was gone.

After ten days of captivity, fear and uncertainty, I searched for an opportunity where I could once again control my own destiny. The weak, frightened foreigner who had been so easy to intimidate during those first days of captivity would be gone. For though my body had endured a lack of nutrition and physical abuse, my spirit was rising inside to fortify me with a new inner strength. And now, with a little rest, I was confident, both physically and mentally, that I could execute my plan of escape.

That night I could hardly sleep from the excitement of what was to come. Even so I tried to rest so that I could get up around 4:00 or 5:00 in the morning. Finally, with hope and determination in my heart, sleep came.

But my escape was not to be. Not long after I had fallen asleep, Andong kicked me awake. He unlocked the shackles on my ankle and wrist and ordered me to my feet. Then he and Eddy grabbed me roughly by the arms and led me out of the hut and to the other end of the camp. *What is going on? How can they possibly know about my plans to get away?* I was confused and only half-awake. But the disappointment of not being able to execute my plan of escape was quickly replaced by the familiar fear of not knowing what was to come next.

In the darkness Andong led the way to a path running into the jungle. It was not a well-worn path so we had to walk slowly and carefully picking our way through thorny bushes and tall grass. As we wound down the mountain my heart began pumping faster and faster. I dreaded the worst. They must be planning to kill me. Why else would they take me away in the middle of the night? The adrenaline rush of terror pushed my feeble body forward. Where were they taking me?

As we journeyed deeper and deeper into the thick underbrush, I hesitated for a moment trying to protect my face from the plants whipping across my eyes. *KA-POW!* A boot kicked me hard in the rear, almost lifting me off of the ground. As I fell forward a hand pushed me from the back almost putting me into a nosedive to the ground. I turned to see Eddy scowling at me and pointing forward. Each time our progress was slowed by the dense and dark jungle in front of us, Eddy kicked me and pushed me forward, not allowing me to rest. I had not walked in days and my legs felt soft and lifeless.

At one point I fell to one knee and then was knocked to the ground by a vicious kick from Eddy's foot. As Eddy yanked me up by my arm I noticed that Joseph, the interpreter, was also following us just a few yards behind Eddy. Seeing me glance at Joseph, Eddy grunted something and pushed me forward again.

In the cool evening air as we pushed through the tangle of vegetation, I looked up once to see another clear, starry evening sky. The sky was thick with millions of stars spread across the dark blue heavens above us. Rather than feeling its beauty this time the sight made me feel small and helpless like a speck of sand in a sea of blue water.

Finally we reached a ridge and began edging sideways around the mountainside. The ridge became thinner and narrower as we carefully moved along the rocky path. Then suddenly we had to stop. We had come to a dead end and were perched on a rocky ledge. I looked down and for the first time in days I could see the ocean, surrounding the island like a dark blue blanket in the night.

Suddenly there was a rustling in the bushes behind us. I turned to see where the sound was coming from and was startled to see Abu emerge like a phantom from the mountainside. Pushing aside a dense wall of vines, Abu stepped from the darkness and onto the ledge in front of us. He looked at me with a strange smirk on his face. His eyes were glazed and wild looking. *Where did he come from?* For a minute I thought my eyes were playing tricks on me or I was hallucinating.

Then Abu barked something to Eddy and disappeared again into the abyss from which he had come. Once again Eddy pushed me forward and Joseph, who now was standing next to him, motioned to me to follow him past the wall of hanging vines and into the dark mouth of a tunnel. As I ducked my head to enter it I saw an old, rusty iron gate that was almost hidden by the thick vegetation. It appeared to be stuck open, long forgotten and unused.

Ahead of us in the blackness was a curved rock wall which we soon rounded and then we could see a lantern hanging from the wall. Nearby stood Abu, his face dimly lit with a spooky yellowish glow.

As we inched forward in the shadows the musty smell and dampness accosted me. I thought about the old rusted gate at the entrance and realized there was little chance of anyone finding me even if they were searching. A strange and unsettling feeling of doom came over me. Then, a new rush of fear took hold of me. My skin prickled at the unmistakable presence of evil in the air. I felt like I had just entered the gates of hell.

As we neared the lantern Abu turned on a large spotlight and pointed to a place on the wall. Eddy pushed me to the spot and then kicked the back of my knee. My legs buckled dropping me to the floor. Eddy grabbed one of my ankles fastening it to an old rusty chain and then, using handcuffs, locked the cuffs with a loud *CLICK*.

Alarmed, I looked around. On the floor a few feet away was an old straw mattress; much like the ones I had seen on the hard beds of the pension at which I stayed. At least I would have a place to sleep. The momentary lift in my spirits at seeing the mattress was shot down quickly as I raised my head to see Abu standing over me wielding the machete. Terror struck me.

Speaking through Joseph, Abu told me he was keeping me in this place for my protection. Lying in the dark, spooky space of this underground dungeon and looking up at him wielding a weapon he'd already used to decapitate someone, I hardly was reassured.

As if trying to confuse me further, Abu told me that if my friends cooperated I would be going home soon. *Does that mean that Remy is still alive? Can it be true that I might be freed because of information that Remy gave them?* Somewhere deep inside of me the stirring of faint hope gave me momentary visions of freedom and returning to Cebu soon.

Suddenly Andong came rushing into the tunnel. A few moments later a heated discussion ensued between Andong and Abu. Then they went rushing out of the tunnel leaving only Eddy to watch me. Pulling up a chair, Eddy put his feet up on an old wooden table in front of him. Fortunately for me, it was not long before he fell asleep.

I crawled the few feet to the mattress and lay there. The emotional ups and downs of the past several days went round and round in my head leaving me feeling confused and unsettled. Did I dare think that I might be free soon? But there was a deep foreboding inside me that dashed any new feelings of optimism. I knew that I could not trust Abu.

In addition this dark, ominous setting belied his words. My gut told me that my situation was not going to improve. But what could I do? My earlier plans of escape and being once again in control of my own life were dashed. Now I could only pray and trust God. I asked Him to be with me in my distress. And I tried to find some comfort in my soft mattress. Weary, I finally drifted off to sleep.

The next morning I learned more about my new surroundings. Sometime in the past I had heard stories about the warrens of tunnels in the Philippines that were engineered by the Japanese during World War II. Some fifty years earlier, these tunnels were part of an elaborate network of defenses the Japanese had used to frustrate the advancing American forces in the Pacific. How strange that I, an American, was here now being held captive.

Turning my head I saw a bit of sunlight seeping deep into the tunnel by way of airshafts of some kind. Together with the lantern lighting the chamber in the tunnel, I thought I could almost make out the way to the outer end of the tunnel.

After this, as I sat there contemplating what might happen to me next, I tried to calm my nerves by visually exploring as much of the tunnel as I could. Near the lantern on the wall there was a table and two chairs made of an old, splintered wood. A few feet down the wall of the tunnel I could make out what appeared to be buckets of water, probably brought in from outside. I twisted my body on the straw mattress, which had seemed heaven sent for my poor aching body. It was damp and mildewed. But I did not care.

Reaching into my pocket, I felt about to retrieve the mangled spoon. *It was not there! Where had it gone?* My heart sank with disappointment. I thought back to Eddy kicking me on our way to the tunnel. It must have fallen out of my pocket then.

I could not believe my bad luck! I could only hope that no one had seen the spoon when it fell out of my pocket. They surely would figure out that I had been using it as a tool to aid in an escape plan. I would be punished severely, I felt certain, if they found out that I had it in my possession. In any case, I would have to come up with a new scheme if I had any hopes of escaping soon.

I looked around. My eyes were becoming accustomed to the darkness around me. I could now see more clearly and studied my new prison.

The walls of the tunnel were porous coral rock, yellow and gray in color with some areas covered in a black soot-like dust. I wondered what kind of machines might have been here many years ago and what method of lighting they might have used. There were some areas where I could see flat, shelf-like ledges that had been chiseled out of the coral walls. But I could see nothing that I might be able to use to pry loose the handcuff from my ankle.

However, a sudden urgency was stirring inside me to act quickly and get away from this ominous place before my captors did something terrible to me. It was as if I could sense something awful was about to happen. Like a trapped animal I began to feel restless and nervous. My eyes searched every part of the tunnel, floor to ceiling, hoping to find something that could aid me in freeing myself.

As I looked closely, I could see that all around me were indications that human beings once had been here. I saw old wooden struts hanging from the walls where a cabinet or piece of equipment once was located. I could also see rusted bolts in linear positions in the wall indicating where things were once fastened.

From the moldy old mattress on which I sat, I could see the chain that connected me to a rusted old metal bolt was sunk deep into the coral wall of the tunnel. The metal handcuff around my right ankle felt very tight and the skin underneath had blistered and was bleeding. I worried that I could just as easily die from an infection as at the hands of these vicious men.

A wave of depression swept over me. I slumped onto my mattress and sobbed silently, but no tears came. I was so dehydrated that even tears were now impossible.

I kept thinking about how close I had come to making my escape. *Did they suspect? Why? Why did they decide to move me here?* I had to start all over again finding a way to get away.

Weak, helpless and feeling sorry for myself trapped like an animal, I fell asleep again weeping silent, invisible tears. Only in sleep was there any peace. And only in my dreams did I feel like a human being again.

I dreamed about the night that I had received an award naming me one of the best managers in the southeast United States. I had been working sixty-hour work weeks for nearly two years at a small hospital in Alabama on the Florida border. I thought no one in management had noticed the effort I was putting forth when I found myself nominated for several different awards.

Drifting further into a deep sleep, I was transported back to that awards dinner in Alabama.

> *I turned to an executive sitting next to me. "Just being nominated is such an honor," I told him. He nodded. I went on to tell him I had always been happy and at home amidst the many good people I had worked with in the company. But I was taken completely by surprise when they nominated me for the top award: Best in ALL categories of managerial success. What a happy surprise!*
>
> *"Well, Greg, no one deserves it more than you," he replied kindly.*
>
> *I looked around my table. Almost everyone sitting there was a manager or executive. As I was about to take a bite of my steak, I heard my name called out. I didn't immediately get up, disbelieving that I had actually won. The executive next to me whispered, "Greg, get up. Go on stage!" I was in a delirious fog of shock and happiness. I slowly walked up to the stage to the sound of hundreds of people clapping.*
>
> *It was a milestone in my career. I felt like I was floating on air as the crowd applauded and the spotlight shined on me. I was a dream come true.*
>
> *I felt elation warm me all over. The future was mine for the taking. I was so blessed to be in a*

business where I was doing God's work—helping
people, both employees and patients—in the hospi-
tals that I served.

How good I felt about myself, really good, as I
soaked up the warmth of that spotlight, holding my
award in my hand and smiling. I was a good man.
People loved me, people respected me. I was blessed.

Then suddenly everything faded away. My
boss strode up to me and grabbed the award from
my hands. I was startled, "What? What are you
doing?" I asked as he walked away into an unlit
hallway clutching my prize.

In an instant the room turned totally dark and
eerily quiet; then it disappeared completely. I
looked around and was no longer in the banquet
hall. I was in the hospital standing in my office, the
same hospital where I had my accident. My boss,
still holding my award, was frowning at me. "You
will not get this back until you have told me
exactly what you were doing on your vacation!"

I felt like crying, Why is this all happening to
me? *My boss ran away with my award. I tried to*
run after him, but my feet were rooted to the
ground. "Come back! Come back!" I shouted. "You
cannot do this to me, it's not fair!"

My dream ended abruptly. With a lump in my throat I
awoke on the old mattress in the tunnel. I was whimpering;
strange noises were coming from my throat. Laying in the
gloomy tunnel with the emotions of the dream still gripping me,

I realized I had awakened from a nightmare only to face a reality that was far worse. "Why me?" I murmured. "Why do these terrible things keep happening to me?"

My dream had reminded me that there was treachery and unfairness in the world no matter where you dwelled. And then I realized that the real pain I had suffered in my old life was due to the material things upon which I had placed so much importance.

It was time for me to rise above such petty desires and put my faith in God. I had to trust him with my fate. This was the next step that I had to take.

I closed my eyes and quietly prayed, "Lord, I know you will not forsake me." I continued praying, trying to reassure myself that I was not alone. "I know there is a reason for all this tragedy in my life. Please help me to understand the wisdom I should gain from all of this." And with a final sigh I softly added, "I am yours Lord: do with me what you will. My life is in your hands."

A foot suddenly kicked my leg. I looked up and saw it was Eddy. He had some rice for me. I sat up. "Thank you," I said humbly, grateful for this gift. Eddy, despite his gruffness at times, surprised me with his compassion. Perhaps he was a decent guy who just followed orders. Maybe I could reach him somehow? Maybe he would be my key to freedom?

Satisfying my hunger, the rice tasted better than the most kingly of meals. I felt blessed again by just this one small act of kindness. But even as my spirits grew, my body continued to wither.

Although the pains in my back and shoulder were not as agonizing as they had been earlier, they still throbbed dully. My lips had numerous sores and my mouth was cracked at the corners, infected and bleeding often as did my gums. My arms and legs were covered with dirt, bug bites and numerous bloody scratches from bushes and rocks. The open wound where my tooth had once been was infected also.

As I sat there taking inventory of so many different wounds I realized that I was getting thirsty. I asked Eddy for some water from the buckets I had seen along the wall. "Tubig?"

I said as I motioned with my hands as if I was drinking something. Eddy looked at me confused. "Tubig?" I tried to pronounce it more clearly this time. I pointed at the buckets of water a few yards down the tunnel. Eddy looked at me and then walked down to peer at the buckets.

Then, somehow understanding, Eddy returned to the table at which he had been sitting and retrieved a small tin cup he had been using. He dunked the cup in one of the buckets a couple of times to rinse it. I wondered how clean this water would be, but I was not about to be picky; I needed water to survive. After I had drunk two cupfuls of it, I lay back on the mattress half asleep.

Suddenly there was commotion in the tunnel. I rolled over to see a light coming around the corner and two figures following close behind it. It was Abu and Joseph holding a lantern.

Eddy, Abu and Joseph stood talking for a few minutes and then approached me. Eddy pulled me roughly to my feet, his earlier kindnesses to me evaporated as he wrenched one of my arms. Abu began barking out short sentences that Joseph then interpreted for me. "Where your missionary friends?" Joseph demanded, reflecting the same sharp tone of voice that was coming from Abu.

"I don't know?" I responded, shrugging my shoulders.

"You know!" Joseph shouted. "Where were you going with them?"

I looked at the men sheepishly and feigned stupidity. "I am not sure," I said. "I don't remember the name of the place." Joseph turned around and rapidly translated what I had said for Abu.

Angry Abu jumped forward and hit me hard in the mouth with his fist. I staggered back against the wall. Before I had a chance to recover, Abu kicked me, digging his boot into my groin. The pain from this kick momentarily paralyzed me as I bent forward, knees together, cupping my genitals with my hands. I fell to my knees moaning, trying to catch my breath as my body curled into a fetal position.

Standing above me, Abu shouted something. Eddy began to drag me up but then Abu kicked me again in the chest, toppling me over and out of Eddy's grip. Joseph rushed forward yelling at me. At first I could not understand what he was saying, I just stared up at him with tears filling my eyes. Then Joseph screamed "Not so! You know it! Not so!" My groin was on fire with agony and I could not catch my breath.

Abu was enraged. I had never seen him this angry. He stomped over to the wooden table and slammed a small bag down on it. Eddy pulled me to my feet again and Abu shouted to Joseph. Joseph turned to me again and screamed, "Tell me! Where your missionaries! Tell me now!" I stood there bent over in pain still unable to speak. Then suddenly Abu jumped forward again and punched me hard in the stomach. Eddy grabbed me, pulling my arms back and pinning them behind me. *THWACK!* Abu punched me again in the face, this time the blow glanced off my cheekbone. *THHHUUMP!* Abu punched me hard in the stomach again.

A moment later Joseph screamed again "Tell me! Where are they?" I tried to mouth a few words but nothing came out. *SMACK!* Abu punched me again in the face this time splitting my lip. Now I tasted the blood in my mouth. I tried vainly to pull my arm away from Eddy and wipe away the blood dripping down my chin.

But Eddy only pulled my arms tighter, straightening my body again for another blow. *THHUUUMP!* Abu punched me again in the stomach. The muscles in my gut spasmed and cramped as my body tried once again to curl into a fetal position.

Joseph screamed louder. "Tell me now! Now!" Abu turned his back and walked away.

I looked at Joseph. "Please stop," I begged. "I don't know. Really, I do not know!" I pleaded with Joseph.

Abu returned with his assault rifle swinging the butt end of it into my midsection. *POW!* The blow threw me backwards into the wall of the cave just as Eddy let me go and got out of the way of the swinging rifle. I slumped to my knees in pain, breathless from the blow. *CRACK!* The last thing I saw out of the corner of my eye was the rifle butt coming toward my head. Then darkness.

I sputtered, water filling my mouth. I blinked my eyes, trying to clear the fog from my mind. Slowly, I began to remember where I was and what had happened. As my eyes opened wider, I saw Eddy and Joseph standing over me. Eddy splashed more water on my face. "Utt utt," Eddy grunted. He motioned for me to get up.

Joseph looked at me and angrily shouted, "You know, now! Tell now!"

"Please, I don't." As I tried to shake the dizziness from my brain my hands automatically moved to my face, feeling for damage. The left side of my face was so swollen I could hardly touch it. My left eye was beginning to close. My stomach and head throbbed.

And so the worst of hell befell me. It was approximately the eleventh day of my captivity when the new phase of torture began. Now kept in a place with no sunlight, I found it nearly impossible to know day from night. Only by watching my captors' sleep cycles was I able to estimate the passing of time.

When they beat me during my first week in captivity and when they hung me from the tree I thought that I knew what real agony was. I did not yet know that the next few days of torture would redefine for me the meaning of pain and terror.

Chapter Eleven

Facing Evil

Abu returned again and again punching, kicking and beating me with his rifle until there was no place on my body that was free from pain or swelling. My face and eyes were blackened; my mouth and nose bled constantly. Two more teeth were dislodged by the butt of his rifle.

Most of the time I was dazed, unable to even cry out against the pain and violence inflicted upon me. I honestly had no information to give even had I wanted to. I really did not know where the Blind Prophet's crusade could be. *Should I make something up?* My mind searched for an answer that would end my suffering. But I could not come up with a place, even a fictitious one. I simply could not remember the names of any of the islands except for Cebu.

At one point Abu stopped beating me and left for a few minutes. When he returned he said to me in broken English, "Tell us where Prophet is and you go home." I was surprised not only by his command of English, albeit rudimentary, but by this sudden offer of freedom. Yet I was skeptical as well.

A moment later Abu's face changed dramatically, becoming sympathetic as if he understood my pain. "Would you like something to eat?" he asked compassionately. I was taken aback by his offer, but I quickly decided he simply was trying a new tactic, thinking that maybe he could seduce me with sweetness. Yet I knew he was not sincere; he simply was not believable as a kind person.

As I looked into his eyes I realized that I was still looking into the eyes of the same evil snake I had earlier seen mutilate a man he had just killed. His outward appearance had changed for the moment, but I was not fooled into believing that he suddenly developed empathy or compassion. *The devil has many faces*, I thought. *Don't be fooled by him.*

"Yes, please, and water also," I told him, hoping he might actually make good on his offer. At any rate I wanted to see how far he would go though I guessed in the end he would renege. He smiled and turned to say something to Eddy. Then as he started down the long dark space of the tunnel he suddenly turned and looked at me again. The pale yellow light from the lamp lit his face as he stared at me. His smile quickly faded like the false front that it was and then he turned and left.

I shuddered, feeling as if it had been the very first time in my life that I had actually faced evil. Beguiling and seductive, Abu's face could still not hide the heart-stopping wicked presence of his damned soul. About him was an aura of evil as powerful, it seemed to me at that moment, as was the goodness of Jesus Christ. *Does that make Abu the devil?* I wondered.

I was beginning to understand the full scope of Satan's energy in mankind. Facing evil, I either had to succumb or make a stand. This was my moment of truth, my day of reckoning and I could not hide from the battle. Only the strength of my faith would determine the outcome of this ultimate challenge. My life and my soul now depended on it.

As I had suspected, the devil was only toying with my emotions. Abu deceived me again; Eddy did not bring me food or water. There was a method to his madness, his psychological torture of me. He was demonstrating to me again that I had no power. Only he had the power to give or take away the things that I needed most. He was in control. This was his message in almost everything that he and his thugs did to me.

By the end of this cycle of torture I had been beaten unconscious twice. Each time I was doused with water to wake me up again. They would not even allow me the comfort of unconsciousness.

Finally, the beatings ceased, but they still did not bring me food. I was too exhausted and in too much pain to do anything but lie on my straw mattress and pass into and out of consciousness. Little did I know that the worst was yet to come.

When I awakened I saw that Joseph and Abu had left. But a short time later they returned. Perhaps, I surmised, they had gone somewhere to eat for they returned with food for Eddy.

Starving, I watched in agony. These men were doing everything they could to break my will and it was working. Feeling weak and losing hope of any resolution to this nightmare, I actually began thinking of ways to kill myself to end the suffering. Fortunately, I was too weak to do anything. And I knew God would not forgive me for such a sin.

Seeking some comfort and reassurance I asked God for courage to face this terror. I prayed for strength of will and spirit to survive the violence and pain I was now experiencing. Then, to my surprise, I found myself praying also for my captors. I asked God to touch Abu, Andong, Eddy and Joseph and change their poisoned hearts. I asked Him to somehow enlighten them and lead them to the path of peace and tolerance. And I prayed for the ability to forgive them all for what they had done, were doing and undoubtedly still planned to do to me.

But on what I assumed to be the next day, the intense torture resumed and my spirits fell. I begged and begged for water having no pride left and I felt like a wounded animal, devoid of any redeeming human characteristics. Finally, I received a half cup of water.

When Abu and Joseph entered the tunnel they were accompanied by Andong. All of them were laughing and jovial. I could not imagine why unless maybe someone, Remy perhaps, had given them the answers that they wanted. I asked Joseph about Remy. "Where is Remy? Is he still alive?"

Joseph just answered quietly, "I don't know about your Filipino."

That was when Abu, Andong and Joseph, who was translating for me, launched into a tirade about the "Whites." I assumed he was referring to people like me, people of Anglo descent. "Who do you think you are?" Joseph said angrily. "You whites think you are better than we. You are weak and spoiled and ugly," Joseph went on. "Look at you now." He laughed.

Abu and Andong kept shouting while Joseph interpreted. "Christians are corrupt and deserve to die; their religion is our enemy." I was surprised by the last comment; I had no idea that Muslims viewed Christians in this way. It was the first time in the Philippines that I had heard this kind of anger expressed toward

Christians and foreigners. But it would not be the last time that I would hear this venom of hatred spewing from my captors' mouths.

Abu, Andong and Joseph traded hateful remarks and then pointed at me and laughed. They mocked me and belittled my faith. Anger began to stir inside me as they again tried to intimidate me with their fists and rifles. Each time they moved toward me I recoiled like a dog that has been kicked too many times, but inside I was screaming in rebellion against the injustice.

A little later Abu grabbed me by the throat and looked me straight in the eye spewing angry words at me. I had the overwhelming urge to spit in his face, but I knew he might use this act as an excuse to maim or kill me.

His breath was sour and his eyes were bloodshot and glazed as if he was drunk or high on something. His eyes were empty pools of darkness as if no soul lurked beneath. I blinked, frightened by his malevolence. The strength of his evil suddenly gripped me, sending shudders through my body and mind. It was as if I were looking into the eyes of the devil himself.

Suddenly, Abu reached up and with his hand behind my head pulled me over to the old wooden table. *Ka-Thump!* Abu smashed my head into the table almost knocking me out. *Ka-thump!* Again he smashed my head, forehead first, into the table. Just as quickly, Andong kicked my feet out from under me and I fell backwards into one of the wooden chairs being held by Joseph.

Abu barked some orders to Eddy and he stepped forward grabbing my hands and pinning them to the table. Then he separated my hands as far from each other as he could with the handcuffs on and held my hands flat, holding each one by the wrist. *What are they planning to do?* I looked up and saw Abu standing across the table with a fiendish grin on his face. Joseph stood next to him smiling also.

Abu began barking instructions to Joseph again. Joseph stared at me menacingly and yelled, "Where your American friends?" I shook my head to indicate that I didn't know without actually saying anything. "Where your missionary friends?" The tone of his voice increased in volume as well as anger with each word. My gut told me more torture was soon coming.

Abu abruptly reached across the table and drove a large knife into the wood, just inches from my right hand. My heart started pounding and the familiar gut wrenching feeling of fear and helplessness gripped me again. Abu walked slowly to the side, sneering at me, his face twisted with a vicious intensity.

Then with another quick move, Abu drove a long, sharp needle of some kind into the table next to my left hand. *Oh my God,* I thought to myself. *What is he going to do with that?* Moving to the right side again Abu shouted something to Eddy. Letting go of my left wrist he grabbed my right hand and spread it out, flat on the table. In one swift move Abu pulled the knife from the table in front of me and plunged it quickly between my thumb and forefinger, barely missing them both.

I looked up at Andong and Abu. I could see devilish delight in their eyes. This was a game to them, a game in which they could up the stakes by threatening to sever one of my fingers. It was mental as well as physical torture. It was like a scene from a horror movie. I could not believe that this was really happening to me.

Abu moved coyly to my left side again. This time Andong came around and held down my left hand, spreading it flat out on the table. Another swift move and Abu plunged the sharp looking needle between my pinky finger and ring finger on my left hand. My pulse raced and I felt sweat began to bead on my forehead. I was weak and dehydrated and had not sweated in days. But this terror was flushing sweat I didn't even know I still had from my pores.

Slowly they plunged these sharp instruments between my fingers. First on my right hand traveling from my thumb to my pinky. Then, on my left hand traveling from my pinky toward my thumb.

Abu grunted something to Joseph. Then reaching over again he laid the knife near my right hand and thrust it into the wood between my forefinger and middle finger. Joseph leaned over and whispered in my ear "You tell us where your friends are, yes?" I didn't move; my mind raced trying to think of something to say to placate them.

The game continued and mere seconds seemed like hours. Each time Abu plunged the knife or needle close to my next finger, Joseph whispered in my ear, "Which finger you miss more?" I did not answer.

At this point I recognized the needle that Abu was using to scare me. It appeared to be a long injection type of needle with a metal cylinder that a farmer might use to inject livestock.

The next time Abu plunged the knife between my thumb and forefinger of my right hand I began to wonder if he was just threatening me or if I would barely survive this terrorizing encounter—with extensive injuries and blood loss.

Then Joseph told me something I never forgot. He stopped whispering in my ear and said in a very matter of fact manner, "You no talk, you lose something."

My heart throbbed with fear and I began to silently pray. *Please God, help me*! I closed my eyes and prayed. *Please God, stop them*! I was sure without God's interference now that I was going to lose a finger if not more.

Suddenly there was quick and violent movement to my left and I felt a sharp, intense pain in the middle finger of my left hand. Saliva dripped from my mouth from the fright of it and I opened my eyes to see that Abu had driven the needle through my finger at the first knuckle below the fingernail. He lifted the needle, pulling my entire hand up off the table in the process as my finger was still attached to the piercing needle. In shock, I reacted instinctively, pulling my hand away from him. And with that one instinctive reflex my hand came free of the needle.

I looked down at the knuckle of the finger that had been speared. It was swelling and purple, but surprisingly, not bleeding that much. Andong grabbed my left hand again and flattened it out on the table. I thought now they were going to sever a finger.

Instead, Abu sat down at the other end of the table and held the needle above my thumb. I turned my face away thinking Abu was going to stab me again. Eddy smacked the side of my face, forcing my eyes back to the table. Next, Andong held my left hand and Eddy held my right hand as Abu began jumping the needle between the fingers of my left hand. Only this time he stopped and landed on top of one of my fingers. Each time he did this he pressed the needle into the skin of the finger, acting like he was going to puncture another knuckle.

As he always did, Joseph stood by and watched while Eddy and Andong restrained me, only speaking to translate what Abu was saying. Like Eddy, Joseph only seemed to be aggressive when he was in the presence of Abu. He stood somewhat apart from the others, only the yellow lamplight lighting his face as he observed Abu's every move.

I watched with dread as Abu played out his little game. He was succeeding in intimidating me, not just physically, but also mentally. My mind searched for some kind of answer that would stop this horrific agony.

Joseph looked at me and raised his eyebrows as if to say, *Well, what do you have to say?* At that point I started to believe that just making up a name might save me from more harm.

Meanwhile the needle hopped between my fingers again and came to rest on the thumb of my left hand. As Abu pressed it menacingly into the side of the knuckle I finally broke under the strain and threw out the only name that came to mind. "I think they are at Mindanao!" I blurted out. Both of them stopped and looked me in the eye. Then they looked at each other and laughed.

Joseph looked at me and suddenly turned serious saying, "Not so, no whites there!"

I wondered how the name had popped into my mind. It had been in the news sometimes over the years as a battleground for rebels. Nevertheless, I hadn't remembered it before this. But what I didn't know was that those rebels were communists not Muslims. I had given these men the wrong answer.

Abu sneered at me and drove the needle into the side of my thumb. When I screamed, he slowly and deliberately moved it to inflict maximum pain. Blood oozed out of my thumb. "Aahhhhhhhhh!" This was much more painful than the quick, shocking penetration of the needle through my knuckle that he'd inflicted earlier. Abu did not impale my thumb as he had my middle finger; he just jabbed and dug at my thumb creating the horrible feeling of being stabbed over and over again.

I closed my eyes, trying to lessen the impact of the pain by not seeing what was going on. Then suddenly it stopped. When I opened my eyes I saw that Abu had left the table, walking a few feet away to drink some water. Joseph and Eddy released my hands and joined him while I sat there cradling my wounded left hand.

I did not know why he so abruptly ceased torturing me. I didn't care. I was just happy that the torture, for the time being, was over. The four of them stood in a huddled group mumbling and drinking water. I waited, watching them, fearful that they were about to return. But Abu, Andong and Joseph did not. Instead grabbing a light, they disappeared out of the tunnel.

I breathed a sigh of relief; my whole body, which had been so tense, went limp. Eddy walked slowly back to me and brought me a cup of water. I was surprised by this gesture of kindness. But as soon as I had finished the water, he pulled me out of the chair and pushed me back down onto the mattress. At least for now the torture was over; I had survived another round.

I slept as though unconscious that night—or at least I think it was night. Maybe it was from the mental exhaustion of what they had put me through; maybe it was just because my body was so weak from the lack of food. I estimated that it had been two days since I had eaten. Only a few cups of water had sustained me during that time.

A long interval passed. Then Andong brought some rice and fish to Eddy. I was amazed that after Andong left, Eddy shared some of his rice with me. But maybe he was just doing his duty. I used some of the water he gave me to drink to wash and clean my wounded left hand as I was worried about infection. After that I had a brief period of peace and rested, sleeping a long time.

But they were not finished with me. Later Andong returned and the intimidation started again. I was relieved at first to see that Abu was not with them. However, my spirits sank when Andong and Joseph suddenly produced a finger and threw it on the mattress in front of me. I looked closely; it appeared to be the finger of a dark skinned Filipino which seemed to have been recently severed. Fresh blood was dripping from the inside of it and the bone and tendons had been cut cleanly straight through.

Of course, this renewed my fear that I would be the next to suffer this fate. I was sure that this was the purpose of the macabre gift. I could not help but wonder if it might be Remy's finger or even the cab driver's. "Whose finger is this, Joseph?" I asked somberly.

Joseph's next words brought further fear, "Your friend's, yours now."

Andong and Eddy lifted me again from the mattress and marched me over to the table. "Why you not tell us the truth?" Joseph asked me.

"Because I don't really know," I replied.

"No money, soon you die," Joseph said. His words shook me and a feeling of impending doom began to consume me again. I could not take the strain of this torment any longer.

Then, just like an executioner, Abu came strolling down the tunnel, lantern in hand. His eyes glistened as if with a drug-induced glaze; his mouth curled in a wicked smile. He began immediately shouting at Andong and Eddy. They pushed me down into the chair and spread my hands on the table. With Andong on one side and Eddy on the other they held my wrists flat again spreading the fingers of each of my hands.

This time Abu walked up to the table with his rifle and drew back as if he would strike me with the butt of the weapon. I flinched and ducked my head. They all laughed. It was true, they had broken me. I now was a weak, shaking cowering animal. I knew it and so did they.

Abu shouted threats. "You want to die little by little?" Joseph translated. Andong babbled on, spewing words. Despite my weak and timid state their insults began to bring up the anger deep within me.

Suddenly, I could no longer contain my rage, "You are strong only because you have guns!" I shouted at Abu. Abu and Andong looked shocked for a moment as Joseph translated what I had said to them. But it definitely felt good to me to have finally spoken what I felt. I looked them defiantly in the eyes.

Abu jumped toward me and brought the butt of his rifle crashing down on the pinky finger of my right hand. "Aaooooooooooo!" I screamed in pain. Instinctively I tried to withdraw my hand from the table. But Eddy slammed my hand back onto the table. My finger began to swell and turn purple. I could see that the top part of the finger was pointing at a forty-five-degree angle. I wanted to grab it and pull it straight, but before I could summon the energy Abu brought the rifle butt down on it again. "Aaaaaaaahhhhhhh!" The pain was intense. My finger was now bleeding around the fingernail.

"Damn you!" I cried out, losing control again. With that Abu swung his rifle butt again, cracking me along the right side of my head just above my ear. I went crashing to the floor while Andong and Eddy jumped back to avoid Abu's vicious swing. For a moment I lay there on the mud floor of the tunnel too dizzy to move. My vision was blurred; I could not tell up from down.

I thought I was going to pass out. But a splash of water to the side of my head kept me from slipping into unconsciousness. I became aware of someone yanking me by my arms and pushing me back into the chair. Then someone slapped me in the face. *SPLASH!* Another barrage of water hit me. I was temporarily blinded. *SLAP!* I was slapped again as water dripped down my face. "You tell us! You tell us now!" I heard Joseph's voice say. But I could not find my voice to speak.

As I sat there trying to clear my head they began screaming at me. Joseph was yelling in English and Abu and Andong in their own language. I tried to focus my eyes as I listened to this new angry tirade. "You will die!" I heard Joseph shout. "You lie," he went on even louder. "What you say, not so!" he yelled even more forcibly. I just shook my head afraid whatever I said would invite more abuse from them.

That's when Abu sat down across the table from me and grabbed my left hand. He pulled out a pair of what appeared to be old pliers. Then he reached down to his side and produced the hunting knife that he had secured to his military style belt. Suddenly my head was clear. As I watched in horror he took the tip of his knife and jammed it under the fingernail of my left thumb. The pain was excruciating, my mouth dropped open and I gasped in pain. "Aaaaaaaaahhhhhhhhh!" He wiggled the knife deeper under the nail and I screamed again. Then he withdrew the knife and slammed it into the wooden table.

Picking up the pliers, he grasped the loose nail from my bleeding finger and began slowly prying it up and out of my finger. *Oh my God*, this was agonizing as he pried and twisted the fingernail slowly from my finger! I could do nothing but scream from the torment.

Even through the agony I was enduring I could hear the devilish laugh of Abu taunting me. At each new infliction my screams rose and Abu seemed to congratulate himself.

His eyes burned with fire and his voice rumbled like the thunder of hell as he watched me squirming. There was no doubt that he was enjoying what he was doing. And he voiced his approval of my screams with more sinister laughter reflecting his fiendish delight.

Why is he doing this to me? Does he really think I will tell him where the Prophet's crusade is? Or is he just amusing himself with my torture? Whatever his reasons I could see he was capable of anything and everything vicious and cruel.

The heat of his evil stare wilted what courage I had left in my heart as he continued inflicting pain to one of my fingers, then the next. Whenever I tried to look away Eddy grabbed me by the hair and violently whipped my head around to face Abu again.

I would have run, if I could, not caring anymore if they shot me in the back. Anything would have been better than the torture I was enduring. But they held me firmly in place, face forward, looking into the cold cruel eyes of my tormentor.

Each time the pulling stopped Abu started digging again with his knife under my nail cutting into the sensitive tissue below it. My body jumped and twisted as I tried to deal with the pain he was inflicting upon me. My eyes filled with tears and I became delirious from the agony, but he did not stop.

One by one he repeated the awful digging and pulling of each fingernail from one finger to the next on my left hand. Both Andong and Eddy had to grip my left arm and hand as my body spasmed and jerked in reaction to this torment. I could not have answered his questions now even if I had wanted to.

As he went from finger to finger everything around me began to blur in the dim yellow light of the tunnel. The searing pain of flesh as it ripped open, the smell of blood mixed with sweat, the sounds of vicious laughter and my own screams made me dizzy. I gasped for breath.

Suddenly everything went quiet. There was a swirl of lights and color surrounding me, but no sound. Then instead of everything going black, as I expected, the air around me glowed with the soft, white light of a dream. I felt somehow detached from my body floating into space moving high above the violence around me. At that moment I looked down and saw myself and the others. I thought it odd to be watching myself from afar. The silence was peaceful and I felt no pain. *What is this? Am I dying?*

Looking away from my face and the bloody sight of my fingers I saw the faces of Abu and Andong. They looked little and mean, desperate for attention. I felt sorry for them. They were the real tortured souls. They appeared to be unhappy and full of hate. It was so sad.

In that atmosphere of strange calm, I realized that they were the truly weak ones. They were cowards who could face no one alone and needed a gang of men and weapons to make up for their own insecurities and emptiness. Violence was their poor attempt at feeling strong and in control.

In those moments of spiritual clarity my very being hovered on the realization of truth, my spirit strengthened, I had risen above all earthly weaknesses. I was wrapped in sweet serenity as I soared above the frenzied creatures below me, my spirit surrounded by a cocoon of warmth and enlightenment.

These poor men were the faithless ones. They had no real inner fortitude. My heart revived for those moments; if only they could have lasted.

But then my perspective abruptly changed again as I watched Abu and Andong walk away from the table. An instant later I was back in my body holding my bloody, throbbing left hand. Pain returned and loud sounds vibrated in my ears as I sat there looking in disbelief at my mangled hand. I heard Abu and Andong cursing and grumbling and watched as they left the tunnel.

I was alone. Joseph, Abu and Andong had disappeared. Eddy was drinking water from the buckets in the distance.

I managed to lift myself from the chair and fall onto the mattress. I was drained physically and emotionally. But as I drifted off to sleep I felt better. Despite the pain, the blood and the exhaustion, I felt stronger. An inner strength, a moment of grace had revived my spirit.

Chapter Twelve

A Worthless Hostage

I never knew when the beatings would start or finish. It was an unending cycle of pain. However, in the rare quiet moments lying on the mattress, I tried to rejoice. I told myself I had faced pain and terror and with God's help, when they returned I would overcome them again.

But there were still questions that kept haunting me. *How long will it be before my captors realize that I know nothing and am both poverty stricken and friendless? What will they do to me then?* And I also agonized about Remy. *Is he still alive? Was that his severed finger they brought to me?*

In the hours following the last torture, Abu and Andong returned to the tunnel and began drinking heavily and doing drugs again as they had earlier at the camp. Later they and Eddy openly snorted the powder they'd used before, placing it on the table in front of me. Once in a while they made attempts to threaten me, but for whatever reason, they did not torture me

again at that interval. They appeared distracted and stupefied. I
relished the little oasis of peace and quiet their disoriented state
brought me.

In this interval Eddy surprised me again with small gifts
of rice and some other vegetable that looked like another kind of
root from a tree. This made me feel again as though Eddy might
be someone with whom I could reason. But, unfortunately, there
still was the problem that I could not communicate effectively
with him.

Making myself comfortable on my moldy old mattress,
I finally slept like a baby, feeling for the first time somewhat safe
and unmolested. I awoke feeling rested and ate as much food as
I could get from Eddy hoping it would help some of my bruises
heal. Then I tried to tend to my injuries.

The fingernails on my left hand were now mostly gone,
leaving bloody open wounds. I tore the cleanest piece of cloth
that I could find from my shirt and used it to wrap my left hand.
Washing the hand with water as often as I could, I tried to keep
the wounds on my thumb and fingers from getting dirt in them.
My fingers were slowly scabbing which I felt was a good sign,
but the deep hole in my thumb from the needle was becoming
infected. All I could do was clean and squeeze the puss from it.

After what seemed to be many hours, perhaps it was
even night, I fell back asleep and had another vivid dream.

I was transported back to a time when my life
was successful and fulfilling. On the first day of my
job as the director of a hospital housekeeping depart-
ment, I walked with purpose and pride through the

*hallways, taking time to stop and introduce myself
to nursing staff and hospital employees.*

*I experienced again the thrill of new begin-
nings. I had always loved starting a new job and
the wonderful honeymoon period of the first few
months. Walking the floors and getting to know the
many employees was fun and sometimes challenging. It was a fresh start with new people and a new
set of goals.*

*As I walked down a long hallway, I
approached one of my new employees. She was
preparing her equipment for the day ahead. A
pleasant-looking, middle-aged, black woman, she
looked at me with a combination of curiosity and
trepidation. Trying to put her at ease, I told her my
name and a little about myself. We began a polite
discussion about our work, our families and our
lives. We exchanged our views on what our careers
meant to us and what motivated us in our lives.*

*Then she said something to me that I would
never forget. Looking into my eyes her face beam-
ing she said to me, "I can tell you are a man of
God." She smiled and added, "That's why I know
I will enjoy working for you." Taken aback by this
beautiful comment, I thanked her and told her
that I felt the same about her look of dedication
and commitment. It was one of those wonderful
moments in one's life when all feels right in your
world. I was flattered and happy that someone*

actually recognized in me the role model of
Christian humanity to which I aspired. I felt
happy and fulfilled.

I wasn't sure why I dreamed about that event on that particular night and I wondered about its meaning. Was it a sign that even at this terrible moment in my life there was still hope? It seemed to me to be a reminder that the noble and dignified person I had hoped to be still existed.

The dream stuck with me, even after I woke up feeling weak and thirsty. I felt touched by the woman's reassuring words all over again. I had the feeling again that the Lord was there with me, reminding me through this dream/memory to never lose faith. I prayed again and expressed my gratitude that I had once touched someone else's life in a positive way. I felt blessed and determined to make my life worthwhile even in this most dire of circumstances.

However, this mood of reverence was dissipated over the next hours when I became spectator to an orgy of debauched partying that swirled around me. Abu and Andong had invited some others into the tunnel to drink and get high on drugs. Many of the young boys I had seen in camp came to participate. They drank, taunted and gawked at me.

In addition, I suddenly noticed the gang's numbers were growing. There were a lot of kids with AK-47s I had never seen before. They brought more lights, chairs, tables and food. Along with them came teenage girls no more than sixteen years old who stared and pointed at me like I was a gorilla.

Drinking beer, rum and smoking a pungent substance they laughed, joked and stared at me while acting like the proud owners of an animal they had captured and caged. The tunnel was now like a smoke-filled, rowdy all night zoo which everyone visited to gawk at their prize captive. I could not sleep because of the noise, fumes and the poking and loud taunting.

Twice young teenage girls came close and touched my face, acting surprised by my skin color and long beard. It was obvious that some of these young girls and boys had never seen a white man before.

For hours more and more people visited the tunnel chamber. Sometimes the smoke from cigarettes and aroma of drugs was so heavy I thought I would choke to death. At these times I lay down trying to breathe the cool damp air close to the mud floor. Surprisingly, no one harmed me; there were cruel taunts and an occasional rifle pointed at me, but the non-stop partying went on and on.

To get away from the scene at least mentally, I tried desperately to replay my best memories over and over in my head. I tried to take my mind off of the perverse activities around me. But by then, perhaps because of the second hand smoke, I was becoming less and less able to sustain clarity in both my memories and my thoughts.

As the activity wound down I saw the crowd begin to thin out. Soon Andong brought three young girls into the tunnel. They were about fourteen to sixteen years old. It was obvious that Andong and Joseph were showing me off like some kind of trophy. The girls began drinking beer and snorting drugs while they watched me intently. Then, becoming high or drunk they laughed and talked loudly.

The group partied until everyone passed out. But then, several hours later, I was awakened by the unmistakable sound of people having sex. At first I heard a few whimpers, whispers and the sounds of clothes being shed. But those sounds were soon replaced by rhythmic grunting and whining.

There was only one light on and it was dark in the direction of the sounds I couldn't help but hear. I assumed that it must have been the same teenage girls that were partying earlier. At least this time it seemed that the girls were willing participants and not being brutally raped. Covering my ears, I slowly fell back to sleep as the men and girls continued grunting and moaning in the darkness.

When I woke up, Abu, Andong and the teenage girls were nowhere to be seen. But Eddy and some of the young boys from camp were drinking beer and acting rowdy again. Joseph and Greasy soon joined them. This was the first time that I had seen Joseph without Abu or Andong. As he talked with Eddy and Greasy he seemed more normal—like one of the guys.

My tunnel prison was now strewn with beer bottles and trash from the many partyers who had come and gone in the last two days. The scent of smoke, stale beer and urine hung heavy in the air. The dark, damp confines of my dungeon now smelled like a garbage pit.

Hoping my captors would not become preoccupied with torturing me again, I stayed curled up on my mattress trying to keep my head close to the mud floor of the tunnel. Perhaps they would not notice me and I would be left alone.

Unfortunately, soon after Joseph and Greasy sat down and began drinking, they turned their attention to me again. After a few beers Joseph strode over, questioning me at the request of the others. I was surprised that this time his inquiries were mostly benign, having to do with the United States and what life was like there.

He also asked on the boys' behalf, he said, about Michael Jordan and the Chicago Bulls basketball team. Basketball was a big sport in the Philippines, as I had learned earlier, and they were big fans of Michael Jordan. He went on about boxing, running off names that I had never heard of before. Joseph kept giving me Filipino sports stars and team names and asking me if I knew of them. Of course I didn't; they must have been Filipino basketball and boxing personalities. But soon the talk turned to politics and religion.

At first I was uncomfortable, because I did not want to provoke any more violence against me. Slowly and cautiously I began to participate in the discussion. It turned out to be the first civilized conversation I had experienced since being taken hostage.

After a while most of the boys became bored and left us. Soon there was only Joseph, Eddy, Greasy and I discussing our philosophies on life, love and family with Joseph translating. I became aware that there was not that big a difference in how we all viewed life in general. And I could tell that for that short period they were genuinely interested in me as a person rather than an enemy.

Thereafter we all shared a simple dinner of rice, vegetables and water. Not long after that Eddy and Greasy fell asleep and the last of the boys left the tunnel to go home, leaving only Joseph and me still absorbed in our discussion of politics, religion and family.

Several times during our conversation Joseph took issue with what I said and we exchanged opinions about what the most important things were in each of our lives.

For the first time in my captivity I was engaged in a real conversation with another human being. It was exciting to be speaking with someone who understood my language. In this unique moment, we shared our feelings and listened to each other, instead of my being attacked. We communicated peacefully, without the threat of violence. For a while we spoke of dispassionate things.

I asked Joseph, "How many different languages are there in the Philippines?"

He replied, "Although Tagalog is the national language, almost every island has its own native dialects. Some islands still speak Spanish, because the Philippines was once a colony of Spain."

I nodded. "What is your native language, because I do not understand it?"

"Tausug is the language spoken most prominently on the islands around us," he explained. "But I learned English in school while I was studying to become a teacher." I was surprised to find out that over the last ten years English was now replacing Spanish as the second language of the Philippines.

Then Joseph and I began talking more about the history of the Philippines. It was interesting to get his perspective on the many years that the Philippines had been ruled by other nations. Even thought he was grateful like many Filipinos that the United States had freed them from the Japanese in World War II, the continued military presence of the United States had caused anger.

I asked Joseph about the history of the tunnel in which we were sitting and he told me, "I know it was built by the

Japanese during World War II." Still chained to the wall, I followed Joseph until the chain stopped me while he pointed out with a flashlight some Japanese writing on the wall. I was intrigued by these old Japanese markings. We both stood there for several minutes trying to figure out what this writing said. Was it military instructions of some kind or just some personal graffiti scribbled by a lonely Japanese soldier? We could not decide.

Then Joseph asked me, "Why are you in Pila-peens?"

"To help people," I replied.

"You think your religion helps us?" he asked, his face grim.

"Yes," I said. "Showing people how they can have a relationship with God helps them resist the bad things in life."

Joseph laughed and then said sarcastically, "Ah, your religion is better than ours?" I could see the resentment in his eyes.

"There are good and bad people in all races and religions. We want them to become aware that God is merciful and forgiving," I said, trying to make him understand where I was coming from.

"Our God gives us strength to fight the infidels," Joseph said proudly.

"Who are the infidels?" I questioned him.

"All those who do not believe in our God," he said defiantly.

"Really?" I said with surprise. "So you believe that all people who do not embrace your religion are bad?"

"Yes," he said. "All non-believers are infidels."

"I believe that all people have a choice whether to be bad or good," I asserted. "But God is compassionate and forgiving and loves all his children even when they make mistakes."

Joseph gave me a serious look and said, "That is why your religion is weak, because you accept even the bad people. It corrupts your believers."

"No, I don't believe that," I told Joseph. "Forgiveness and love are much more powerful than the violence and ignorance of this world. It is those who love, forgive and help others who do God's will."

"Our God believes it is necessary to destroy the infidels and fight a Jihad against our enemies," Joseph blurted out.

"But Joseph," I said, "We are all God's children. Why would our God want us to kill part of our own family?"

The question puzzled Joseph. For a moment he pondered what I had said, but I could tell he did not quite accept my thinking. "If your brother is your enemy then you must destroy him," Joseph said.

"Why would you destroy rather than forgive and help him to change?" I asked.

Joseph looked surprised by my question. "Jihad is a holy war against all infidels, even when they are part of your family."

I shook my head. "Are you telling me that you would kill your own brother or sister if they did not have your same beliefs?" I challenged Joseph.

"If God wills it, yes!" he responded.

I looked Joseph in the eye, "You do not seem like a man who could kill a member of his own family."

He did not answer.

I went on, "What is the most important thing to you on this earth Joseph?"

"On this earth?" he repeated.

"Yes, what is the most important thing to you on this earth, in our world?"

Joseph thought for a moment and said, "My children." Then he asked me, "And what is your most important thing on this earth?"

"My family," I said with a smile, "especially my children."

For the first time since I had known Joseph, he broke into a big smile. His faced beamed with pride and joy as he added, "Yes, my children are my heart." I could see that he loved his children just as much as I did mine. It was the one thing that both of us agreed on completely.

For a few minutes we talked about our offspring and proudly traded stories about them. Despite our circumstances, through that exchange, we bonded as fathers. I told him, "We are not so different, you and I."

Joseph smiled and agreed saying, "Fathers are same, children same also."

Then I asked, "What kind of future do you want for your children?"

His smile faded as he seriously pondered the question I posed. Finally, he said, "I want my sons to be good fathers and my daughters to be good wives."

I was caught off guard by the simple nature of his answer. Was this really all he could hope for in his children's futures? I pressed on. "What do you hope your sons will do? For a living I mean."

"I want them to be honest, hard workers and good providers for their families," he said quite plainly.

Again, I was surprised by the modest expectations he seemed to have for his children. I looked in his eyes again and probed further. "Do your children know what you do for Abu and Andong?"

Joseph fidgeted uncomfortably and, for a moment, I thought he might end our talk. "No, they do not," he finally said with a sigh.

I could not help but push this opening. "What do you think your children would think about Abu and Andong? Do you believe they would be good examples for your children?"

Suddenly Joseph glared at me; he was clearly angry.

But, unable to stop myself, I went on, not waiting for a reply. "Would you want your children to grow up to be like Abu and Andong?"

Joseph's face reddened and he finally spoke, "No! But if they must, to fulfill God's will, they must!"

I shook my head. "I think you want to be a good example to your children. I cannot see you raising them to be violent like Abu." His face relaxed a bit at my compliment, but he said nothing.

After that heated exchange Joseph became more withdrawn and we went on to talk more generally about the difficulties of providing for a family. I was saddened that our earlier connection seemed to have broken. I felt that I had probably blown a good opportunity to become much closer to Joseph and possibly get some kind of help from him. I knew I had probably pushed him too far and chastised myself for being too aggressive about expressing my own beliefs.

But I told myself that despite the uneasiness that now had crept in again between us, we had openly expressed our deepest feelings and I felt that Joseph and I seemed to have gained mutual respect. Most importantly, he had not walked away. We continued to talk into the night. On the issues of family and life in general, Joseph at least was willing to hear me out. Respectfully listening to each other, I was surprised to find that we had as many things in common as we had differences.

Our biggest difference was our divergent beliefs about the use of violence to achieve a goal. I finally asked Joseph what he thought would be accomplished for the Muslims of the Philippines if they continued to kill Christians and hold people hostage. He stopped and thought about my words and I could tell that he had not really fully considered the long-range consequences of such actions. Yet he conveyed the depth of his emotions.

"If we do not fight for what is ours, it will not be given!" Joseph stated insistently.

"Do you think robbing and killing people will give you the respect and prosperity you are looking for?" I questioned him.

"Yes, the infidels only respect guns and power," Joseph responded.

I looked at Joseph and shook my head. "No, that's not true!" I told him. "Violence and hate only breed more violence and hate and you and your people will never have peace that way!"

Joseph's voice was stern, "There is no other way for my people to gain justice and live our own lives," he said emphatically.

"I don't believe that," I shot back at Joseph. "People of all races and religions can live together. My country is a good example of that."

"Maybe, but here it is not possible," Joseph lamented.

"Why not?" I questioned him.

"The Christians treat us like animals!" Joseph said angrily.

"All Christians?" I asked, questioning his generalization. Joseph did not respond.

"It is the ignorance and hatred of people like Abu and Andong that affects your view of the world, Joseph. I think you are better than that," I told him. Joseph remained silent. "If more people would share their views peacefully like you and I are doing now, then there would be less ignorance and hatred of each other's beliefs and more tolerance for each others' lifestyles. How can you say that people's political or religious beliefs are good reasons to kill and rob them? I don't believe that our God would approve of such evil acts."

I stopped and looked at Joseph, waiting for a response. Finally Joseph broke his silence. "I am sure you would kill me if you had the chance," he said sarcastically.

"No, why would I do that?" I responded, surprised by his sudden blunt accusation.

"You are angry with us, because you are our prisoner," he said.

"I don't hate you or even Abu and Andong," I replied. "I have already prayed for you and for the strength to forgive you."

"You have?" Joseph said with astonishment.

"Yes," I said, reassuring him. "I don't think that you are the same kind of man that Abu is. I believe you are a decent man."

"Decent?" he questioned me. Joseph did not understand the word.

"Yes, I believe you are a good man." Joseph looked in my eyes suspiciously. He seemed confused as to why I would be so forgiving.

For a long moment we both simply took each other's measure. I was the one who finally broke the silence, "I have learned a lot about you and your people during the last two weeks. I understand a lot more than I did before." My statement surprised Joseph again; his face took on a quizzical look of amazement.

"Oh, what do you understand about us?" he said, testing me.

"I understand a lot more about the poverty here in the Philippines and how people in such circumstances are desperate not to let their families starve. They fight by any means they can."

"Yes," Joseph nodded. "Poverty causes those who endure it to find a way, any way to help their families survive."

And with that the anger and resentment between us dissipated. I felt Joseph and I were truly communicating. I had not let my antagonism toward Abu and Andong cloud my view of him. It was true; I did understand him and his people much better now.

Like many poor Filipinos I had seen, his primary concern each day was just finding the next meal for his family and keeping them clothed. Despite his vitriolic thoughts on his religion justifying a holy war against the infidels, he was still living day-to-day, concerned first and foremost with attaining the basic necessities of life.

However, I had to take his interpretation of his faith's views seriously for he made it plain. "I am not afraid to die for my beliefs; it is honorable to do so," he said proudly. "Christians are afraid to die!" he added in a tone of superiority.

"Why do you think that?" I questioned him. "Do you think that because we value life and do not believe in killing and suicide?" Joseph shrugged and did not respond.

After a pause he challenged me about my own moral vitality. "Christianity is based on love and forgiveness," I said slowly. "But I am not afraid to die." I looked in his eyes. "After all, I believe that by accepting Christ into my heart, living a life that is harmonious and loving my fellow man, I will live with peace of mind and soul in this life and the next."

I explained to him that living a life in which I must turn the other cheek even when attacked made me a stronger and more fulfilled part of God's creation, giving me a spirit that could never be destroyed by the hands of man.

Though at times I felt completely inadequate explaining the Christian faith to him, I tried anyway. And for the first time since my captivity I had an opportunity to talk about the strength of my faith.

Speaking calmly but forcefully, I tried to convey that my faith was both mighty and peaceful in nature.

Turning to another subject, Joseph asked me about my childhood in the United States and also shared with me memories of his childhood on this island that he called home. He spoke with happiness of the loving mother and father who had raised him and how he had found so many fun things to do with his brothers and sisters on the island.

He also related to me the sadness of losing one brother who drowned and a sister who became ill and died. It was a very simple life he had led, but he had also become a fiercely spiritual person because of it.

"Fishing and farming were my family's only means of support for several generations and with each year the land and the sea yielded less and less food for them." I now understood why his people felt threatened and how ignorance and fear was driving their hatred of foreigners and Christians. Like so many other tragic situations in the world it was poverty that had propelled them into a militaristic state of mind. And it was the hate and lack of morals of men like Abu who had galvanized whole communities together in the name of survival. How sad it was that they used religion to divide people rather than bring them together.

As we talked about the good aspects of our faiths it was apparent again that we both sought the same things. Muslim and Christian alike, we really only wanted peace and prosperity for our families. But I could not help pointing out to Joseph again, "People like Abu are not helping your situation by breeding violence and intolerance of others." I could see in his eyes that he agreed with some of what I was saying, but he would not admit it.

Both yawning, we finally gave in to our exhaustion and Joseph left. The tunnel was quiet again. Eddy was the only one left guarding me. While I attended my wounds, Eddy began cleaning up the mess in the tunnel.

As I watched Eddy sweep the bottles and trash further and further down the tunnel I realized with dismay that I had missed a golden opportunity. *How stupid!* I murmured to myself. I could have hidden away a broken bottle or something in the trash to use later to dig or pry with. Surely, there could have been something in the trash brought in by all the visitors that I could have used to dig, bend or even pick my way to freedom. I was angry with myself for not being alert enough during all the chaos to grab something that might help me escape. It was another opportunity lost.

Since I believed Joseph would not be disloyal to his leaders, my thoughts turned again to persuading Eddy to help me. Though I could not communicate with him as I had with Joseph, he was not cruel like Andong or Abu. He did bring me small gifts of food, so perhaps there was kindness in him I could cultivate. Yes, he could be violent on command when Abu and Andong were around, but he was much less menacing when we were alone. It was too bad that he did not speak English, because he might be the only one I could influence to help me escape.

The thought of escape was beginning to be a constant one. After all, I knew that it was only a matter of time before Abu and Andong realized I had no wealthy friends or supporters. In fact, if the truth were known, I had no one who cared about me but my children. My time had to be running out.

But what if I could not persuade Eddy to help me? Since I spoke only a few words of his language, I knew that my chances to get him to help me were not good. Nevertheless, I would have to try again to get his attention and use sign language.

I thought about the spoon that I once had which I now needed so desperately to help me dig. But it had been lost while I was transferred from the hut to the tunnel. There was no use longing for it now. It was gone. I needed to find something else that I could use. I began to look around again for items within my reach that I could use to pry or dig myself free. "There has to be something!" I told myself. I scoured my surroundings over and over again. But I didn't find anything near enough to me that I could use. Except for the trash and bottles that Eddy had swept out of my reach, I could find nothing. Finally, exhausted by my search, I fell asleep.

Early the next morning I opened my eyes to see a flurry of activity. Several men were standing over me talking to each other in sharp bursts of words while Eddy unlocked the handcuffs securing my ankle to the chain in the wall.

Slowly, still half asleep, I sat up and felt my hands being pulled together. Eddy clicked both cuffs tightly around my wrists securing them together in front of me.

Then I saw Joseph whose demeanor had completely changed from the preceding day and night. He spat out, "Get up." Eddy pulled me to my feet. My heart froze with dread as I saw Abu. *Is this it, is my time up? What are they going to do to me?* I felt suddenly helpless again as fear gripped me, my legs buckling.

Abu then shouted something to Eddy who began pushing me forward through the tunnel. Holding a flashlight, Abu went ahead of us leading the way, while Joseph pulled me along by the handcuffs around my wrists. Soon I saw a faint gray light at the end of the tunnel. When we reached the opening

Joseph pushed through the curtain of green vines and bushes that covered the tunnel entrance, pulling me with him into the morning air.

The morning light blinded me. Unable to focus I stopped, covered my eyes and squinted vainly trying to see ahead of me. Days of being kept in the darkness of the tunnel had taken their toll. It took a while for my eyes to get used to the light. But as Eddy pushed me forward again I smelled a fresh ocean breeze.

The fresh salty air seemed like a bouquet of flowers as we stepped out onto the rocky ledge. And then I noticed that it was beginning to rain. The early morning sky became overcast as gray clouds blew in from the ocean and cooling sprinkles fell. It was a light rain, falling in short bursts, making a pitter patter sound on the leaves of the trees and plants around us. For a moment I just stood there in the rain, enjoying the feel of it.

Then I heard voices to my right. I turned to look down the rocky path. A group of armed men were trudging toward us. There appeared to be about eight of them crowded onto the narrow path moving slowly up the ravine.

As their forms became clearer I tried to make out their identities. As they came closer I saw Andong and behind him, being pulled along by a rope, was Remy. His hands were bound in front of him. When he was only a few feet from me, I saw that Remy's lip was bleeding and his bruised eyes were swollen to tiny slits. I tried to smile and catch his attention, happy to see him at last. He was alive! For a moment I felt hope that he might be joining me in the tunnel. At last my friend and I could talk. That had to make us both feel reassured.

But when Remy looked back at me I saw his swollen eyes were filled with fear. He acknowledged my presence with a weak smile that faded quickly. The anguished look on his face told me that something was very wrong.

Looking around I saw that the cab driver was not with the group, so I said to Joseph "Where is the other man?" Joseph turned to Andong asking about the cab driver. Andong replied with a snappy answer and then wickedly smiled. The men and boys around us laughed nervously at Andong's reply.

"What did he say?" I asked Joseph.

After hesitating for a moment, Joseph curtly replied, "The man seems to have lost his head." He then quickly translated his comment into Tausug and the others laughed uproariously. As Abu stepped from behind me with the old machete in his hands the group quieted. Horrified, I looked at Abu again. In his hand the gleaming sharp edge of the machete was smeared with blood.

Oh, My God, I thought, *They have killed the cab driver, and we are next!* Now I felt Remy's terror. My legs started to shake and my heart constricted. I stared at Remy. We both understood what was happening. We stood there frozen in fear, looking helplessly at each other.

Abu yelled something to Joseph who turned to me, "Where are the missionaries?"

"I don't know," I said helplessly. He translated my words for Abu and Andong.

Suddenly Abu and Andong sprang in front of me and begin screaming in my face, their bloodshot eyes had the unmistakable glaze of a drug-filled night. As they jumped up and down in front of me, yelling like two wild men and waving their weapons at me, Joseph translated. "They do not believe you. They know you were with the blind woman. You must tell us now where she is!"

I looked at Joseph with pleading eyes. "How can I do that? I already told you I don't know."

Led by Abu, the men and boys around us now began chanting and pumping their weapons into the air. Then Andong grabbed Remy and screamed something, waving his rifle in a threatening manner. Remy could only shake his head no, too terrified to speak. Joseph then turned to me. Pointing to Remy, he shouted, "I know he was with the blind woman; he must speak!" I could see the frustration on Joseph's face as he looked first at Remy and then back at me. "Your friend will not speak!" Joseph shouted at me again. "You must or you will both die!" he added, his voice shrill with exasperation.

The sound and the fury around us was fast reaching a crescendo. The chanting from the crowd of armed men had become deafening and was punctuated with wild, angry screaming words coming from Abu, Andong and Joseph. "What are they saying?" I yelled to Joseph. "Time has come; time has come!" Joseph replied in an icy tone.

I tried to step back away from the angry faces and frenzied yells but Eddy and Joseph grabbed me and held me tightly so I could not move.

Then I saw the machete in Abu's hand rising, its sharp, bloody edge gleaming in the morning light. Abu moved closer to me, waving the machete near my head. As he screamed into my face, I flinched, seeing his round, baby face red and twisted in rage.

Suddenly, signaling Eddy to follow, Abu backed away from me and strode toward Remy. Time stood still. I watched in horror as slow motion violence played out before my eyes in graphic second-by-second detail.

Eddy stopped behind Remy and grabbing his shoulders, pushed Remy to his knees in front of me. A moment later Andong moved to my side where he and Joseph held me motionless, looking down at the left side of Remy's face. Abu stepped up behind Remy. Then Eddy grabbed Remy by the hair and pulled his head up. Remy turned his head and glanced at me, a look of sheer terror in his eyes.

Suddenly, with two quick movements, Eddy yanked again on Remy's hair, pulling Remy's head and neck straight up, almost lifting him off his knees. In a split second Abu stepped forward and swung the machete through the base of Remy's neck severing his head from his body. Reacting to the vicious blow Eddy let go of Remy's head to avoid being struck by the machete. Remy's severed head pitched into the air as Eddy's hand let go of it and tumbled to the ground, first rolling and then disappearing over the ledge in front of us.

I tried to look away as Remy's body twitched for a moment and then toppled forward, convulsing on the ground, but they would not let me. A pool of dark blood formed quickly around the stump of his neck. Andong held my head taut to make sure that I could not turn away, so that I watched every last movement of life leave Remy's body.

Standing there staring at the gory sight before me, I was transfixed, stunned by the sudden finality of the act. I gazed in shock not only at death, but man's inhumanity to man.

Chapter Thirteen

Delaying the Inevitable

As I stood there in shock and disbelief at the horror I had just witnessed, the air around us grew thick with the sickening odor of fresh blood. I retched, overcome with the urge to vomit as nausea coursed through my body.

Smiling, Abu raised the machete into the air in triumph and the men around us began cheering. My legs shook and then gave way, but Joseph and Andong held me up, keeping me from doubling over onto the ground.

So this is how I will die, I thought looking at the headless body before me. I knew I was next. As if he heard my thought, Abu pointed the machete at me and yelled something to Joseph.

"You speak now or you die," Joseph said in a cold, almost casual way. I stared at him remembering the Joseph who had shared emotional and spiritual moments with me the evening before. I wondered if he remembered too or had Joseph wiped that exchange completely from his mind and heart.

My mind searched frantically trying to find something that I might say to save my life. At that moment, it was all that mattered. I wanted to live.

Then, like a miracle, I remembered a city that I had heard both Remy and the Blind Prophet refer to once. It had a quaint, rustic sounding name. I prayed the missionaries were not there. "I think they are in a place called Dumeguete."

Joseph looked at me intently and asked, *"Seguro?"* ("Are you sure?")

I tried to look confident as I met Joseph's eyes. "Yes, *Seguro!* I am sure!" I replied, lying to him in a pitiful attempt to save my life.

Joseph turned to Abu and they spoke for a couple of minutes. "We will see," Joseph said. Andong reached around in front of me and began leading me by the handcuffs back into the tunnel. The relief that I felt was counteracted by a feeling of shame. I had broken under their threats; I had resorted to lying just to stay alive. Yet I told myself that despite my conflicted emotions, my delaying tactic had worked. I was happy to have bought some time. I was ashamed but thankful to be alive.

Later I could not sleep. I tossed and turned. It was only a matter of time before they would realize that my words weren't true. All night I was troubled that I was trapped with no way out.

When I woke the next morning I realized that I had only delayed the inevitable. There was little time left. I had to find a way to escape. But how? I had barely the energy or the strength to walk and I did not know the island terrain. I felt empty and bereft.

They had done a very good job of breaking me down physically and mentally. I not only doubted my physical stamina, but my will to live was also ebbing away.

A battle began within me between a desire to give up, to let death release me from the pain and heartache I was suffering and the natural instinct we all have for self-preservation.

I began to believe that a quick death, once they discovered my deception or if they caught me escaping, would be more merciful than suffering several more days of torture only to die in the horrible way Remy had. But how could I escape? I was too weak to swim. I had been here long enough to know that the people on this island were bound together by poverty and their Muslim faith. I doubted that anyone would help me escape by boat. And even if someone did, I had no idea where I was or how to get to safety.

But in the back of my mind emerged the images of my two little boys, reminding me that I had to persevere for them. My desire to survive was again buoyed by my love for them. I could not leave them the legacy of a father who had run away and disappeared.

Again, an undeniable fact returned. My life was not my own. My life was truly in God's hands. Could I accept it and put my faith completely in His hands? My mind was clouded with fear and doubt.

So I prayed. I prayed for a way out of this situation. And I prayed in order to reach down deep inside myself to find out who I really was. Was I the person, the one I remembered from the past, who was committed to finding a way to help people and had the strength of will to succeed no matter the impediments?

Or was I the person who had failed so badly not only at being a family man, but at the work he had once loved and at which he had been so successful? Could it be that I was just a weak person who was not spiritually strong enough to face his own death with dignity?

These and many other questions began passing through my mind. I struggled to reach a state that I had been unable to attain during the course of my lifetime. Was I worthy of heaven?

Who was I and what was my destiny? This was the ever-present question and the identity crisis from which I had suffered all of my life. And at this very critical moment I found myself drowning in doubt and the same old questions and fears.

In the midst of this storm of self-doubt and despair, calming words began to creep into my mind. Just as I began to feel overwhelmed with depression and fear, the words of the twenty-third Psalm came back to me. To draw comfort I repeated them aloud.

Even though I walk through the valley of the shadow of death,
I fear no Evil; for thou art with me;
Thy rod and thy staff, they comfort me.

Thou preparest a table before me in the presence of my enemies;

Thou anointest my head with oil, my cup overflows.

Surely goodness and mercy shall follow me all
the days of my life;
*   and I shall dwell in the house of the Lord for-*
ever.

As waves of fear washed over me, I kept repeating the words of the psalm in my head over and over and over. Each time I recited those words my spirit and faith strengthened.

In the following hours there was an eerie stillness in the tunnel. Eddy managed to bring me more rice and roots to eat and I tried to rest to gain some energy. As time passed I tried to figure out a way that I could influence Eddy to help me. If only he understood English. I knew that I could be persuasive if I could just communicate with him. I knew I had to try.

When Eddy brought me some water, I tried to hold his attention. Pointing to him, I used my arms to signify holding a baby, asking him if he had any children. He was confused at first, but after I acted the idea out several times his stern look-ing face broke into a smile. Without saying a word, he shook his head up and down, indicating yes.

I pointed to myself and then used two fingers to indicate to him that I had two children. He responded by raising his fin-gers and indicating that he had three. I was encouraged that finally I was finding a way to get through to him. Maybe, just maybe, I could get him to relate to me as a father and as a human being. Then maybe I could persuade him to help me escape.

But before I could continue using this approach with Eddy, Andong and one of the boys entered the tunnel, inter-rupting our primitive communication. As people continued to come and go that day, bringing food and beer, Eddy was never again alone long enough for me to reengage him in a conversation.

I had to find a solution to my dilemma. I tried to think of ways that I could make an escape by freeing myself from the chain around my leg. The chain was strong and though I carefully felt each segment, I could find no weak links or rusted connections.

I also searched for a way that I could slowly wiggle or dig the bolt out of the coral wall of the tunnel. It appeared that someone, who had been there before me, had tried digging around it. But with nothing hard or sharp that I could get my hands on, it was fruitless to attempt digging. The coral rock was porous but very solid. And the old rusting bolt was sunk very deep into the wall.

If only I could get my hands on something, even a rock, that could assist me in breaking the chain or cuffs holding the chain to my ankle. I seriously considered the idea of finding a way to break or sever my ankle in order to slip from the cuffs. If I had been able to get my hands on a machete, I believe that at that desperate moment, I would have cut off my foot to escape.

I even wondered how long it would take to actually chew through my own flesh, like an animal caught in a trap, without it becoming too bloody or obvious to Eddy. Unfortunately, because of my back problem, there was no way I could bend my head down low enough to reach my ankle with my teeth. It was simply not an option.

The next evening, after Eddy fell asleep, I roamed the floor of the tunnel as far as the chain binding me would allow. I managed to find a small bone, it appeared to be a chicken bone, about two inches in length. I began slowly and quietly digging around the bolt in the wall, being careful not to break the bone. It was very slow and tedious work, but I was making some progress.

When Eddy or someone else was around, I tried to sit or lie in front of the bolt so that the person could not see the freshly dug groove around it that was beginning to show. *If I have enough time*, I thought, *maybe I can slowly work this bolt loose.* That was my plan.

While Eddy slept I worked diligently at the rock with my chicken bone. Then the bone snapped. I picked up the biggest remaining piece and tried to continue on, but it was no use. I was not going to move that bolt from the wall with tiny fragmented pieces of bone.

Then I had another idea. While I sat there staring at the small pieces of chicken bone it occurred to me that I had to find something stronger. "Why not a tooth! Or better yet, why not a crown!" I muttered.

They had already knocked out several of my teeth and even though I no longer had them there were other teeth that were loose from the beatings I had received. I tried to remember which of my teeth had crowns on them. Maybe I could work one of those crowns out and use it to dig with. Yes, a crown had a metallic core with a very hard porcelain coating! That might be something I could use to remove the coral rock from around the bolt.

I began using my fingers and tongue to find the hard, telltale rim of a crown within my mouth. I finally decided on a large tooth on the left side of my mouth that I was able to jiggle. The tooth felt like it could have a crown. There was a certain round, smooth, artificial feel to it.

I tried to clean my fingers the best I could and then inserted them into my mouth trying to get a grip on the tooth. The corners of my mouth, which were already dry and chapped, split open and bled as I tried to get most of my hand in my mouth. Now wasn't a time to worry about a little blood, I told myself.

Using my thumb and forefinger I began to work on the tooth. I had hoped that the crown itself was loose so I could pry it from the top of my tooth. But I discovered that my whole tooth was loose. To get to the crown, I would have to remove the entire tooth from its roots; something that I could already tell would be very painful.

I wished I had some rum to use as an anesthetic. Of course, I had nothing. And so I began to wiggle and pry my tooth loose, all for the purpose of getting to the crown that was firmly seated on top of the tooth.

I began to make progress, but as I loosened the tooth, my pain also increased and blood began to spurt out. Nevertheless, I continued pushing, prying and pulling the tooth, trying to keep a good grip on it long enough to pull it out. But it was no use. Even as I wiggled the tooth loose my fingers kept slipping from the spit and blood filling my mouth.

Finally I decided to tear off a piece of my shirt and use it to get a grip on the tooth. I no longer cared if I infected my whole mouth because of the dirty cloth. I felt an urgency deep in my stomach that was warning me the little time I had left was ebbing. I had to make a move now!

I spit out all the blood and saliva from my mouth and, using the dry cloth between my fingers, I got a good grip on my tooth and pulled hard.

Once, then twice I pulled and the tooth finally was almost totally uprooted from the gum. Ignoring the pain and blood that rushed to the hole I was creating, I pulled again with all my strength and ripped the tooth free. "Ouuhhh," a moan of pain came gurgling from my throat as pain seared into my jaw.

My other hand reached up to clutch my face at the spot where my tooth used to be. While holding my tooth in my right hand and looking at it, I used my left hand to rub the burning in my jaw on the left side of my face.

I could not believe it. Despite the pain, I had done it! Like a cavemen I had pulled my own tooth with brute strength. My eyes watered as more pain coursed through my jaw. I felt a need to spit the blood from my mouth that was collecting there, but in my starving state I decided it was best to swallow it for nourishment. For a few minutes I sat there thinking about the animalistic impulses I now acted from, wondering what I had become.

Then I looked at the tooth and I saw that it did have a crown on it. What luck! I had pulled the right tooth. At that point my observations ceased. This was life or death. I needed to begin working immediately with my new tool while Eddy still slept.

I worked into the early morning hours using my left molar to dig deeper into the coral rock around the bolt. I was making progress and I began to feel like I had some hope again.

With the pain in the joint of my right shoulder slowing me down and the knuckles of both my hands becoming bloody I finally stopped my digging and fell asleep.

The next day I watched Eddy carefully, hoping he would take a nap or turn his attention elsewhere so that I could resume my work on the coral rock around the bolt. But I was frustrated time and time again throughout the day, as he always seemed to find a reason to stay put at his table.

Eddy even tried talking to me again. But our communication was stymied by our lack of understanding of each other's language.

During one of our exchanges that day I showed Eddy my bloody, blistered ankle where the handcuff had been rubbing the skin raw. I pointed to my ankle and then to the water barrel and made a motion like I was washing it. He understood right away and brought me a bowl of water in order to clean my wound. But when I showed him that I needed him to undo the handcuff around my ankle he immediately motioned to me an emphatic "No!"

I tried again showing him that I needed to wash it with a rag that I had used on my now scabbed fingers. He looked at me sympathetically and for a moment I thought he might do it.

But a grim look came into his eyes as he motioned at the other end of the tunnel. Then he took his knife out of its holder and ran it across his throat, again pointing to the end of the tunnel.

I understood what he was saying. He was telling me that if he loosened or unlocked the handcuff on my ankle he would be killed by Abu or Andong. For a moment I almost felt sorry for him. I knew that he was right. But then my own need to survive took over as I tried to persuade him to unlock the handcuff.

I kept prodding him, even at the risk of getting him angry with me, for I had to make my move now. Remy was gone. I would be next. But my pleas did not persuade Eddy. He finally turned and walked away from me to escape my begging.

I must have been getting to him, because why would he just walk away out of frustration? Maybe if I found another way to win his sympathy he might just help me. If my own attempts didn't succeed I would have to try pleading with Eddy again.

Later, Eddy finally took a nap and I was able to work a little more on the bolt in the wall.

I was determined to keep both of my options for escape open. When Eddy was awake I would keep working on him for help. When he was asleep I would work on loosening the bolt in the wall. But neither option, at that point, was coming through.

That evening, Eddy had some visitors. One of the young teenage boys delivered some food and a bottle of rum to Eddy and brought a girl along with him. The boy and girl talked and stared at me giggling and making jokes. Eddy shared his rum with the young man who looked like he could not have been more than fourteen.

Eddy also offered rum to the young girl, who seemed the same age as the boy, but she refused. Soon Eddy and the boy became drunk and began singing and laughing. I began to worry that I would have to endure another rape scene with them taking advantage of the young girl.

But instead they huddled together for a couple of minutes with the girl and then came walking over to me. All three of them were smiling broadly as they approached me. *What are they up to?* I wondered.

Eddy took a sip from the bottle of rum in his hand and then pointed at the girl. "You like?" he asked looking me in the eyes. I hesitated, knowing that it was probably a loaded question and I did not want to cause any harm to the girl.

The boy pointed to the girl and, like Eddy, said, "You like?"

I looked at the girl who was still smiling innocently at me and finally said, "Yes, *guapa*." I knew that the Spanish word *guapa*, meaning pretty, was commonly used by Filipinos to describe an attractive girl and I did not want to hurt her feelings or bring on the rage of one of my captors for insulting her.

She was dark-skinned with pretty eyes and long hair, but her face was not particularly beautiful. She looked like a farmer's daughter. She was obviously a young girl who had probably spent most of her childhood laboring in the fields for her family. Being at what I suspected to be early adolescence, her body was obviously blossoming but her looks were still at the adolescent, ugly duckling stage.

All three of them giggled at my answer and looked at her approvingly. Then Eddy and the boy did something that surprised me. Together, as if they had planned it, they both reached down and pulled the girls shirt up to her chin revealing two young breasts.

I stared in shock, then looked at the boy and Eddy. They were smiling dumbly. The girl did not protest, which told me that this had been their plan all along. They were trying to tease me. I should have known this was coming.

Eddy reached up with his dirty hands and grasped one of the breasts just under its bulk and thrust it upward.

"You like," Eddy repeated again, beginning to laugh out loud.

Then the boy suddenly pulled down the shorts the girl was wearing revealing a pair of torn, white panties. She yelped and scolded them both as she tried desperately to pull her shorts back up and then laughed along with them anyway.

I moved to face the wall, turning my back on them. They all laughed, including the girl, as they felt satisfied that their little prank had embarrassed me.

Yes, I was embarrassed, but it also angered me. Did they really think that I was in any condition to be turned on by this tawdry display? Sex was the last thing on my mind. I was beaten and bloodied and sickly from dehydration and malnutrition. There was no way this little prank could have affected me except to make me disgusted and angry.

The three of them continued with their drunken singing and playing around, often looking at me to gauge my reaction to their antics. Their loud and obnoxious behavior went on for another hour or two until Eddy passed out drunk and collapsed on the floor.

The young man and the girl helped Eddy onto his chair and finally left. Eddy did not even check on me before he put his feet up onto another chair and fell into a drunken stupor.

I waited for about thirty minutes, making sure that Eddy wasn't going to wake up. Then I again began my digging around the bolt with my tooth. The work was slow and tedious, but I continued to make progress. I noticed that the tooth itself was also beginning to wear down and I wondered how long it could last.

I kept alternating my hands and using different sides of the tooth as I worked slowly inside the groove that I had created around the bolt. There was now a pronounced circle cleared out and I could almost grasp the bolt to begin wiggling or prying it loose. I kept going, convinced that I was going to complete my task either that night or the next.

As I dug and scraped, the monotony overtook me and I began to daydream. My mind took me away again to better times. I remembered another day that I spent with my children, after my wife and I separated.

I awoke on a beautiful Saturday, happy to have taken the day off from work. I picked up my boys and took them to an arcade which had great games and rides, as well as an obstacle course that my younger son loved to play in for hours.

We took turns playing one of the games in which we tried to throw balls through small holes. My boys were excited when all three of us won. We received tickets which could be turned in at the cashier and exchanged for an actual prize.

After the boys each chose a prize, we ate pizza for lunch. Afterward, I rested and watched the boys laugh and enjoy various mechanical rides at the arcade. I wished I could freeze the moment forever. It was one of those fleeting, special moments where I truly felt the satisfaction of being a good father I

*loved my boys so much. Watching the joy on their
smiling faces, tears began to form in my eyes as a I
realized I would soon have to take each of them
back home to their mothers. It was hard knowing
that I could only enjoy a few, brief hours of their
companionship before they would be gone again,
leaving me alone and full of guilt. How I longed to
spend more time with both of them. I wanted to
make sure that they always knew how much their
father loved them.*

Suddenly, I was ripped from my daydream by someone violently grabbing my arm. It was Eddy. He had woken up and discovered me digging into the wall! A rush of fear ran through my veins as he spun me around, gripping my left arm tightly.

He reached out and pulled my hand open revealing the tooth I had been using to dig with. Pulling my tooth from my hand he looked curiously at it. But the anger on his face told me that I was in big trouble. Would he tell Abu? My heart sank as I realized that I might have brought about the end I feared.

Eddy looked at my tooth and then at me and broke into a smile. *What is so funny?* I thought, waiting for his reaction. But Eddy just shook his head and smiled, looking at me like I was crazy. I suppose he could not believe that I was so desperate as to think that I could escape using a tooth as a digging tool. Without a word, he threw my tooth away. Then he knelt down and reaching into his pocket pulled out a set of keys.

I was surprised by this. I had thought that only Abu and Andong had the key to my handcuffs. But what was Eddy going to do? I watched him fearfully, hoping that I was not going to be tied up again in a more painful position.

Eddy unlocked the handcuff around my ankle and then pulled me by the arm down into the dark tunnel. After walking a few yards, just far enough to be out of the lamplight, he stopped and backhanded me across the face with his hand, sending me flying against the wall and sliding to the ground. I sat there dazed for a moment trying to focus my eyes again. *Here it comes!* I thought. *Here comes my punishment.*

He walked up to me and then kneeled again. He fumbled around in the darkness for a moment with one hand and then reached over and pulled me next to him with his other hand.

There were two more chains, each one very short in length, hanging from the wall. Eddy took the handcuffs and locked them around my ankle and then to one of the chains.

I had no way of knowing if he did it on purpose, but he moved the handcuff to my other ankle, thereby freeing the raw ankle that had been handcuffed from further irritation. Now I was chained flush with the wall of the tunnel; there was little room to maneuver. I wiggled uncomfortably into a sitting position, hugging the damp coral wall.

Afterward I watched as Eddy walked down into the lamp lit area of the tunnel and returned, throwing the straw mattress down in front of me. He turned around and walked back to the table, this time sitting down in the chair facing me.

I was now sitting in the dark peering down the tunnel at the distant yellow spot of lamplight where Eddy sat. Rubbing my now swollen face, I took a deep breath grateful that Eddy had not become more angry and taken it out on me. Or worse, gone to fetch the others.

Eddy was angry, but he had not lost control. And he had been compassionate enough to bring me the mattress to sleep on. But now a new worry dominated my thoughts. *Will Eddy tell Abu or Andong about my escape attempt?*

Helpless and vulnerable, I realized that not only was my first option gone, but Eddy certainly would not help me escape now. What could I do? I tried to bring up the soothing memories of my children. But this time I could not hold them in my mind for long and I could not sleep. My body and mind were tormented by fear and anxiety.

"Lord, help me find a way!" I prayed. "So many times in my life You have helped me find a path!" But doubts clouded even these hopeful entreaties. What other options were left?

What would happen to me now? Had my luck just run out? Finally, despairing but exhausted, I fell asleep, knowing that any hope of escape was now probably gone. It was only a matter of time before my captors realized that I was worthless and ended their deadly game of cat and mouse.

Chapter Fourteen

Darkness and Light

The next morning the inevitable happened. I awoke to someone kicking me in the ribs. "Aoooww!" I protested trying to move away. My eyes flew open to see Andong, Joseph and Eddy standing over me.

All three of them stared at me with angry, malevolent looks. "They can not find the blind woman," Joseph said. "They say you lie," he added. I looked blankly at Joseph, not knowing how to reply. There was a long silence as they glowered at me. Before I could think of another excuse to divert them, Joseph and Andong started to walk away from me.

I looked at Eddy to see if he knew what was going on. Eddy looked away from me and called out to Andong. They exchanged words for a short time. Then Andong walked away heading out of the tunnel, flashlight in hand.

What a relief! Obviously Eddy had not told Andong about my escape attempt. Otherwise I would have been severely punished. But my feeling of relief was short lived. Joseph whipped around and strode back to me, his face grim. "Tomorrow you die."

My jaw dropped and my heart throbbed. "What?" I asked hoarsely. "Why?" I blurted out.

"They angry with you, make you warning to other whites!" Joseph said as he hurried to follow Andong.

"But…but," I stopped.

Joseph heard me stammering, turned around for a moment and gazed at me. "Your head…tomorrow to Cebu. Abu here at dawn," Joseph said in a somber tone. Then he disappeared into the darkness following Andong.

I sat there stunned, as the shock of his words swept through me. I wanted to cry but no tears came. I peered at Eddy, searching for a sign of sympathy or hope in his face. But Eddy would not meet my eyes. He knew I was a dead man. He did not want to be involved.

"Help me. Please!" I beseeched Eddy. But he just turned his back and walked toward the end of the tunnel to get some water and escape my pleading voice.

My heart thumped in my chest; I could not move. I was overwhelmed with the desolate feeling of sinking into a cold, dark abyss. Misery and hopelessness filled me. I was utterly alone. I would die a horrible death very soon. The thought of it horrified me.

I sat there trying to absorb that reality. There were no more postponements; my time in this world had come to an end. And I knew that no one would come to my aid. Abu would be there in the morning and the boys would have another show.

Even more revolting was the idea that my head would be used as a trophy to warn other foreigners to pay or die.

I did not want to be remembered that way. But worst of all, my family would probably never know what had happened to me. No one, including my children, would ever know how and why I had disappeared. The thought of that hurt me more than the thought of dying.

A sudden jolt of panic ran through me as I realized that I could wait no longer if I was to try and escape. I had to take action immediately. I began hurriedly wiggling the chain and the bolt that was anchored into the wall. Hoping against hope I frantically pulled and twisted the bolt with a new energy born out of horror. Maybe I could wiggle it loose! I had to try! I kept glancing over my shoulder, looking to see if Eddy would try to stop me.

But he didn't. He paid no attention to me, pretending that I did not even exist. In desperation I used what strength I had left to twist and wiggle the bolt, then using my legs to gain leverage, I attempted to pry the bolt loose from the wall. But my efforts were in vain; it would not budge.

Finally, I admitted to myself it was useless. I just sat there and cried in frustration. But another burst of panic hit me and again I began figuring out ways that I could break my ankle and slip my foot through the handcuffs. First I tried to gather the chain to wrap it around my ankle so I could twist it in an attempt to break my ankle. But there was just not enough chain. I was flush against the wall of the tunnel, the new chain to which I was attached being so short in length.

Then, out of the darkness, I heard footsteps coming down the tunnel. I turned and saw Eddy coming toward me.

I could only see the shadow of his body silhouetted against the lamplight behind him. He must have heard me trying to loosen the chains. Now he was coming to punish me. He stood there in front of me for a minute not saying a word.

He moved closer and I flinched, curling up against the wall to protect myself from an imaginary kick or punch.

"You wan' caaaa," he stammered. He was trying to speak English; it was the first time I had heard him attempt it.

"What?" I said trying to get him to speak louder.

"You wan' ciirrrrrr," he said again.

"What are you trying to say?" I asked him.

This time he leaned forward and pointed his finger at me saying, "You wan' cirl."

"I still don't understand," I repeated, confused.

He moved closer and I jumped again, afraid this was some kind of sneak attack like the ones I had experienced with Greasy and Berto. But instead his hand gently touched my arm. *What is he trying to do?* I asked myself.

Eddy pointed his finger again. "You," he said softly, "wan' cirl?" This time he accentuated the words he was saying with a motion using both of his hands. He then repeated the words again moving his hands as if they were outlining a statue.

Then it hit me; he was asking me if I wanted a girl. *Why is he asking me that?* I was still confused. "A girl? You mean a woman?"

Eddy immediately stopped what he was doing with his hands and acknowledged what I said. "Ya, a cirl," he repeated, his tone of voice telling me that I had guessed what he was saying correctly.

"What do you mean?"

"A cirl, one time," he said stuttering. "One time, lass time," he said again. Then I realized he was asking me if I wanted a girl, in order to have sex one last time before I was executed.

Silence filled the air. What a strange last offer. Yet the thought of it tempted me. *Why not?* I asked myself. Part of me argued that feeling the pleasure of physical love again would dull my fear. The other part of me felt it would be a violation of every spiritual step forward I had made while imprisoned. I would be surrendering to the weaknesses of the physical world again, the empty pleasure of a meaningless sexual experience.

All my life, sex had been a driving force. And now, at the one moment that I needed to be spiritually strong someone was tempting me, asking if I wanted sex as my last wish. I could not help but inwardly smile at the irony. A moment later I took a deep breath trying to clear my mind. It was then I realized it was something I could not do. I was touched by Eddy's gesture, but dismayed that he thought a few moments of pleasure with a stranger would ease the horror I was facing on this my last night on earth. It was a bizarre and yet heartfelt offer.

Finally I said, "No, no thank you." His face darkened. Suddenly I remembered someone telling me when I was in Manila that to refuse an overture from a Filipino was to insult him. But this was not the kind of gift that I had expected.

After an awkward pause, Eddy slowly turned around and walked back to his table and chair. From a distance I watched as Eddy opened a bottle of Tanduay rum and began drinking it down. I guessed this was his way of handling another execution. Still, I was grateful for his last gesture of compassion.

I sat there in the darkness wondering what kind of life Eddy would lead after I was gone. It was a strange thought, but I was actually worried about how the next morning would affect him.

I prayed for Eddy, hoping that God would find a way to reach him and save him from the violent life that he was now leading. And then I prayed for myself, asking God to accept me as I was.

Finally, I rolled over and lay there staring at the shadows forming on the wall. I could not sleep. Like clouds drifting in the wind, thoughts came and went beyond my control. In my ears the deafening silence pulsed around me.

Sadness welled up inside me again and the familiar agony of loneliness returned to my heart. Never had I felt such utter helplessness and desperation.

As I lay there, whirled in a sea of emotional turmoil, no answers came as to how I could save myself. Tears formed in my eyes and I wept.

"Why me, Lord?" I murmured. "What have I done so badly in my life to bring me this terrible death?" I felt abandoned by life and by God.

Abandoned. That word seemed to typify the story of my life. In this, the dark night of my soul, I could not help but reflect on my two failed marriages. Why had I failed? Why did both of my ex-wives choose to abandon me? Was I that terrible a husband? My mind flooded with memories of those two marriages, as I walked again the well-worn paths of self-doubt and shame. And my heart ached again with the agony of being separated from my children.

My mind spun to other days when, physically broken, I had lost everything. Then I thought of the evening when I had answered the call to minister in the Philippines. I also recalled how my parents and brother had treated me, as if I was running away from my responsibilities. At one point, I had begun to believe they were right. Throughout my life I had always found a way to turn bad things into good, yet when my marriage and job failed and I had been stricken with paralysis and depression, these obstacles had proved to be too much for me. Why had I failed so miserably when there were children depending on me? The pain of that guilt split my heart open again.

Guilt was something ingrained so deeply in me that I doubted that even death could free me from it. I felt betrayed by my own body, my own spirit. I could not help but relive the day I'd gotten the back injury and felt that this was the trigger catapulting me into failure. After that injury I was never the same. I lost my confidence, my health, my family and my friends.

I lay there asking myself the same old questions over and over again. I wanted to blame someone for this terrible ending to my life. But I could only blame myself.

I was the one who had been physically challenged for the first time in my life because of my injury and could not physically or mentally recover. Yes, I was the one who had become so depressed that I no longer had hope.

I was the one who could not pick myself up and land again on my feet. I was the one who was responsible for choosing to go to this far away land to find answers. And now it was I alone who would face a terrifying death.

How many times had I considered suicide because of the seemingly insurmountable problems I was facing? And how many times did I realize just in time that death by my own hands would never be acceptable to God? And in how many instances did my heart reveal that no matter how bad things became for me, I simply could not leave my children in that way?

Like a child who continues to play with fire and burn himself, I had to learn over and over that there was only one answer to my questions: that I must finally accept that I had to trust the Lord with my fate completely.

And so, in the gloomy, foreboding confines of the tunnel which was my prison, I got to my knees still crying and prayed, thinking of how much I had learned in this agonizing time about myself and my relationship with God. For that, I realized, I was thankful. I also knew then how blessed I was to have known the power and the grace of the Lord. I prayed intensely for about an hour, calling on God to help me face this final crisis.

Finally, my eyes swollen and burning, I lay down and tried to rest. Lying there with my eyes closed, something magical happened.

A bright, warm glow of light penetrated my eyelids, entering my mind and surrounding me, illuminating my body and soul. Approaching me with a warm and understanding smile, I saw Jesus.

I thanked him for his love and his mercy. He did not speak, but as he embraced me I was enveloped in his aura. My body and mind soaked up the sweet and loving power of his heart.

Not words but thoughts caressed my weary head. Do not be afraid, He said without moving His lips. All will be well. In my heart I knew He was right. I believed in Him. It did not matter anymore what happened to me in the physical world. Pain and death had no more meaning.

It was all clear to me now. I knew at that moment, it was better to die with courage than live in fear. What was truly important was the salvation of my soul.

Unlike the cowardly, lost souls who held me captive and brutalized me, I was the one who had been called upon to choose the high ground. And in doing so, all my mistakes of the past would be forgiven. Yes, it was so clear to me now. My victory would be in facing death with dignity if that was God's will, content in the knowledge that my passing would free me from the clutches of evil. In this world or in the next, I would be forever happy and at peace. Of this I was sure. I fell into a deep and tranquil sleep.

Suddenly, I felt a hand gripped tightly over my mouth. Startled, my eyelids opened a little as I tried to cry out, afraid that I was being smothered. "Shhhhhh," a voice whispered. I looked up and saw with surprise it was Joseph. *Why is he here? Is it time already?* Joseph lifted one finger to his lips, signaling me to be quiet before loosening his grip.

I was confused. *What is he doing?* Then, as I lay there half-awake staring at him, Joseph moved slowly down the tunnel and over to Eddy, who was sleeping with his legs propped on a wooden chair. Amazed I watched as Joseph slowly and carefully bent down and pulled a key ring from Eddy's belt. *Is this a dream?* I wondered as I opened my eyes wide and looked again. No, it was real. Then as my heart began to race with trepidation, I asked myself, *Can it be true that Joseph is going to help me escape?* I rolled to a sitting position and watched in disbelief as he slowly walked back to me. I could hardly believe my eyes. I wanted to ask him why he was doing this for me, but there was no time.

Joseph saw the excitement on my face and reminded me again to not make any noise by putting his finger to his mouth. Slowly and quietly he unlocked the cuffs around my ankle. I was free! I could not believe my good fortune! Not wanting to anger Joseph, I murmured under my breath, "Thank you, Lord!"

Joseph had turned on his small flashlight. Motioning to me to follow, he led me past Eddy and began slowly walking deeper into the tunnel. I hesitated. *Why is he going farther into the tunnel instead of toward the entrance?* I wondered. Joseph saw my puzzled look, came back to me and whispered, "I know way." That was good enough for me. I followed him.

As we began walking into the unused end of the tunnel, spider webs got in our faces, mouths and hair. Several times we had to stop and quietly spit the webbing from our mouths as our heads became coated with the dusty, dangling threads. I did not even want to think about the type of spiders that might be lurking nearby. I put that thought out of my mind as we continued on.

Then we reached an area of the tunnel that began to narrow in height and size. At a fork we slowly proceeded to the right which led to a space with ceilings so low we could no longer stand. Getting down on our hands and knees we began to crawl forward. I could not help asking myself if Joseph really knew where he was going. I tapped him on the shoulder. He turned and saw the concern on my face. Again he whispered to me, "I go here when boy." Then he pointed ahead of us.

Toward the end of the narrow crawlspace, I could see a small shaft of gray, pre-dawn light. Soon we were wiggling on our stomachs into an area that seemed to be a natural crack between the floor and the wall of the tunnel.

Now the space became no bigger than the size of our heads. We could hardly breathe and had to move sideways into this natural gap, which appeared to have been formed by an ancient underground stream. As we were squeezing through it, Joseph suddenly stopped. With some difficulty he reached back and into his pants' pocket. I watched intently as he pulled out a small pocketknife and worked his arm back around in front of him.

Carefully turning my head, I looked back to see if I could make out a light or anyone coming. I could hear the pounding of my heart as I scrutinized the darkness. No, there was no sign of anything amiss. I turned back to Joseph.

I could not see what he was doing, but I tried to be patient while he began cutting at something in front of him. I knew we had to hurry. Each moment we tarried brought more danger to this daring escape. I cleared away some dirt that had been kicked into my eyes by his feet. Then, I tried to steady my breathing which had become ragged and short from the physical exertion and the fear of being caught.

The minutes inched by feeling like hours. Finally Joseph moved up and to the side and I saw what he was working on. There was a natural opening to the outside, but it was covered by decades of vines and overgrowth. I had to admire Joseph. He was cutting away with that little knife, opening little by little the dense curtain of vegetation that had grown over this thin opening.

Suddenly, I thought I heard footsteps behind me. Filled with terror I stared back into the darkness of the tunnel trying to focus my eyes. I listened carefully hoping that the noise that had caught my attention was not someone coming to get us. But I heard nothing else scrambling or making crunching noises in the tunnel, only the rasping sound of Joseph's knife against the plants he was trying to cut through.

Did I imagine the footsteps? Maybe it was just a rat. My mind searched for some reassurance that no one was behind us. My heart pounded in the darkness, loud and fast from the momentary panic that gripped me. I took another deep breath, trying to calm my labored breathing and the frantic beating of my heart.

Meanwhile Joseph worked deliberately at his task. I watched as he made progress cutting a hole through the layers of plants and vines, asking myself why he was doing this for me. Dim light began to shine through, lighting the crevice around us. My heart jumped this time with joy as I began to think that we just might get out of there alive.

Slowly Joseph pushed forward until he was halfway out of the hole. I ducked as he turned over on his back and began digging his feet into the dirt in front of me. At the same time he began pulling away the vines that were surrounding his waist. Then he wiggled his way out and pointed the flashlight back into the hole so I could see my way.

"Now, now," he called to me as I inched forward and tried to pull myself through the hole. As I pulled my waist and rear through the hole, I realized just how much weight I had lost.

"What an irony," I muttered. If I had not been starved so long by my captors I would never have been able to fit through the narrow opening.

I wanted to pause and thank God for that miraculous moment. I knew that somehow He had powered the chain of events that were now leading me to freedom. But before I could, Joseph tapped me on the shoulder and said something in his own tongue. As I turned and took in his body language, I understood the meaning of what he was saying. We had to hurry. He helped me to my feet, but my legs shook and wobbled from weeks of malnutrition as I tried to find my balance. For a moment I glanced back.

We had emerged from a tiny hole in the mountainside that no one could have known was there. It must have been a long forgotten airshaft to the tunnel complex or perhaps just a natural crack in the tunnel wall. Turning, I began to follow Joseph. The vegetation and trees around us were so thick that I could barely see him though he was only a few feet in front of me. But the fresh air was exhilarating, thick with the smell of plants and earth.

I looked up at the rock face of a cliff that rose high above me. My eyes soared above the shadow of the mountain peak above us and into the gray morning sky. "Thank you," I said in a whisper. At that moment a shooting star pierced the earth's atmosphere overhead.

Then, with a smile on my face, I moved through the trees toward Joseph. As we slowly made our way down the mountainside, the trees became sparser, but I was still able to move from one to the other, using the trees to keep me upright on my wobbly legs.

Around us the jungle was waking to a new day. The sounds of birds and animals echoed in the morning air. The sky peeking through the jungle canopy above us was growing pink, glowing with the impending sunrise. It was a wonderful moment of liberation.

As I took it all in my senses were more alert and sensitive to the beauty around me then they'd ever been in the past. The leaves appeared greener, the flowers more colorful and the air more fragrant as my eyes skipped from one beautiful sight to another. I was free.

Suddenly I heard Joseph call to me. "Psssssssssst! Come here!" I followed his voice until I finally saw him waiting between two trees. He was perspiring heavily and had a very serious look in his eyes. "We must get away quickly."

Despite his warning, even Joseph had to stop several times, as he ran downhill through the jungle, because I, with my rubbery legs was like the bouncing ball of a pinball machine quivering and lunging as I went from tree to tree trying to keep myself from falling, mustering all my strength to stay on my feet.

As Joseph hurried farther ahead of me my giddy mood changed. I could not help thinking of Eddy and Abu. Did they know I was gone yet? Had anyone seen Joseph enter the tunnel? Fear pumped adrenalin through my body and helped me quicken my pace. Finally we came upon a path in the jungle. Motioning with his hands and reminding me not to speak, Joseph urged me on.

But I was moving too slowly. Joseph finally came to me and threw my left arm over his shoulder and half-carried me the rest of the way down the rocky slope.

We followed the path downward, slipping and sliding on the dewy, moist mud and wet grass. As the dense foliage around us began to thin, the steep incline of the ground beneath us also leveled out. Joseph and I stopped for a moment to catch our breath as sweat dripped from our faces. Joseph looked worried and I knew that I was not completely liberated yet. I looked around, fearful my captors might be coming, and saw we were in a grove of palm trees, spaced close enough to provide shade to the flat, grassy field. Tied to one of the trees was a huge, black ox with wide, sharp horns. He had an intimidating stare, but after all I'd been through I didn't even react. Then Joseph pointed to our right, saying, "My home over there."

I looked down a path that led into another clearing where I saw a house on stilts of fairly good size. There was a line strung from the house to a nearby tree from which hung dripping wet clothes. In front of the house were two women squatting over large plastic tubs washing more clothes.

I followed Joseph down the path to the house. Suddenly one of the women stood up and stared at us. Then she waved to Joseph and smiled. He turned to me and said proudly, "My wife."

In seconds, we were surrounded by about six children, ranging in age from two to eighteen. Joseph politely introduced me to each one of them. They all giggled and stared at me, wide-eyed with amazement. I was probably the first foreigner they had ever seen. Again I heard the words "Mercano? Mercano?" as they quizzed their father about me.

Joseph's wife motioned for me to sit down on one of the two wooden benches outside the entrance of their home. I did so quickly, gratefully resting my tired legs. While I sat there

Joseph's children gathered around me and smiled at me with impish delight. One of the older girls, maybe twelve years of age, brought me an old plastic cup full of water. I drank it quickly thinking nothing had ever tasted so good and she offered me another.

Joseph spoke to his wife while I rested and then approached me with a young girl of about eighteen at his side. Her skin was smooth and tawny-colored. She was very beautiful.

"Go with my daughter, Anna," Joseph said. "She is leaving today to live with her auntie."

Anna smiled sweetly and then in perfect English said, "We will be going soon on a boat." I was surprised that her pronunciation was even better than Joseph's.

I turned to him and asked, "Are you going to be okay?" I was worried about his safety if my captors found out that he had helped me escape.

"No, no worry," he said. "Nobody see me."

I felt relieved to hear his words. And suddenly I was overwhelmed with gratitude.

This man had risked his life and probably his beautiful family to save mine. How could I ever repay him? Despite the days of torture and brutality, my faith in mankind had been restored by this wonderful act of bravery and kindness. I was in awe of this simple, honorable man.

Joseph turned and said something in his native tongue to Anna. She ran into the house and brought back an old, worn, beat up suitcase with rusted hinges. It was just the right size for her to carry. Wrapped around her head was a pink and white scarf. Smiling at me again, Anna said, "We must go now. The boat is waiting."

I stood up and walked over to Joseph. I put my arms around him and hugged him. He seemed taken aback by my emotional display, but patted me politely on the back and then pulled away. "Happy trip," he said smiling.

"I shall never be able to express the depth of my gratitude to you for helping me," I told him. Anna said good-bye to her mother and I started to follow her. But I could not go just yet. I turned back, looked Joseph in the eyes and asked him the one question to which I had to have an answer: "Why did you risk your life for me?"

Joseph looked embarrassed, he stepped towards me, thrust out his hand to shake mine saying, "You influence me."

Puzzled, I looked at him and said, "In what way?"

Joseph smiled shyly. "You have good spirit, strong faith. I believe we are brothers under the same God." With that he looked proudly into the sky above us.

I was stunned by his answer. Here was a man, a Muslim, telling me that he believed that we were both of one family under the same God. And I realized I believed it as well.

When his eyes returned to mine, they beamed with the look of pride. "Go now," he said abruptly. "Be well." And with that he waved good-bye as I turned and followed Anna into the jungle. I felt as if I had just witnessed a miracle and joy filled my heart.

As Anna led the way down another jungle path I thought about Joseph. I knew the lesson I had learned today would stay with me forever: Faith is a universal power. It is a power that can overcome all evil among us.

The world felt like a whole new place to me. I was part of the brotherhood of man. For the second time in my life, I felt reborn.

As we continued Anna turned around several times to help me through thick vines and bushes. I was still very weak and could barely lift my feet to keep from tripping over the roots and vines on the jungle floor. Then, suddenly, we emerged onto a beach, shaded by several tall trees.

At the waters' edge was a fishing boat. It was big enough for five or six people and had a plywood roof supported by four bamboo poles and pontoons attached to each side of the boat for stability. It was a typical Filipino fishing boat covered with colorful markings.

A man in shorts, no shirt and a cone shaped hat sat on one edge of the boat. I tensed seeing him. But Anna sensed my fear and turned to me saying, "It's okay. He is my cousin."

After we settled down in the boat, Anna's cousin pushed us out into the ocean until he was almost waist deep in water. Then he hopped aboard and using an old-fashioned rope pulley, started the small engine at the back of the boat. Soon we were chugging out into the ocean.

I turned around to take one last look at the place where I had endured so much pain. The sun was rising from behind the island producing another colorful, picture postcard setting.

The powder blue sky glowed with yellow and pink streaks as the sun rose. The island, dark green and misty from the early morning fog, slowly grew smaller as we headed out to sea leaving it behind. Even the ocean around us had a soft mist hovering above it as the warm tropical water met the cool, early morning air.

As I stared at the beautiful scene behind us, Anna began asking me questions. "Where are you from?" she asked.

"Illinois," I responded. My back was to her as I watched the island disappear.

"U.S.A.?" she asked. "You Mercano?"

I turned to look at her and said, "Yes, I am an American."

Anna stared at me with the curiosity and innocence of a child and said, "I would like to know your country." Then she asked, "Are you married?"

I laughed at her sweet and innocent probing, "No, divorced." I turned away again to marvel at the colors of the sun rise.

"You looking for real love?" she continued.

"Maybe," I said, chuckling at the question. "Maybe in the future."

At that moment I was struck by the realization that I still had a future. Never again would I doubt the many ways that God touches us all or the miracles in life that demonstrate to us His existence.

Then, as Anna's gentle questioning continued, I realized something else. I did not feel the kind of relief or exhilaration that I thought I would experience having escaped from such a terrible ordeal. Instead, I felt very grounded, calm and secure. And I had the strangest intuition that this was actually the beginning of something new and wonderful in my life. In my heart was peace and confidence that the best was yet to come.

Afterword

Feelings of peace and contentment filled me, as if I had no reason to fear anything, anywhere, anymore. The power of God's Grace and my deliverance from the evil of the men who had brutalized me inspired me to pursue a life serving God's will.

The day of my escape, with Anna's help, I found my way back to Cebu. My first stop was the pension to reclaim my baggage and some valuables—including my passport, my watch and a little money—I had left behind. The owners of the pension took pity on me allowing me to use their facilities to shower and change my clothing one last time before I left. Immediately after that, Anna accompanied me to a local clinic to have my most serious wounds and injuries checked. While we waited for my antibiotic prescription to be filled, I went over in my mind the harrowing encounter I had experienced and a wave of different emotions engulfed me.

I was, of course, relieved and happy to be alive and free. There also was, however, sadness in my heart because of the loss of my friend Remy and a haunting feeling of guilt that his wife and child no longer had a loving husband or father to provide for them. Though he had been a part of the Blind Prophet's entourage when Remy and I met, I still somehow felt responsible, so I resolved to try and track down his family.

I do not know what became of the cab driver, although I suspect that he was beheaded in front of Remy in an attempt to get him to talk.

For several weeks, and with Anna's help, we ran down tips and an endless flow of bad information in search of Remy's family. But our search bore no fruit; we never found them. Perhaps they somehow heard we had been kidnapped and fled for their own safety. Knowing that his wife and child will never know what happened to Remy is still a sorrowful ache that has never left my heart.

I made an attempt to report my kidnapping to the police while I was in Cebu. But after getting the runaround from the Philippine authorities in Cebu, I became discouraged. I was ill, as well as running out of time and money. Besides, I loved the Filipino people and since I was now free, I did not want to create an international incident, because I happened to be in the wrong place at the wrong time. Nor did I really want to disturb the serene and content feeling that God had put in my heart. But most importantly, I was afraid that if the story of my kidnapping and escape hit the local newspapers, Joseph, Anna and their entire family would be in grave danger and very possibly, they would be killed. My tormentors must have realized someone helped me and if they took revenge on Joseph, I would never forgive myself. God only knows what happened to poor Eddy when Abu discovered I was gone.

When our search for Remy's family led nowhere, at Anna's insistence I accompanied her to the small, college town on the island of Bohol where she was living with her aunt. Tagbilaran City was much less populated and polluted than Cebu. I somehow thought that this might be the little town that the Blind Prophet was heading to when we were abducted. So I followed Anna there hoping to find the Blind Prophet and her companions.

On my first weekend in Tagbilaran I attended Easter services at an old Catholic church in the town's center. Afterwards I stopped at a bakeshop to sample the Philippine style donuts that were sold there and to watch the people in their Easter Sunday best parade by.

It was there that I met my future wife, Nheni, and her daughter, Mercy Grace, who happened to sit down at the same table where I was eating. Although I didn't see them again during my remaining weeks there, we miraculously bumped into each other on a street corner the very night I was to leave the Philippines. I firmly believe that just as God saved me, He brought us together.

That night, we connected on a spiritual level and discovered that we had many things in common, especially our love of God and Jesus Christ. I learned that she was planning to graduate from a theological school in Cebu as a pastor. We agreed to write to each other when I left the Philippines. Little did I know then that she would become yet another one of God's gifts in my life.

Anna convinced me not to leave just yet and helped me find a cheap place to stay in Tagbilaran. There I got to enjoy the hospitality of the easygoing natives of Bohol. Determined to take care of me and take my mind off the trauma of being held hostage, Anna became my guide, friend and caretaker.

As Anna tried to help me regain my strength and good health over the next several weeks, I discovered that the disabilities that had kept me from working in the United States had deteriorated further due to the horrific treatment I endured in captivity. Although I had been given antibiotics at the clinic and the wounds on my hands, head and mouth began to heal rapidly, my right shoulder hung limply and without strength. I could not raise my right arm out enough to even shake someone's hand. The cycle of pain and paralysis in my back and left leg was now constant and beginning to affect some of my internal organs. The few painkillers I had left in my luggage were dwindling fast. Whenever we went out, gentle Anna acted as my human cane, giving the left side of my body added stability as I limped along.

Our search for the Blind Prophet in Tagbilaran also ended in failure. I never did see or hear from the Blind Prophet or her followers again. I often wonder if they ever knew what happened to Remy and me.

Anna became homesick and I saw an opportunity to reward the people who had saved my life. Without telling her, I cashed in my return airline ticket to have the money to send Anna home to see her family. There was a little extra money left so I gave that also to Anna to take with her as a gift for Joseph and his large family. She was surprised and delighted by my generous gift and said she and her family would never forget me.

Before she left, she asked if she could borrow my camera to take some pictures.

"Sure, bring it home with you and take some photos of your father and your family to send to me in America."

"I will…proudly," she said with a smile.

As Anna headed south on the ferry for the reunion with her family, I headed back to Cebu to update my immigration status and find out the cost of a new airline ticket.

I felt good about using my scant funds to help Joseph, Anna and their family. It was the least I could do for the man who saved my life. I later learned they stretched the money to give a little financial help to Anna's auntie in Tagbilaran who was desperately trying to save her husband's life from kidney failure.

By the time Anna returned from her trip I was busy selling my last few possessions to raise enough money to pay for my immigration fees and new airline ticket. Even after selling my watch, high school ring and sunglasses I was only able to come up with enough money to get a ticket to Hawaii. I wanted desperately to return to Florida to see my children, but a ticket to Florida would have been twice the cost of going to Hawaii; I just did not have the funds to get there. Unfortunately, my health problems were growing worse each day and even if I could get to Florida, all I could do was live on the streets. I simply had no home to which to return.

And so I left the Philippines in May of 1996 and arrived in Honolulu, Hawaii, hopeful that I could make enough money there to return to Florida. I never did meet or speak to Pastor Sumrall in Manila. But I did have two new pen pals. Both Anna and Nheni had promised to write to me in Hawaii. Unfortunately, after receiving one letter filled with photographs from Anna, I never heard from her again. I surmised she feared reprisals for her family if the Abu Sayyaf found out. Nheni, on the other hand, wrote to me regularly.

I lasted only about two months in Honolulu working part-time jobs and trying to save money there. One afternoon after work, I was walking back to my room at the YMCA when the severe pain in my back and leg intensified. I only made it a few blocks before my left leg gave out. This time I could not walk at all. I ended up in a hospital emergency room. Later that evening, they gave me my first cane before discharging me.

Unable to continue working, I called my family for advice and some moral support. My father graciously offered to help me fly back to Rockford, Illinois, where I could live with my brother. I didn't like having to beg for help again, but I had nowhere else to turn.

After arriving in Rockford, with my brother's help for which I'll always be grateful, I finally received some much needed medical care that literally got me back on my feet again. And within a month after settling into an apartment with him, I received a letter from Nheni. With a sense of destiny, my relationship with Nheni grew. Love letters and scripture connected us for the next year. Despite the many miles that separated us we established a true and loving relationship and recognized God's plan for us to be together.

In 1997, after my health had improved, I proposed to Nheni and moved to Florida so I could be close to my children. My plan was to make a new life there once Nheni and I were married. I was again hopeful that I could start over in Florida, sure that I could work in one of the many hotels near the various tourist attractions.

I finally got to see my beloved sons, but again my body failed me and my recovery was short-lived. Only months after finding work in a hotel in Orlando, my health deteriorated leaving me unable to walk and with internal complications. I soon found myself with only unemployment compensation as a dwindling source of income.

My doctors made it clear that I was now permanently disabled and would never be able to work again in a normal capacity. Taking my doctors advice, I filed for disability benefits and began a difficult legal battle to win the benefits that were supposed to be mine.

My now fiancé, Nheni, suggested, since she was a pastor at a church there, that I travel back to the Philippines. Though I didn't want to leave my boys again, I knew I couldn't support myself or my dependents if I stayed in Florida. So I went along with Nheni's suggestion.

Nheni and I were married in the Philippines on December 14, 1997 and, despite my precarious health and loneliness for my children, we settled into a wonderfully peaceful life in the tropical paradise of Tagbilaran City, Bohol. Living with Nheni, my happiness and contentment grew knowing that God brought us together to live a spiritual life.

During the time I lived with Nheni in Tagbilaran, I ran into Anna's auntie and got an update on Anna. She told me that Anna had moved to another island, was married and expecting a baby. Fortunately, I shall always have the photos that Anna took during her trip home. They remind me that there are far more good people in the world than bad.

For two years Nheni and I lived happily and very simply in our island paradise becoming heavily involved in our church's

Praise and Worship music team. Encouraged to play the drums again by our Filipino pastors there, I relished my new role in serving God together with my wife.

During those two years, I traveled back and forth to the United States collecting insurance settlements and fighting a long legal battle to receive my disability benefits. At the same time I was also forced to fight for my rights to see my children. When I told my ex-wives that I was unable to pay child support payments until I received my benefits, they did not believe me and refused to let me communicate with my children.

With God's help and the loving support of my wife I persevered and continued my legal battles while waiting to receive disability benefits in the United States. My island home became my sanctuary and it was our church and our many friends in Tagbilaran City in the Philippines that became my source of strength and family during those times.

The bliss of our Christian life in the Philippines was interrupted in 1999 when I was diagnosed with cancer and was told I might have only months to live. Choosing to stay with my wife, I elected to have surgery in Bohol to remove tumors from my chest and underwent chemotherapy there also.

In 2000, I was finally granted my disability benefits and was able to resume child support payments again for both my sons. I also returned to Rockford, Illinois, in order to address my continuing health concerns, to heal my still strained relationship with my parents and to be with them during their senior years. Only after seeing my doctor's reports did my family finally realize the extent and truth of all that I had been through and we became close again.

Learning to forgive and overcoming numerous physical and emotional challenges, I have triumphed over all of those problems by the will of God while settling down to a peaceful life in Rockford, Illinois, with Nheni. I am once again part of a caring family and best of all I am now able to communicate with my children again.

During the years since the kidnapping I have gradually learned more from Anna, Nheni and others about the radical Islamic group called the Abu Sayyaf which had taken me hostage. One of the things I learned from Anna was that the Abu Sayyaf operated from the island of Basilan, where her family lived and they spoke a unique island dialect called Tausug, the dialect that Joseph had mentioned in one of our conversations in the tunnel.

However, it was not until the kidnapping of European tourists in 2000 and American missionaries in 2001 that I actually saw photos and film of several of the individuals that I recognized as my captors. These reports and pictures flashed on the national news, confirming for me that it was indeed the Abu Sayyaf who had captured me. I was able to recognize at least four of those men; Abu Sabaya, Andong, Berto and Greasy. The investigation into the terrible events of September 11, 2001 confirmed that the Abu Sayyaf had links to al Qaeda.

While following the news and praying for those who were now their captives, I began having terrible flashbacks, nightmares and anxiety attacks. However, God's hand once again touched me and urged me to begin writing about my own experience as therapy for the Post Traumatic Stress Disorder I was suffering. Although it was sometimes very painful emotionally, the process of writing about my experience has proved to be very therapeutic and spiritually cleansing.

Abu Sabaya was reportedly killed in June of 2002 when he was ambushed at sea by Philippine marines. However, as of 2003, the Abu Sayyaf gang which has perpetrated the terrorist bombing of Davao Airport in the southern Philippines as well as other heinous acts, is still being hunted by the Philippine military.

By the grace of God, I am now telling my story as a witness to the victory of God's awesome power and how he touches people of all races and cultures. With Nheni at my side, we are now moved to spread a powerful message of hope to all people. We tell all that regardless of their religious convictions, there is no reason to fear the cowardice and evil that the Abu Sayyaf and Osama bin Laden embody in our world today. Whatever our faith, we are all brothers and sisters.

My wife and I now enjoy a simple existence in Rockford, Illinois, while waiting for her daughter, Mercy Grace, to join us soon. We are actively involved with the Christian ministry both in the United States and the Philippines, spreading the Good News of God's strength, love, mercy and powers of healing—a message which has changed my life.

Glossary

Abu Sayyaf – A Muslim extremist guerrilla group based in the southern islands of the Philippines, but linked with al Qaeda and other international terrorist organizations. The group is known for kidnapping and holding hostage Westerners and Christian missionaries for ransom as well as the bombing of public places to achieve their ultimate goals: which include an independent Muslim state in the southern Philippines.

carenderia – an inexpensive restaurant, often buffet style

Cebu – a large island in the southern Philippines

guapa – pretty

jeepney – a bus-like vehicle used for public transportation in the Philippines

malamig – Cold or refrigerated

Maayong Buntag – a greeting meaning "Good morning"

Negritos – A group of dark-skinned people of small stature that originated in Africa believed to be the earliest inhabitants of the Philippine islands

Raja – an Indian or Malay prince or chief

sari sari – an inexpensive variety store in the Philippines similar to the American five-and-dime store

shabu – a cocaine-like substance used in the Philippines

Super Cat – a large, modern, jet-powered catamaran style sea-faring vessel used commercially to transport people from island to island

Tagalog – the national language of the Philippines

Tausug – a language dialect spoken on Basilan and surrounding islands of the Southern Philippines

tubig – water

Visayan – a group of many islands in the Central Philippines including Bohol, Cebu and Samar; a person from any of the Visayan islands; any of the languages spoken on these islands